Twelve Best Books by African Women

This series of publications on Africa, Latin America, Southeast Asia, and Global and Comparative Studies is designed to present significant research, translation, and opinion to area specialists and to a wide community of persons interested in world affairs. The editor seeks manuscripts of quality on any subject and can usually make a decision regarding publication within three months of receipt of the original work. Production methods generally permit a work to appear within one year of acceptance. The editor works closely with authors to produce a high-quality book. The series appears in a paperback format and is distributed worldwide. For more information, contact the executive editor at Ohio University Press, 19 Circle Drive, The Ridges, Athens, Ohio 45701.

Executive editor: Gillian Berchowitz
AREA CONSULTANTS
Africa: Diane M. Ciekawy
Latin America: Brad Jokisch, Patrick Barr-Melej, and Rafael Obregon
Southeast Asia: William H. Frederick

The Ohio University Research in International Studies series is published for the Center for International Studies by Ohio University Press. The views expressed in individual volumes are those of the authors and should not be considered to represent the policies or beliefs of the Center for International Studies, Ohio University Press, or Ohio University.

Twelve Best Books by African Women

CRITICAL READINGS

Edited by Chikwenye Okonjo Ogunyemi
and Tuzyline Jita Allan

Ohio University Research in International Studies
Africa Series No. 88
Ohio University Press
Athens

To obtain permission to quote, reprint, or otherwise reproduce or
distribute material from Ohio University Press publications, please
contact our rights and permissions department at (740) 593-1154 or
(740) 593-4536 (fax).
www.ohioswallow.com

Printed in the United States of America
The books in the Ohio University Research in International Studies Series
are printed on acid-free paper ⊚ ™

18 17 16 15 14 13 12 11 10 09   5 4 3 2 1

Library of Congress Cataloging-in-Publication Data

Twelve best books by African women : critical readings / edited by
Chikwenye Okonjo Ogunyemi and Tuzyline Jita Allan.
    p. cm. — (Ohio University research in international studies, Africa
series ; no. 88)
    Includes bibliographical references and index.
    ISBN 978-0-89680-266-7 (pb : alk. paper)
    1. African fiction—Women authors—History and criticism. 2. Women
and literature—Africa—History—20th century. 3. Women in literature.
4. Africa—In literature. I. Ogunyemi, Chikwenye Okonjo. II. Allan,
Tuzyline Jita.
    PN849.A35T64 2009
    823'.91099287—dc22
                                    2009014870

We dedicate this book to all the African women writers and scholars, past and present, who have written the nation into consciousness, reproduced the self into awareness, and crafted the community into resilience and responsiveness.

Contents

vii

Part 3. Regeneration:
Labor Pains and Tentative Steps toward Independence

Acknowledgments

Our sincere appreciation goes to Sarah Lawrence College for a sabbatical leave for Chikwenye Okonjo Ogunyemi, and to Dean Barbara Kaplan and the Faculty Writing Group of Sarah Lawrence College, Bronxville, New York, for nurturing an intellectual environment that made the production of this book possible. A Sarah Lawrence College grant expedited the process.

We also thank Dean Myrna Chase of the Weissman School of Arts and Sciences and Dr. Thomas Hayes, chairperson of the English Department, for their support of Tuzyline Jita Allan's sabbatical leave in the spring semester of 2007 when this project was completed.

Prolepsis

Twelve Telling Tales by African Women

Chikwenye Okonjo Ogunyemi

> This introduction is dedicated to the Zimbabwe International
> Book Fair, whose maternal resilience in the midst of
> socioeconomic upheavals is inspiriting.

In 2002, the Zimbabwe International Book Fair, supported by Professor Ali Mazrui, enabled the selection of "Africa's 100 Best Books
of the Twentieth Century" regardless of the race of the writer and
the language in which the book was written; it sparked off an African,
millennial, can-do spirit. The move countered the sense of déjà lu–
déjà vu aroused by the exclusivity of some Western lists of "100
Great English Books of the Twentieth Century," even if it could not
undo the slight offered when Africans were left off such lists. Infused
with this invigorating attitude, two women scholars, including Nana
Wilson-Tagoe, one of the contributors to this volume, joined fourteen
male colleagues to constitute the committee mandated to pick out the
books. The committee's choice of twelve fictional works and one play
by women among the one hundred "best" books acknowledges female
literary endeavor, bringing it into a privileged circle. This point of
departure of including women at a celebratory moment is noteworthy
for officially establishing a female literary canon.

Here are the writers and the works that were singled out, arranged
chronologically for those interested in questions of intertextuality
and intersubjectivity.[1]

Ama Ata Aidoo (Ghana), *Anowa* (a play) (1970)
Bessie Head (South Africa–Botswana), *A Question of Power* (1974)
Nawal El Saadawi (Egypt), *Imraa Inda Nuktat Al Sifr* (original in
    Arabic; *Woman at Point Zero*) (1975)

Aminata Sow Fall (Senegal), *La Grève des bàttu* (original in French; *The Beggars' Strike*) (1979)
Nadine Gordimer (South Africa), *Burger's Daughter* (1979)
Buchi Emecheta (Nigeria), *The Joys of Motherhood* (1979)

Mariama Bâ (Senegal), *Une si longue lettre* (original in French; *So Long a Letter*) (1980)
Assia Djebar (née Fatima-Zohra Imalhagene) (Algeria), *L'Amour, la fantasia* (original in French; *Fantasia: An Algerian Cavalcade*) (1983)
Tsitsi Dangarembga (Zimbabwe), *Nervous Conditions* (1988)
Sindiwe Magona (South Africa), *Living, Loving, and Lying Awake at Night* (1991)
Yvonne Vera (Zimbabwe), *Butterfly Burning* (1998)
Ken Bugul (née Mariètou M'Baye) (Senegal), *Riwan ou le chemin de sable* (original in French) (1999)

When the one hundred best books were chosen, the committee had another select list comprising what they considered to be the top twelve works. In spite of the contentious nature of categorizing works as "best" and the arbitrariness of having a list within a list, this model is emulated in the decision to concentrate on twelve of the thirteen texts in *Twelve Best Books by African Women: Critical Readings*. Elsa Joubert's *Die Swerfjare van Poppie Nongena* was left out because of controversy surrounding the mediated status of the telling.[2]

The twelve works neatly map the continent and span the last three decades of the twentieth century, which gives the erroneous impression that nothing valuable predates them. Further, with its colonial frame of mind, the idea of a list is problematic, as it already hierarchizes, unwittingly mimicking the fractious, debilitating, Western exclusionism that marginalizes other invaluable works by these and other writers. I am fully conscious of the Catch-22 situation of compiling essays structured around the list-making I am criticizing.

The creative texts spring from a long writing tradition based on an oral fundament dating back to such globally recognized foremothers as the biblical Queen of Sheba—Ethiopia's Makeda[3]—and the legendary raconteuse, Scheherazade. Also important in this dialogic affiliation are Egypt's women activists, for example, Huda Sha'rawi and Nabaweya Moussa, who thrived early in the twentieth century. Nigeria's first woman novelist, Flora Nwapa, Kenya's Grace Ogot, and her compatriot, Rebeka Njau, who tackled women's mystical powers fictionally, provide antecedents in English.

Serendipitously shoring up the female literary terrain, the twelve texts are telling for their candor and encyclopedic coverage in three Africanized lingua francas (Arabic, English, and French) that globalize women's conversations with the heterogeneous continent. The writers tackle the hierarchies of power (in all the regions of Africa, North, West, South, and East) arising in gender matters, different religious and political affiliations, diverse races, ethnicities, and cultures. In the process, they traverse three historical phases. To bypass the rigidities and alien nature of colonial chronology, I refer to the initial phase as *the reconfiguration*. This covers early, internal migrations, fueled by wars and economic deprivations, across borders, which have remained porous. The attendant turmoil instituted by these indigenous displacements and the outsiders' intrusions and remapping led to the vulnerability that enabled the slave trade and the official scramble for Africa toward the end of the nineteenth century. The second phase I see as *the resistance* throughout the continent. This refers to the widespread wars against the colonizers and their local stooges and imitators in the twentieth century. The last phase is the fin de siècle, *the rebirth*, amidst the millennial hope cultured in the ancestral blood sacrifice throughout the ages.[4]

I use this division to place the books. *Anowa* and *Fantasia*, with their historical sweep, location, and bewilderment, feature under *reconfiguration*. Preoccupation with female fighters who become casualties of an undeclared internal war places *Woman at Point Zero, Burger's Daughter, The Joys of Motherhood*, and *Butterfly Burning* under the category *resistance*. *Rebirth*, with its labor pains implicit in the interrogations of the status quo and the joyously mixed outcome, is the thrust of *A Question of Power; The Beggars' Strike; So Long a Letter; Nervous Conditions; Living, Loving, and Lying Awake at Night*; and *Riwan ou le chemin de sable*.

These books memorialize the past, circling painful memories that prompt the reshaping of the continent for an economically just Africa. Their global circulation has catalytically helped in giving birth to the appearance of women as leaders in the public domain, notably Kenya's Nobel laureate Wangari Maathai, Liberia's President Ellen Johnson-Sirleaf, Tanzania's Asha-Rose Migiro, as the United Nations' deputy secretary-general, and Nigeria's Ngozi Okonjo-Iweala, as a World Bank managing director. The placement of women in intellectual, social, and political positions of power bodes well for the future, just as this literary canon opens fresh vistas for new, award-winning, creative writers in the twenty-first century, such as the light bearer, Nigeria's Chimamanda Ngozi Adichie, Ghana's Armah Darko, and Senegal's Fatou Diome. In the chaotic orderliness of Africa, I imagine the selection of a list of "100 Best Books by African Women" that would include these emerging women and, most importantly, the prolific Nigerian playwright, Tess Onwueme, and Cameroon's Calixthe Beyala.

The diverse trajectories emanating from the creative works have also prompted the critical response in this book, one that looks at familiar material with new eyes. In their thickly layered, revelatory scripts and distinct thrusts, the women writers place Africans, especially women who have endured failed male leadership, at the center of their storytelling. This subjectivity and narrative power to tell the self is at the core of such voiced texts as *A Question of Power, Woman at Point Zero, Nervous Conditions, So Long a Letter,* and *Riwan,* works that are psychically energizing. The women writers address those areas their male counterparts left out in pursuing their version of nation and the fight for its realization; remarkably, they present their female characters as daughters with inalienable rights to participate in reconstructing the nation as partners, not mere dependents. This revisionary history and storytelling demonstrate that women have always actively participated as citizens, daughters, sisters, wives, othermothers, and mothers in the reproduction and evolution of the self, family, community, and nation. By concentrating on these aspects and on the private world as it impinges on the public, the writers deal with the bedrock of nation building, foundational matters for a healthy continent.

Their interests are wide-ranging: the moral, spiritual, political, and economic issues rooted in the slave trade and slavery as reproduced in contemporary versions of democratic capitalism; gender in the scheme of African affairs; indigence; educating the modern woman-child; revising historical documentation to include women; ethnic, racial, class, and caste diversities; (mental) health problems; polygyny; motherhood and the childless woman; prostitution; migrations, especially the "been-to," that doubly exposed migrant who has traveled out and returned home. Considering these trajectories, how can women be seen not merely as a problem while making optimal use of their strength for African development? By reframing issues, amnesic or concealed, the writers publicly reach out to a large constituency, bringing to light key matters of twentieth-century African diaspora life that encourage critical thinking. These topical concerns constitute the core of an African women's literary tradition—the fare for college courses with a womanist thrust, as a look at the twelve texts demonstrates.

Following the committee's open acknowledgment of women's contribution to African literatures, the works now deservedly have pride of place in literature curricula throughout Africa and the diaspora, most especially in women's literary studies. This fine literature forms the core of a female literary canon which includes other books by these same writers and many others that did not make the "100 best" list.[5] Yet there is a problematic paucity of scholarly material to support teachers and students at the graduate, undergraduate, and advanced secondary levels that want to and should study these and other works by African women. *Twelve Best Books by African Women: Critical Readings*, a collaborative effort in the true African spirit, remedies the situation.

After Tuzyline Jita Allan consented to be a coeditor, both of us were moved by the haunting theme of being an African, critical in the committee's commitment. This led to a significant point of departure in the process of selecting the participating scholars. We compiled a list of ten African women we knew intellectually: fellow collaborators, colleagues, and former students. For a diversity of approach, we chose scholars—African, African Arab, and African European—located in different institutions and different parts of the globe: Botswana, Canada, Egypt, England, Nigeria, South Africa, and the United States.

Since these scholars are not outside observers but participants in the burgeoning of the continent, putting the book together became a heroic act, for African women reading African texts in a scholarly fashion with the particular visions they bring to the reading is revitalizing. The multifaceted thrust, I believe, contributes immensely to spearheading the serious reading and teaching of African women's creative works. The twelve contributors' suggestions for the book title reminded me of the communal Yoruba naming ceremony. The divergent details embedded in the titles show a community pool, deep and broad, that attempts to represent African diversity. The different points of view indicated in their suggestions demonstrate not just the scholars' intellectual responses to the literature but the multiple mothering of the resultant text.[6]

The literary tradition that the scholars unveil speaks to the plight of an indigent underclass, particularly the majority of women excluded from full participation in nation building; the psychological repercussions of ignoring the wounding from the past, when the continent was humiliatingly occupied and nearly denuded; the trauma and indeterminacy attendant on a continuingly failed African leadership that still allows the continent to be milked; the divisive issues of race, ethnicity, gender, caste, culture, language, and religion; and the closed, colonized, distrusting mentality operating vulnerably in a complex global scene.

Following the rethinking of the historical schema noted earlier, part 1 of *Twelve Best Books by African Women: Critical Readings* concentrates on the spatial and philosophical movement toward modernity and nation formation. *Anowa* and *Fantasia* address this reconfigured Africa.

Ama Ata Aidoo's *Anowa* captures a historical moment through a marriage (standing in for Ghanaian/African union) rocked by the couple's participation in the horrendous trans-Atlantic slave trade and the African version of slavery. The ensuing psychological disenabling speaks to African male political and entrepreneurial leadership, for through the disoriented wife, Anowa, Aidoo presents woman as the conscience of the continent. In this cautionary drama, selling one's people (past and present) is counterproductive and suicidal. In "Modernity, Gender, and Agency in Ama Ata Aidoo's *Anowa*," Nana Wilson-Tagoe reconceptualizes the idea of modernity. Referring to the play as a "drama of marriage," she looks at unequally yoked couples debating issues in a communal context. Anowa's unstable marriage doubles as the troubling mixing of Akan and European cultures that birthed Ghanaian modernity in the nineteenth century. As the modern woman, Anowa, interrogates the self, the power dynamics between women and men, the issue of agency, the nature of capitalism, the link between internal slavery and the slave trade, all unfold. These conversations with the self and the other provide the philosophical base for the movement toward modernity and the idea of the Ghanaian (African) nation.

Historian, novelist, and film producer Assia Djebar circumvents a babel of languages (Berber, Turkish, Arabic, and French), creating a fantasia of opposing voices that translate the oral/aural, the visual, and the remembered into the written in *Fantasia: An Algerian Cavalcade*. Invading metropolitan spaces as she raids the archives of colonizing countries, interrogating and revising their accounts, she writes women into Algerian (African) history, from the ancestral and nomadic to the national, acknowledging their contribution to wars of liberation. "Charting the Nation/Charting History: The Power of Language in Assia Djebar's *Fantasia: An Algerian Cavalcade*" is Nada Halloway's mapping of Djebar's struggle with the French language and the rewriting of Algerian history from a female perspective. Djebar's 2006 induction into the Académie Française creates hope for newness in this male bastion that controls normative language usage. Halloway reads the French language as a war zone: liberating as well as oppressive, it provides a space for subjectivity for silenced women. Djebar the historian uses this inimical language to rewrite French (and other) versions of Algerian (and African) history that make her account wholesome.

Part 2, which focuses on the casualties resulting from differing attempts at resistance, is composed of essays on *Woman at Point Zero, Burger's Daughter, The Joys of Motherhood,* and *Butterfly Burning.* The texts establish women's momentous lives and the inexorable journey to the end. By harnessing patriarchy and other forms of domination, the texts act as oppositional sites that demonstrate women's power in the face of apparent injustices.

From an African Arab, female perspective, the Egyptian Islamic world unfolds as a prison in Nawal El Saadawi's *Woman at Point Zero.* Through economic, sexual, and sociopolitical lenses the psychoanalyst-turned-novelist brings into focus the plight of her ironically named Firdaus (Paradise), a prostitute and murderer languishing in the web of an unrelentingly patriarchal religious world. Amira Nowaira's "Nawal El Saadawi's *Woman at Point Zero* within the Context of Arab Feminist Discourse" deals with feminism and women's place in the nation in an Egypt that straddles Africa and the Arab world. She presents the text as groundbreaking in its advocacy rather than condemnation of Firdaus as a prostitute. El Saadawi's feminist, liberatory zeal speaks to the situation of women as a confined group, zeroing in on women's underdevelopment because of incapacitating sexual, socioeconomic, and religious inequalities. This emphasis distinguishes her from her upper-class female predecessors, who focused, like their male contemporaries, on national liberation, ignoring gender matters and women's place in the nation.

Dealing with imprisonment and death in prison from Egypt to South Africa, El Saadawi and Nadine Gordimer see women as freedom fighters. In a complementary move that acknowledges her bold compatriot, Bessie Head, Gordimer homes in on the politics of South African antiapartheid whites in *Burger's Daughter.* She stakes a claim for the inclusion of whites in a new South Africa, examining this heritage from the perspective of a daughter who returns, after her flirtatious European sojourn, to a home not yet ready for white embracement of Africanness. Nobantu L. Rasebotsa looks at the intersection of the personal and the political in "Nadine Gordimer's *Burger's Daughter:* Consciousness, Identity, and Autonomy." Operating in multiple cultures affected by gender, sexuality, and race in African and European contexts, Rosa's self-scrutiny vis-à-vis her parents, who conscientiously resist the extremely oppressive, racist climate, drives her sociopolitical metamorphosis. To Rasebotsa, Rosa's activism, evolving through her changed perception, her growing awareness of the need for genuine South African liberation, and her consciousness of the processes at work, constitute the core of her reeducation—Gordimer's seed for a new white South Africa.

Contrastingly, Buchi Emecheta's *The Joys of Motherhood*, set in a Nigeria under siege, focuses on an extended family (Africa) reeling from the turmoil of coping with crippling poverty, alien and confining urban spaces, and destabilizing polygyny—familial and national, as the country struggles under an invisible British mistress, controlling yet controlled. True to her calling as a sociologist, Emecheta expands the discourse by incorporating women's unappreciated and unrewarding role as caregivers who reproduce the family and nation at the expense of self. Tuzyline Jita Allan's "Dreams of (Dis)order: Competing Visions of Colonial Nigeria in Buchi Emecheta's *The Joys of Motherhood*" addresses the issue of indirect rule, the British dream of invisibly and effortlessly controlling its empire. The locals, especially Nnu Ego, the archetypal mother, have their different dreams, whose treacherous deferment leads to dreadful consequences for all involved.

Yvonne Vera, like Emecheta, chooses the life of a woman to target a moment in a national history. Her *Butterfly Burning* centers on a fatherless black Rhodesian girl and the roles of men and the fatherland in her development. Without access to the nursing profession because of her (pregnant) body, Phephelaphi represents the African woman denied social mobility; thus, her potential contribution to African health and development remains unexploited. These acts of omission are abortive, a miscarriage of fair play, ending in premature deaths, though the dawn, Vera reminds the reader, holds a new promise for Zimbabwe. Sisi Maqagi's "In the Pauses of the Historian's Narrative: Yvonne Vera's *Butterfly Burning*" highlights the torment generated by changes in gender roles as they intertwine with the psychological devastation resulting from white control, manifested in the lack of black land ownership. These traumas, with their racist and sexist undertones, find temporary relief in the rejuvenating spirit of kwela music. Phephelaphi's rebellion against patriarchal appropriation of her body through pregnancy and the sexist, racist stifling of her professional ambition to participate in nursing the community/ nation back to health becomes tragically manifested in abortion and suicide. To Maqagi, Vera rejects the totalizing tendencies of historians by telling the stories of marginalized women, who must be commemorated in order for there to be a new national beginning.

Part 3 of *Twelve Best Books by African Women* pinpoints the pains of rebirth, the resilience, and the tentative movement toward a meaningful, revisionary, African approach to regenerating power in different walks of life—a precursor to national rehabilitation for all areas of governance. The works in this category are *A Question of Power; The Beggars' Strike; So Long a Letter; Nervous Conditions; Living, Loving, and Lying Awake at Night;* and *Riwan ou le chemin de sable.*

Bessie Head's autobiografiction, *A Question of Power,* depicts apartheid South Africa's psychological and spiritual chaos as experienced by its biracial product, Elizabeth. Migrating to Botswana, she exhibits her internalized schizophrenic heritage, hallucinating dysfunctions emanating from global and historical economic, political, religious, and racial inequalities. *Question* is a psychic release, artistically framed for the therapeutic outcome necessary in caring for African lives out of whack. In "Mapping a Female Mind: Bessie Head's *A Question of Power* and the Unscrambling of Africa," I trace Elizabeth's critical reappraisal of male discourses on power. Elizabeth, the activist, stands in for an Africa resisting under siege, manifested in her schizophrenia, outsider status, poverty, and gender. Head reinstates her as a revolutionary writer and intellectual in those spheres from which she was excluded or where she was rendered ineffectual, rewriting the racial, psychoanalytic, economic, and religious scripts by presenting the recuperating Elizabeth as a new type of pan-Africanist prophet, the bearer of the gospel of an assuaged, humanized Africa. Head's interrogation and feminizing of religion—African Traditional Religions, Buddhism, Judaism, Christianity, and Islam—accentuate a sense of belonging.

Islam is equally critical in the Senegalese imbroglio of gender, capitalism, politics, and a leadership indifferent to the masses; these aspects form the core of Aminata Sow Fall's *The Beggars' Strike*. Sow Fall contrasts modern government with the more inclusive governance to be found among the novel's beggars, ironizing the former's irresponsible attitude toward mendicity and the relief mandated by Islamic almsgiving. With great economy, she simultaneously addresses African poverty and knee-jerk local and global responses. Chioma Opara takes a deconstructive approach in "A Drama of Power: Aminata Sow Fall's *The Beggars' Strike*," dismantling binaries to trace power shifts in governance in the family, the community, and Senegal as a whole. The empowerment of the beggars under female leadership, which institutes changes in the nation's governmental policy, is noteworthy. Opara sees Fall's work as subversively feminist, with the private sphere impinging on the public as the excluded—women and the underclass—indirectly participate in nation building, undermining crass capitalists and leaders who flirt with spiritual figures affiliated with a patriarchal religion that promotes self-serving almsgiving.

Another Senegalese, Mariama Bâ, spotlights in *So Long a Letter* how the society and nation shortchange women emotionally, intellectually, economically, and politically, particularly through the institution of polygyny and status of widowhood. Ramatoulaye fights back by modifying and reinscribing gender roles. Mimicking the authority of the social critic, she promotes herself through writing, simultaneously exposing her self and her sister travelers' lives. Exploring competing meanings of "traverse," Modupe Olaogun, in "Aesthetics, Ethics, Desire, and Necessity in Mariama Bâ's *So Long a Letter*," generates a reading of spaces where aesthetics and ethics intersect and fissures occur in a character, numerous pairings of characters, and incidents. Whether gendered, class- or caste-based, localized or globalized, private or public, philosophical, moral, or political, these splits tend to emphasize difference, glossing over similarities that intensify textual complexity. Ramatoulaye and Aissatou's envisaged reunion is a case in point that deemphasizes their divergent approaches to comparable problems. Further, Ramatoulaye's subjectivity identifies her as a griotte (though she spurns Farmata, the tradition-bound "griot woman"), creating traverse spaces that enhance female solidarity.

Echoing this political thrust in rethinking gender matters, Tsitsi Dangarembga, in *Nervous Conditions*, proposes sisterhood-in-community as a counter to the psychologically debilitating factors of colonization on the black Rhodesian populace. Though she emphasizes the need to guarantee a productive place for the woman-child through equal access to modern education, she alerts us to the limitations of a Western-style model for African development. In the novel, the subaltern gets to tell her story, one which provides an alternative model for intellectual and mental recovery. Rather than interpret *Nervous Conditions* as a straightforward feminist novel, Helen Mugambi's "Reading Masculinities in a Feminist Text: Tsitsi Dangarembga's *Nervous Conditions*" pays close attention to male and female characters whose masculinities and femininities overlap. Mugambi demonstrates the limitations of predictably gendered readings, as neither male nor female characters are necessarily confined by the imagined boundaries conventionally separating them. Dangarembga's characters performatively drift toward unexpected roles, blurring gendered lines and dramatizing the complexities of masculinity and femininity, mandating a creative rethinking of "female" and "male" as categories.

Like Dangarembga, Sindiwe Magona, in *Living, Loving, and Lying Awake at Night*, moves away from Head's and Gordimer's foci on the individual to concentrate on the community, as she explores the sociopolitical implications of black women's work and lives in apartheid South Africa. In this collection of short stories that can be read as a novel, with South African urban communities as a composite central character,[7] black maids in white households and black girls negotiating violent, racist, and sexist cultures get narrative space as they stumble toward liberation. M. J. Daymond's "Sindiwe Magona: Writing, Remembering, Selfhood, and Community in *Living, Loving, and Lying Awake at Night*" focuses on the self as speaker and writer, operating within the confines of the family and community that give it credence. Taking off from Magona's autobiographical works, Daymond locates *Living* in the South African subaltern effort to tell a life-in-the-community, which mimics the traditional stories associated with the family circle. However, the politics of overwhelmed black women working in white households tend to undermine the emergence of a strong community for liberatory purposes. The initiation of young girls into racist and patriarchal systems keeps reproducing violence against women, as the community hesitantly moves forward and ambivalently accepts the end of the pass laws.

Finally, in her Senegalese autobiografiction, evocative of Head's earlier account of migration, Ken Bugul in *Riwan ou le chemin de sable* addresses the intricate role of the "been-to" in the place of origin. The been-to's choice to return home and avoid straddling the schizophrenic African-European divide brings fresh insights into cultural and political awareness, in this instance opening up the discourse on polygyny as the complex politics of re-assimilation and husband-sharing unfold through the returnee's experience. In "Every Choice Is a Renunciation: Cultural Landmarks in Ken Bugul's *Riwan ou le chemin de sable*," Aissata Sidikou charts Bugul's fictionalized autobiographical trajectory as a been-to who returns to Senegal to become spiritually and culturally integrated into her community. Renouncing Europe, she establishes her identity and finds a place of her own, blurring lines that separate the westernized African from others. The central character's marriage into a polygynous household, a rehabilitative return to origins, enables her to interrogate the complexities of monogamy and polygamy, as Bugul advocates international conversations to disrupt discourses from the center.

I hope that the rupture generated by reading these iconic (even if iconoclastic) works and this companion volume will awaken interest in other books by these and other African women creative writers, thereby releasing the magical power of literature to lead the way to affirmation and transformation. On behalf of the contributors, I present to you *Twelve Best Books by African Women: Critical Readings*, a pathbreaking collaborative effort by twelve African women, all cultural been-tos, that is rewardingly provocative and helpful in grappling with these twelve telling tales. Twelve apostolic mothers, imbued with the authority inherent in our predecessors' works, we, as scholars, encourage continued intellectual activism. Spread the word: twelve women (and more) are writing the world.

Notes

1. The following works by women were also chosen for other categories:

Amadiume, Ifi (Nigeria). *Male Daughters, Female Husbands: Gender and Sex in an African Society.*

Doorkenoo, Efua (Ghana). *Cutting the Rose.*

Krog, Antjie (South Africa). *Country of My Skull.*

Mama, Amina (Nigeria). *Beyond the Mask: Race, Gender, and Identity.*

Al-Homi, Hayam Abbas (Egypt). *Adventures of a Breath.*

Tadjo, Veronique (Côte d'Ivoire). *Mamy Watta et le monstre.*

2. For a detailed study of this work, see Margaret Lenta, "A Break in the Silence: *The Long Journey of Poppie Nongena*," in *Momentum: On Recent*

South African Writing, ed. M. J. Daymond, J. U. Jacobs, and Margaret Lenta, 147–58 (Pietermaritzburg: University of Natal Press, 1984). Also, David Schalkwyk, "The Flight from Politics: An Analysis of the South African Reception of 'Poppie Nongena,'" *Journal of Southern African Studies* 12, no. 2 (April 1986): 183–95. Works by South African women writers—Bessie Head (1937–1986; *A Question of Power* [1974]), Nadine Gordimer (1923– ; *July's People* [1981]), and Elsa Joubert (1922– ; *The Long Journey of Poppie Nongena* [1980])—serve as precursors to contemporary, black South African women's writing. See also Ellen Kuzwayo (1914–2006), whose revisionary autobiography *Call Me Woman* (1985) is noteworthy in this context.

3. See 1 Kings 10:1–13 (King James Version) for an account of the visit. The Ethiopian version is in the *Kebra Nagast*: see Ogunyemi's *Juju Fission* (2007).

4. Following the rehabilitative spirit of Djebar's *Fantasia*, I shift from using Europe's economic, political, and cultural interactions with Africa as historical referents, implicit in the terms "precolonial" (consider *Africa reconfigured*), "colonial" (that is, *Africa resists*), and "postcolonial" (or *Africa regenerated*). This removal of Europe from the center of the discourse is necessary for a rebirth that entails trauma and the emergence of a new body.

5. Of particular interest is the Cameroonian Calixthe Beyala, who may have been left out of the "best" list because of the issues of plagiarism compromising her writing career.

6. The range of suggested titles indicates the diversity of the scholarly thrust:

> "African Women Writers and Their Texts: Twelve of the Best"
> "African Women Writers between Self and World: Twelve Best
>   Texts"
> "African Women's Writing: The Twentieth Century's Best"
> "Beyond the Silence: The Twelve Best Books by African Women"
> "A Century of Multiple Voices: Twelve Best Novels by African
>   Women"
> "A Crowning Achievement: The Twelve Best Literary Books by
>   African Women"
> "Daughters of the Words: The Twelve Best Books by African
>   Women"
> "Imagining, Engaging, and Recasting the World: African Women's
>   Twelve Best Literary Books"
> "Jarring Voices, Transforming Visions: Twelve Best Texts by African
>   Women"
> "Making the Cut: The Twelve Best Literary Books by African Women
>   Writers"

"Rethinking African Literature: The Twelve Best Books by African
  Women"
"The Twelve: Spreading the Word: Women Writing the African
  World"
"The Twelve: Spreading the Wor(l)d: The Best in African Women's
  Writing"
"Voices, Politics, and Poetics: Twelve African Female Writings"
"We Live, We Create, and Do Several Things Besides: African
  Women's Twelve Best Literary Books"
"Written into History: African Women's Twelve Best Literary Books"
"Writing the Nation, Self, and Community: The Twelve Best Literary
  Books by African Women"

7. Like Sherwood Anderson's *Winesburg, Ohio* (1919) and Jean Toomer's *Cane* (1923), one can teach *Living* as a collection of short stories or a novel.

Works Cited

Ogunyemi, Chikwenye Okonjo. 2007. *Juju Fission: Women's Alternative Fictions from the Sahara, the Kalahari and the Oases In-Between*. New York: Peter Lang.

Part 1

RECONFIGURATION

Rewriting the Script

1

Modernity, Gender, and Agency in Ama Ata Aidoo's *Anowa*

Nana Wilson-Tagoe

Anowa, Ama Ata Aidoo's drama of marriage in a nineteenth-century Akan world, is rarely explored in terms of the specific modernity of its period.[1] Yet, the play's text itself consistently insists on such a reading and would yield a wealth of insights about colonial modernity in Ghana, if examined within the ambivalent processes of modernity in the coastal Akan regions during the late nineteenth century. A conceptual understanding of historical modernity in a Ghanaian context would be crucial for such an exploration, though one should also heed Tom McCaskie's warning that "such conceptualizations are often a hermeneutics of the present-day [that is] feebly or only very generally rooted in historical evidence" (116). While a mapping of such modernities may admittedly be too elusive to be explored in any linear way, it is still possible to deduce specific historical intersections, the forces at work in these contexts, and the emergent themes in the modernity of particular periods.

A concept of modernity in sub-Saharan Africa is complicated by the fact that modernity is generally perceived as a philosophical concept grounded in European intellectual history and in intersections between modern ideas of individual freedom and a developing industrial world in eighteenth-century Europe. Considered in these purely temporal terms and defined culturally as a specific form of European rationality, "modernity" poses enormous problems for an understanding of African modernities and the nature of African agency in the colonial encounter. For it leaves virtually no conceptual space for other mediating histories, and within its contexts Africans remain just as they were perceived in Enlightenment discourses: as a people outside "the rational and moral culture of modernity" (Gikandi 2002, 137) whose entry into modernity was predicated on their colonization by a hegemonic Europe.

Because such a perspective denies the entire thrust of Africa's precolonial and colonial histories, modernity has been a highly contested concept in African intellectual and literary history. African and Africanist philosophers[2] and writers have redefined it subjectively, seeing it in contrast to its European formulation, that is, as linked to the dynamics of centuries of movement, change, and innovation within Africa itself, while including its more traumatic encounter with Europe. We should see modernity in Africa, then, not only from the point of view of imposed colonial structures and the transformative force of modernization, but also in terms of collisions, struggles, and negotiations between Africa and Europe that threw up their own violence, confusions, tensions, and ambivalences yet ultimately shaped the character of modernity for both Africa and Europe. Such a dynamic, in all its violence and fractures, provides what Albert Paolini calls "a framework of possibilities" that provides "a theater of action and reaction for a whole series of agents and groups it encounters along the way. Not only does it force people to engage with otherness, it requires them to examine their own circumstance and worldview in its march forward, turning the forward back upon itself in the process" (9–10).

Aidoo opens herself to these possibilities when she situates *Anowa* within five centuries of Akan-European encounters in coastal Ghana and in the specific colonial contexts of Akan-British relations in the late nineteenth century. Recreating the silences and unfulfilled potentialities of this past from the vantage position of an uncertain postcolonial present is for Aidoo another way of engaging with modernity and nationhood in postcolonial Ghana. Akan coastal society in the nineteenth century was the focus of a particular convergence of economic and social forces that created the sense of a new modern culture. The activities of European nations within a trading infrastructure created by coastal Akans themselves and by two hundred years of informal relationships before formal colonization meant that Akan-European relations on the coast were largely shaped internally and dictated by events on the coast itself.[3] Within such a unique context, it is possible to see modernity not merely as a narrative of crisis, opposition, and negativity but also as a complex and ambivalent process that could potentially offer communities and subjects access to agency and self-transformation. As Ulf Hannerz has argued persuasively, "modernity may give people access to technologies and symbolic resources for dealing with their own ideas, managing their own culture in new ways" (547). It can in this sense be at least potentially empowering for third world cultures.

In *Anowa*, Aidoo's gaze ensures that the nineteenth-century modern culture on the Akan coast is made contemporaneous with the dilemmas of nation formation in postcolonial Ghana. The play's collective and individual dramas raise questions about cultural processes in times of crisis and examine the Akan community's capacity for agency and self-transformation in the conflictual yet fluid conditions on the coast in the 1870s.[4] It is significant, then, that though the drama centers on the relationship of a husband and wife, it is equally focused on the larger community and is mediated by questions of history, modernity, gender, and sexuality. All these levels of exploration as well as the codes that structure the drama must be interconnected for a fruitful interpretation of the play's multiple meanings.

On the face of it, the story is straightforward and linear: the protagonist, Anowa, insists on choosing her own husband as well as the terms on which she would relate to him as a wife. Buoyed by an egalitarian vision and a sense of newness, the couple, Anowa and Kofi, begin their marriage in great hope as they leave their village to make their fortunes trading with British traders in the developing capitalist economy in coastal Ghana. The marriage falters, however, when Kofi buys slaves to help with their expanding business and counters Anowa's objections by asserting a male dominance and threatening to send her back to the village. Disappointed and disoriented, Anowa now sees a connection between her husband's exploitation of slaves and the greed that made her community complicit with the bigger crime of the slave trade. In a dream, she takes on the historical burden of the slave mother and relives the moments of enslavement as a terrible wrenching and a loss of her community's creative potency. From this illumination she is able to connect Kofi Ako's sexual impotence with his acquisitiveness and greed and to publicly expose him. Shamed, Kofi Ako kills himself, and Anowa, still disoriented and dazed, drowns herself. The tragedy unfolds against the unequal marriage of Anowa's father, Osam, and her mother, Badua, and in the context of a community represented by the opposing views of an old man and an old woman. The two contradictory perspectives—the old woman's fixed ideas about women's place in society and the old man's more fluid view of change and possibility—dramatize the paradoxes within which the play imagines change and transformation in a developing modern world.

On an allegorical level, the play's story—based on the archetypal tale of the beautiful girl who rejects all her suitors only to end up marrying a monster[5]—cautions against flirtations with the unfamiliar and transgressions of normative codes of behavior. In placing this traditional narrative within the new capitalist configuration and reworking it in a different genre, Aidoo signals a dialogue between the Akan community's cultural ethos and the changing modern world on the coast. It is in the play of this dialogism that the drama explores social crisis, the instability of gender discourses, and the possibilities for agency in a modern world tainted by slavery.

The play, then, operates on a far more modernist and discursive level than may appear on the surface. The dialogic relation between the legend structured in the folktale and the modern legend[6] of Anowa ensures that the drama combines three temporalities of the modern: the history of slavery on the Fante coast, the new Fante-British collaboration in the political and economic arena, and the postcolonial period from which Aidoo rewrites the history of modernity in the tragic drama of Anowa and Kofi Ako. All the three periods intersect throughout the drama as connected parts in the narrative of modernity. Indeed, the play's logic demands that the bigger crime of slavery be paralleled with the new collaboration with the British as two sides of a fundamentally exploitative relation that may be explored to yield new meanings.

It is for this reason that the old man's history in the prologue, for all its awareness of fissures in the emerging modernity, may still be seen as flawed, evasive, and incomplete. What Vincent Odamtten sees as the old man's "mythopoetic celebration" (51) of the state of Abura may at another level be judged as complacent and uncritical.[7] His history is thus only one narrative among several in a dramatic structure that forces the entire community in *Anowa* to engage with various narratives and dimensions of its history and culture in a changing world. The objective conditions of modernity should thus not merely be seen in nationalistic terms as the impact of modernization and self-interest on a resisting Fante traditional ethos. It should also be seen in terms of the shifting interpretations of traditional beliefs in a changing modern world.

Odamtten is persuasive when he argues that the old man and the old woman (the mouth that eats pepper and salt) represent the antagonistic contradictions of traditional society (50–51). But our perception of contradiction is heightened even more sharply by the proximity of a developing "modern" world on the coast and by competing interpretations of social reality both in the village and in the new town. The pattern of contrasting perspectives enacted by the old pair is thus repeated in other formations throughout the play. Paired characters present antagonistic perspectives, revealing a much less stable social ethos than may be immediately apparent. For instance, Anowa's parents do not speak with one voice about the responsibilities of a father in the community's matrilineal system. Nor do they hold a unified view of the meaning of a priestess's vocation. Badua (Anowa's mother) interprets the matrilineal system to reinforce paternal responsibility while limiting the boundaries of possibility for women, and Osam undermines this responsibility while still striving for dominance as a husband and a man. Similar competing interpretations in the exchanges of Anowa and Kofi reinforce an ongoing social and ideological flux and suggest that changes in the social and economic order generated by capitalist structures and centuries of trading alliances have had a corresponding impact on other forms of human relationships and on representations of power.

Within this flux, Anowa's vision of marriage presents a competing new meaning that confirms the old man's suggestion that "the heavens might show something to children of a latter day which was hidden from them of [old]" (101). What the vision offers is another definition of marriage in which husband and wife share work, histories, public commitment, and fantasies even in a world caught in new forms of self-interest and power. Aidoo offers this perspective not as a vision divorced from economic and political arrangements but as a novel way of rethinking social reality in terms of gender. For if ideas and values around biological sexual difference originate in a society's history, modes of production, and symbolic order, then seeing the world through these values is also a way of understanding how gender works, how it is linked to politics and power, and how it may change.

As a possibility in the play, however, this vision remains fragile, not only because it competes with changing views of womanhood and an emasculating new capitalist modernity, but also because it must contend with the protagonist's many-layered selves and gendered identity. For only the reader knows at this point that the vision will be tested—that Anowa herself will have to grow up, and that growth will involve both a confrontation with the new modern terrain and a critical perception of the links between colonial modernity and loss of autonomy, between enslavement and impotence, and between a community's gender values and its capacity to transform itself in times of crisis.

The highway as both a physical location and a metaphor of movement is central to Anowa's growth, especially in the way it connects the couple to the economies of the new modern culture and at the same time links them to the discourses of the village. It is thus within the dominant values of colonial modernity *and* the residual elements of a traditional culture in crisis that Anowa's vision must be negotiated. How can an egalitarian conception of marriage (akin to the original terms of Akan matriliny) be sustained in a world that has acquired different markers of value and new languages of power? What risks does this vision take when shared with a man caught confusedly between bourgeois ideas of labor, class, and power and bastardized notions of masculinity in a matrilineal system? The play creates a suitable framework for this negotiation. A dialogic principle runs through the drama buoyed by the interactive character of drama itself. In drama, differentiated speech can be more easily exploited to suggest how meanings struggle against other meanings and how change occurs in specific historical and social contexts.

Such a process occurs continually in *Anowa* and is intensified in the second phase of the play where Anowa and Kofi confront the contingent world of the modern terrain. The world of home and village, however, hovers within the vicinity of the action, and within this juxtaposition the play widens the context of struggle not only to provide a sociocultural referent for assumptions about gender but also to reinterpret discourses of home and identity in the context of the couple's experiences in the new modern space. The dynamics of this struggle stem, then, from contrasting perceptions of modernity and different relations to the community's meaning-constituting system. While Anowa probes the symbolic order and seeks a new language for agency within a new reality, Kofi merely resorts to seemingly normative meanings and is impatient with Anowa's restless search for new meanings: "Where else have you been but here? Why can't you live by what you know, what you see?" (98). Anowa's restlessness, which the play metaphorizes into an all-embracing quest for agency, is thus, in Kofi's view, only the sign of an unfulfilled priestly destiny. Her inability to see herself in the future is, in Kofi's view, a result of her dislocation as a childless woman—rather than, as the play suggests, of her despair at the fragility of her vision in a new world of self-interest and individualism.

Odamtten makes a crucial point about these differing perspectives when he argues that Kofi misreads "the personal and public currents that characterize the confluence of historical streams at which he and Anowa have been caught" (71). But Kofi's problem is not only that he interprets his actions and predicaments only in terms of the power relations between him and his wife and between "colonizer and colonized."[8] It is also his inability to grasp the totality of the currents that constitute the modern context and his failure to rethink his old culture in new ways. The burden of interpreting these larger connections and exploring possibilities for agency falls on Anowa, and it is in her dialogue with other characters and discourses that we can read the relationship between modernity, culture, and agency in *Anowa*. Anowa's confrontations with people and ideas are thus crucial throughout the play, and it is she who echoes the play's central assertion that it is possible to control and shape one's own responses to modernity rather than be contained and driven by its exigencies.

The context of modernity, as the drama is at pains to emphasize, may be potentially empowering, and, as Ulf Hannerz suggests, can provide people with the resources to rethink their culture in new ways. Competing perceptions of social reality are thus crucial throughout *Anowa*. For instance, in her constant struggles with Kofi over meaning and interpretation, Anowa maintains a view of labor as something inseparable from the self, deploying an Akan ethic as an alternative to Kofi's capitalist perception of labor as an exploitable category outside the self. These opposing views acquire a crucial resonance that connects with almost all the major themes in the play.

> Kofi Ako: I do not see the reason why I should go walking forests, climbing mountains and crossing rivers to buy skins when I have bought slaves to do just that for me.

> Anowa: . . . My husband, we did not have to put the strength of our bodies into others. We should not have bought the slaves. (114)

Anowa's insight here, which is also the play's truth, is linked to an old Akan ethic that seems to have been forgotten in the strident self-interest of the new order. Exploiting the labor of others, it is suggested, leads to a depletion of inner resources and energies that can enfeeble the individual, just as slavery itself is, as the old man intimates, "something that is against the natural state of man and the purity of his worship of the gods" (100). The convergence of ideas in the views of Anowa and the old man helps to position Akan ethical concepts in the new modern space as possible mediations in a world that is rapidly acquiring new measures of value. Such interventions work to capture the unrealized potential of the past and posit alternative new meanings for the present and the future.

The link that Anowa makes between capitalist exploitation and slavery in this sense connects the old slavery of the past (the bigger crime) with the individualism and self-interest of the modern culture and with the changing relations between men and women exemplified in the play of masculine power in her own marriage. It is from such contexts that Anowa reimagines her world and explores possibilities for agency. When she constructs herself as a wayfarer (who is not different from any of Kofi's slaves), she assumes the subordinate status and marginality of slaves and women in her world and is therefore able to interpret both the old world and the developing new world from outside the positions of their dominant powers. "The 'right' to signify from the periphery of authorized power and privilege," Homi Bhabha has argued in a different context, "is resourced by the power of tradition to be reinscribed through the conditions of contingency and contradictoriness that attend upon the lives of those who are in the minority" (241). Traditions can be reinscribed and renewed in this way because social symbols and meanings are never fixed, however much normative systems attempt to limit their metaphoric possibilities. Those who feel their subordinate locations within them can challenge and mobilize them in new and different ways to recreate themselves.

Anowa's critique of home is thus at the same time a reinvention of home. For her, what defines and renews "homes and homes" is not (as her father, Osam, believes) the myths and rituals that consolidate the foundations of home and identity, but our ability to confront the multiple configurations of discourse and power that constitute us as subjects and whatever new knowledge or language we can deploy to rethink and reinterpret them. In giving this power of reinvention to

Anowa, Aidoo accepts that the individual's self-reflexivity and powers of perception can become an important basis for renewing a community in which the consensus is already in disarray. Anowa's struggle for agency, especially in the final phase of the drama, becomes, then, part of a wider political and national struggle that is explored through the framework of gender. Commentators on Aidoo's works often remark on the connections that she always makes between gender, history, and economics. But, in *Anowa*, the framework of gender is a much more radical strategy for rethinking the social reality as a prelude to a search for agency.

The notion of agency, whether viewed as an individual or social issue, is never a given essence but rests rather on historical specificities and on how we are constituted as subjects and as a people. Feminist poststructuralists have framed its crucial questions in ways that provide a context within and against which we can examine issues of modernity and agency in *Anowa:* "Given the understanding of our subjection by discourse, can we really take seriously the idea that we are also in turn constitutive of our social world and ourselves or is the idea of the constitutive agent a myth that belongs only in a humanist framework?" (B. Davies, 77) Framing questions of agency in these terms, however, leaves very little conceptual space for exploring those processes of subjectification and sociopolitical transformation central to postcolonial and feminist perspectives. In *Anowa*, Aidoo reframes these poststructuralist questions in provocative and emancipatory terms, recognizing at the same time the conditions against which agency may be claimed in a developing colonial and "patriarchal" context. The drama, particularly in its final phase, turns on how a positive agency may be teased out of a colonial and modern context that might appear to compromise and negate it. How, for instance, would the possibilities of Anowa's vision be negotiated against the discourses that constitute her as colonial and female and through which she perhaps constitutes herself?

The play's final movement provides both a context and a structure for exploring these questions and is thus the most intense and modernist in representation. It seems that the urgent crisis of this modernity cannot be represented only within a straightforward chronological and objective rendering. To understand the crisis of modern culture in this late-nineteenth-century world, characters would need to work backwards through five centuries of history and reckon with suppressed histories, buried memories, and the reflexive power of subjective experience. Simon Gikandi has argued that "modernism was valued by African writers only to the extent that it enabled them to represent their cultures and peoples as entities and subjects that were essentially modern" (2004, 337). Thus, while they eschewed some of the excesses of European modernism, they still had to deal with modern crises that could no longer be explored in straightforward realism.

In A*nowa*, Aidoo faced the challenge of exploring modernity in the genre of drama, a social art that offers a direct representation of its reality and which unlike fiction depends on the power of spectacle to convey minute nuances in meaning. To present the depth of the modern crisis in the play's nineteenth-century community, Aidoo relies as well on other techniques of representation, particularly from modernist fiction. The climactic movements of the drama convey their impact and meanings through the power of dreams, not only to activate memory but also to connect themes by presenting different historical moments synchronically. The combination of modernist strategies and oral dramatic forms is, then, symptomatic of Aidoo's paradoxical presentation of modernity as on one hand a crisis and on the other hand a possibility that presents technologies for reinventing self and culture.

The thrust of the drama in this final movement has to do, therefore, with ways of understanding and negotiating the modern condition. It works toward a communal catharsis, yet invents multiple perspectives, and privileges symbols and subjective experiences as sources of illumination. Commentators on the play have not made enough of the stage directions of this movement as integral expressions of the play's meaning as a performance. Carol Boyce Davies has observed rightly that Kofi's big house in the coastal town of Oguaa is an "external reference for the entrenchment of colonial power and male dominance" (61). But the layout of the house also projects a confused syncretism whose tensions, contradictions, and oppositions appear lost on Kofi even as they provoke serious questions in the audience. There is a sense, then, in which the discourse in this movement is as much about transforming oneself and one's culture in modernity as it is about male dominance. Indeed, the play invites us to see Kofi's new dominance in ironic juxtaposition with his unexamined sense of power in a world already driven by bigger forms of power.

There is a decided irony in the play's strategic positioning of Kofi's portrait, the painting of his totem bird, and the picture of Queen Victoria, for the easy accommodation this parallel placement suggests is also full of antinomies. What is the ritual force of a totem if it exists only as a painting and a decoration? What is the measure of its self-apprehension if it sits unproblematically with the very force that denies its autonomy and history? These questions beg other questions of major thematic relevance: How have Kofi and the community that celebrates him made the transition from the unique situation on the coast prior to 1874[9] to the new colonial context in which Kofi is a powerful player? What is modernity in those colonial conditions "where its imposition is itself the denial of historical freedom, civic autonomy and the 'ethical' choice of refashioning" (Bhabha, 241)?

Aidoo's modernist privileging of subjective experience finds its intensification in this section, and it is Anowa, not Kofi, who is given the discursive space to seize the genealogy of modernity and open it to critique, translation, and reinvention. Thus, throughout this movement, Anowa grows increasingly "possessed" of vision as she grasps and questions the antinomies of the new modern culture. The problematic explored in this nineteenth-century context may be understood, then, from the play's move to examine moments of African-European relations on the coast and their hidden significance. What, for instance, does the drama gain from Anowa's recollection of the big houses of her grandmother's time and from her subsequent dream just at the very moment that Kofi is paraded as the new power on the coast?

In merging two temporalities of the "modern," the drama creates a subtext that rehearses the possibility for agency by opening up and interrogating interlinked modern contexts. Kofi's big house and the big houses of the past are linked to the predatory propensities of global capitalism, to slavery and colonialism, to the community's perverted fertility and the discontinuities in its history. Historical discontinuity is a negative force here not because the drama seeks a simplistic bridging of African and African diaspora history but because discontinuity represents an amnesia about the past which must be broken if the community is to understand its location in modernity and refashion a world out of it.

To refashion a world in modernity is for Aidoo also a search for agency. It involves new ways of imagining community and relationships, new ways of reshaping existing discourses, breaking old restrictive patterns, and inventing new symbols and languages. If gender appears the most apt framework for such explorations, it is because social relations constructed through gender often structure other forms of relationships in economics and politics and have wider application for the entire community. On the face of it, presenting Anowa as the archetypal mother of slaves and the figure of violated motherhood in the play's final section may appear like a rehearsal of the proverbial image of woman as impassive symbol of the violated nation. But Aidoo's is a much more innovative strategy that establishes Anowa as the priestess (wiser now than the wise ones) who can tell her community truths about itself.

In the working out of this symbolism, the relationship between victimhood, motherhood, and agency becomes a far-reaching and radical correlation that moves beyond the agency of the mother as merely the source of human continuity. Naana Banyiwa Horne has explored a particular concept of mothering and agency that moves beyond the ordinary agency of the womb as a source of human continuity. But Horne should have expanded the perceptual, visionary, and political possibilities of her concept, particularly in her discussion of *Anowa*. What she sees as the collapse of the slave mother's maternal agency may be symptomatic of a general failure of motherhood in the play. But Anowa's reliving of this collapse is significant not only because "she mobilizes the dispossessed to strike their oppressor down" (325), but, crucially, because she takes on the much larger burden of repositioning her community in history. The ability to challenge existing discourses and mobilize them in new ways is one of the most forceful acts of agency in history. Anowa's dream experience of violated motherhood is thus not merely a restatement of African motherhood. It is a conduit to a deeper perception of wider currents in history.

In taking on the role of the slave mother, she repossesses the history of the Atlantic slavery as a priestess who can illuminate its wider implications in three centuries of Akan, European, and African diaspora relations. These missing links skew the old man's history in the prologue and stall his understanding of the modern condition. Restating them through Anowa at a crucial moment in the drama allows the community to engage critically with its slave past as part of its new modernity. The play's dramatic action itself enacts this multi-spaced history by inserting a diaspora space and experience within the immediate context of the play, symbolically bridging a historical gap and breaking the amnesia that prevents the community from grasping its location in modernity.

It is possible, then, as Paul Gilroy has argued, "to take the Atlantic as one single, complex unit of analysis" in our discussion of the modern world and "use it to produce an explicitly transnational and intercultural perspective" (15). Aidoo dramatizes this potential of "a black Atlantic world" and would concur with Gilroy's view that a conception of the Atlantic "as a cultural and political system has been forced on black historiography and intellectual history by the historical matrix in which plantation slavery—'capitalism with its clothes off'—was one special moment" (15). Gilroy's problematic, as Aidoo would recognize, is a central and crucial one for understanding the nature of modernity in the black Atlantic world. A mutual exploration of how "ethnicities and political cultures have been made anew" in this matrix would be significant for understanding social and cultural transformations in both Africa and its diaspora. In *The Black Atlantic*, however, Gilroy literally glosses over African transformations, freezing Africa in a premodern time as a cultural ethos that is drastically transformed in the African diaspora and as a category that must be elevated and civilized in the course of the black American's search for selfhood.

It can be argued that Aidoo's focus on modernity in nineteenth-century Ghana works in an opposite direction to Gilroy's by drawing both the Atlantic and the African diaspora into its exploration of modernity and agency in *Anowa*. For why would the play achieve its climactic moment just when the community's amnesia about its slave past is finally broken? I want to argue that this is the occasion when the play's disconnected narratives, isolated symbols, suppressed pasts, and unexamined discourses are finally confronted, illuminated, and thematically connected. Anowa's remembrance becomes a significant subtext that links the symbolism of violated motherhood in the time of slavery to the new images of infertility and impotence in the new modern culture. Linking them in this way presents them as variants of the same dislocation, generated by capitalist modernity and its forms of enslavement and exploitation. In this regard, the link that the drama consistently makes between the status of slave and the new status of woman in the nineteenth-century dispensation forces us to recognize pernicious links between gender, sexuality, and the entire system of social and economic relations within the wider world. The failure to make these crucial connections is, as Aidoo signals, part of the unfulfilled potentialities of Akan history in the nineteenth century. Her drama addresses these in a new reading of the period in which these unrecognized histories are made part of the crisis of modernity both in the nineteenth-century world of *Anowa* and in Aidoo's own postcolonial time.

It is the memory of this history that reminds us of Africa's location both inside and outside capitalist modernity, and this knowledge illuminates how colonial and postcolonial Africans can position themselves in the future as agents and subjects. Naming this history (as Anowa compels her grandmother to do) is also in itself an act of restoration that connects diaspora space and history to the historical narratives of Akan and Ghanaian history. There is a sense, in fact, in which the diaspora theme in *Anowa* is taken up in almost all of Aidoo's writing. In *The Dilemma of a Ghost*, Aidoo's focus is on how diaspora and African pasts can be acknowledged and reinvented in a new pan-African relationship in contemporary times. In *Our Sister Killjoy*, the emphasis is on how the history of slavery can illuminate the postcolonial condition of African and diaspora people caught in new forms of death as migrants in the margins of a new global world.

The perceptual possibilities of these connections are immense. In *Anowa*, they are evident in the clarity and "priestly" insights that Anowa acquires after recalling her childhood memories and her dream. A new reflexive authority seems to drive her actions and utterances from this point on. For instance, in locating the beginnings of women's subordination within marriage and therefore separating a concept of woman from the category of wife, Anowa probes the convergence of an Akan matrilineal system and an acquisitive new modernity on the Akan coast. She hints at possible ruptures that might explain the dominant and oppressive attitudes of Kofi and particularly his anxiety to transform her into his "glorious wife" and "the contented mother of [his] children" (99). "I hear in other lands a woman is nothing. And they let her know this from the day of her birth. But here, O my spirit mother, they let a girl grow up as she pleases until she is married. And then she is like any woman anywhere: in order for her man to be a man, she must not think, she must not talk" (112). Anowa's words encode their own implications. For if in an Akan matrilineal system a woman was always "something," how do we explain the incongruence in the transition from woman to wife? How can this new situation be reexamined and translated in other ways? Odamtten (quoting the sociologist Meyer Fortes) argues rightly that marriage within a matrilineal society was viewed as a contract between equals that "allow[ed] the conjugal relationship to be envisaged as a bundle of separable rights and bonds rather than as a unitary all-or-none tie"

(71). But the anxiety Anowa expresses above has more to do with a new interpretation of manhood that requires the suppression of the range of women's abilities and their capacity to think and question. Molara Ogundipe-Leslie remarks on a similar transformation of woman in marriage. As she argues, "a woman as daughter or sister has greater status in her own lineage. Married she becomes a possession, voiceless and often rightless except for what accrues to her through her children" (501). But Ogundipe-Leslie's critique exposes the contradictions of a patriarchal system whose dynamics have always revolved around such constructions of women. Aidoo's focus in *Anowa* is more on the specific modern conditions that generate transformations in the conception of woman as wife. It is therefore doubly centered on gender and on the struggle between indigenous and modern forces as they affected relations between men and women and on how these can be rethought in imaginative literature.

In *Anowa*, possibilities for grasping this new phenomenon and contesting its implications reside in the way the drama organizes its resolution. While it focuses on and privileges Anowa's inner perceptions, it also presents these in public as part of a communal sharing of experience that achieves a catharsis. As drama, it progresses from Anowa's inner tensions and dialogues with herself to a wider arena of performance in which she co-opts others to bear witness and make judgments. The public exposure of Kofi's impotence becomes a spectacle within which spectators are influenced by the perspectives from which they watch and by Anowa's communication of her side of the conflict. The funeral song played throughout this movement not only suggests links between the ornate house and Kofi's impotence, but also portends the ominous deaths of the protagonists. The power of this spectacle to register both Anowa's desperation and the public dispersal of her private conflicts is often glided over in critical commentaries. Yet, it corroborates another level of presentation in which the uncanny connection made between slavery, capitalist greed, male domination, and creative and sexual death works to reinterpret the dominant and now "normative" discourse of power differently in the new context of drama.

In using the tragedy of Anowa and Kofi to read modernity on the Akan coast in the nineteenth century, Aidoo signals a new legend of the time that may be close in outline to the traditional folktale yet is drastically different in political and social thrust. In reinventing the tale as a social, political, and gender discourse, Aidoo takes the profoundly feminist standpoint of making a woman's vision and subjective experience the channel for reading the political and social terrain. In this, she redefines the very nature of the political, moving it away from its male and public construction as governance and power into the daily relationships between men and women.

To make such a claim is not to suggest that Aidoo locates vision and political authority unproblematically in *Anowa*. The political authority given Anowa in the play is not absolute, since, even as a visionary, she reveals a complex combination of desires that create tensions in the crucial burden she bears as the liminal figure with a political and transformative vision. On the face of it, the explicit social context in the text points to her dominant opposition to Kofi's capitalist ideology and his particular construction of her as a woman and a wife. Yet Anowa's own unconscious desire to be a mother and a wife point to conflicting desires that complicate her dominant ideological position in the play. On one hand, she recognizes the futility of motherhood in a new social order that permits the enslavement of other people's children (112). On the other, she betrays her maternal desires when she gazes longingly and abnormally at another woman's child, and is hesitant to return to the village because she has no child from her marriage. The obvious tension between Anowa's political vision and her maternal longing reveals the extent to which she is both a powerful visionary and at the same time an ordinary Akan woman desirous of seeing her family line continued through a child of her own.

We recognize a similar split between ideology and desire at certain points in the final moments of the play, when we are unsure whether Anowa's disorientation and hysteria derive from her revulsion at Kofi's new capitalist ideology or from disappointment at his rejection of her. Such splits in identity (which can perhaps only be meaningfully interpreted within a framework of psychoanalysis) reveal the complex heterogeneous identity behind Anowa's dominant presence as the main source of vision in the play. To a major extent, they also explain the play's problematic ending, where Anowa uncovers the play's ultimate truth and at the same time betrays her own vulnerability by drowning herself soon after her husband has committed suicide.

The unique configuration of modern culture on the Akan coast in the nineteenth century provides a convenient space for exploring modernity beyond externally imposed colonial structures and local oppositions. For there is another sense in which this context of modernity may be seen as a process of mutual appropriations and negotiations.

In contextualizing the action of *Anowa* in this world from 1870 to 1875, Aidoo explores the ramifications of modernity by showing how changes in the economic and social order impact on other forms of human relations and on representations of power. This period represents two different contexts of Akan relations with the British and thus offers an open space for probing how colonialism mediated the generally fluid and informal relations between the Akans and the British after 1874. Did the unique negotiations of these contexts hold possibilities for a different ordering of the modern world? Aidoo seems to work with such a question and to tease out those unfulfilled potentialities, ones that may throw light on our understanding of postcolonial nation-formation.

In exploring *Anowa* within these sets of questions and from the point of view of gender and agency, this essay examines Aidoo's play as both an imagined history and as a hermeneutics of the present. It reinterprets the social and individual crises of modernity from contemporary perspectives and within wider global contexts that extend their meaning and significance. The logic of *Anowa* itself insists on our reading ruptures and discontinuities in history and the amnesia about them as part of the crisis of modern culture on the Akan coast in the late nineteenth century. My essay has therefore focused considerable attention on the alternative meanings that the play elicits by bridging gaps between different periods of African-European relations, especially as they relate to the Atlantic slavery and the dispersal of African people. The notion of agency that frames my discussion enhances the play's paradoxical conception of modernity as both a crisis and a possibility. I have worked with an understanding of agency as the ability to reposition oneself and one's world, both in history and in discourse, as a way of constructing new subjectivities. The essay's focus on unexamined links between the new prosperity and the violence of the new order creates a critical reading of modernity and suggests at the same time that it is possible to construct one's own relation to it. The framework of gender and the essay's reading of the social world work to illuminate how the ideologies that regulate gender also structure other forms of relationships in economics and politics. This kind of illumination, as I have implied, is not facilitated by the analysis of gender alone but by a feminist political position committed to investigating and rethinking relations of power between men and women.

Notes

1. Vincent Odamtten's *The Art of Ama Ata Aidoo* is a notable exception, though it is much more focused on the historicity of *Anowa* than on the modernity of its context. This particular thrust may explain why the Atlantic world of the African diaspora has very little space in the discussion of the play.

2. See, for instance, Gyekye, *Tradition and Modernity;* Wiredu, *Philosophy and African Culture;* and Rathbone, "West Africa: Modernity and Modernization."

3. See Agbodeka, *African Politics and British Policy in the Gold Coast, 1868–1900,* vii.

4. For a fuller historical account of this period see Priestley, *West African Trade and Coastal Society;* and McCarthy, *Social Change and the Growth of British Power in the Gold Coast.*

5. For a discussion of different appropriations of this common tale, see Opoku-Agyemang, "'A Girl Marries a Monkey.'"

6. In the play's prologue the old "historian" of the community speaks of Anowa in the past tense and in legendary terms, intimating that the ramifications of her tragedy have become a point of reference for the Fante community.

7. Aidoo's allusions to specific dates are more than just chronological markers; they demand the kind of historical literacy that can decipher the underlying ironies behind them. For instance, in the 1870s the state of Abura was in ruins, and this condition requires a much more radical scrutiny of past and present history than the old man is able and prepared to undertake.

8. Odamtten suggests this, but there is no indication in the play that Kofi is ever fully aware of the dynamics of colonial relations. Indeed, his innocence is in line with Aidoo's statement in the stage directions that, unlike Anowa, who grows up, Kofi merely expands.

9. Aidoo appears to be raising the same questions about the unrealized possibilities of this period that historians have raised from different perspectives. For instance, as Priestley (143) asks, "Why when Africans so thoroughly dominated the British at the beginning of the nineteenth century, and in the absence of any military conquest on the part of the British either real or threatened, were the British able to declare themselves to be the government of the Gold Coast colony by 1874?"

Works Cited

Agbodeka, Francis. 1971. *African Politics and British Policy in the Gold Coast, 1868–1900: A Study in the Forms and Force of Protest.* London: Longman.

Aidoo, Ama Ata. 1970/1983. *The Dilemma of a Ghost and Anowa.* London: Longman.

Bhabha, Homi. 1994. *The Location of Culture.* London: Routledge.

Davies, Bronwyn. 2000. *A Body of Writing: 1990–1999.* Lanham, MD: AltaMira.

Davies, Carole Boyce. 1994. *Black Women, Writing and Identity: Migrations of the Subject.* London: Routledge.

Gikandi, Simon. 2002. "Reason, Modernity and the African Crisis." In *African Modernities: Entangled Meanings in Current Debate*, ed. Jan-Georg Deutsch, Peter Probst, and Heike Schmidt, 135–57. Oxford: James Currey.

———. 2004. "Modernity and Modernism." In *Encyclopedia of African Literature*, ed. Simon Gikandi. London: Routledge.

Gilroy, Paul. 1993. *The Black Atlantic: Modernity and Double Consciousness.* London: Verso.

Gyekye, Kwame. 1997. *Tradition and Modernity: Philosophical Reflections on the African Experience.* New York: Oxford University Press.

Hannerz, Ulf. 1987. "The World in Creolization." *Africa* 57 (4): 546–59.

Horne, Naana Banyiwa. 1999. "The Politics of Mothering: Multiple Subjectivities and Gendered Discourse in Aidoo's Plays." In *Emerging Perspectives on Ama Ata Aidoo*, ed. Ada Azodo and Gay Wilentz, 303–31. Trenton, NJ: Africa World Press.

McCarthy, Mary. 1983. *Social Change and the Growth of British Power in the Gold Coast: The Fante State, 1807–1874.* Lanham, MD: University Press of America.

McCaskie, Tom. 2000. *Asante Identities: History and Modernity in an African Village, 1850–1950.* Edinburgh: Edinburgh University Press.

Odamtten, Vincent. 1994. *The Art of Ama Ata Aidoo: Polylectics and Reading against Neocolonialism.* Gainesville: University of Florida Press.

Ogundipe-Leslie, Molara. 1984. "Not Spinning on the Axis of Maleness." In *Sisterhood Is Global*, ed. Robin Morgan, 498–504. New York: Anchor.

Opoku-Agyemang, Naana Jane. 1999. "'A Girl Marries a Monkey': The Folktale as an Expression of Value and Change in Society." In *Arms Akimbo: Africana Women in Contemporary Literature*, ed. Janice Liddell and Yakini Belinda Kemp. Gainesville: University Press of Florida.

Paolini, Albert J. 1999. *Navigating Modernity: Postcolonialism, Identity, and International Relations.* London: Lynne Rienner.

Priestley, Margaret. 1969. *West African Trade and Coastal Society: A Family Study*. London: Oxford University Press.

Rathbone, Richard. 2002. "West Africa: Modernity and Modernization." In *African Modernities: Entangled Meanings in Current Debate*, ed. Jan-Georg Deutsch, Peter Probst, and Heike Schmidt, 19–30. Oxford: James Currey.

Wiredu, Kwasi. 1980. *Philosophy and African Culture*. Cambridge: Cambridge University Press.

2

Charting the Nation/Charting History

The Power of Language in
Assia Djebar's *Fantasia: An Algerian Cavalcade*

Nada Halloway

In the final movements in *Fantasia: An Algerian Cavalcade*, Assia Djebar refers to the French language as the "enemy's language." This language, she continues, "was formerly used to entomb my people. When I write it I feel like the messenger of old who bore a sealed missive which might sentence him to death or to the dungeon" (215). This hostility is tempered, in the early chapters, by the young narrator's perception of French as the language of love and freedom, an idea that was quite common among proponents of negritude. While they would acknowledge its role in the subjugation of the colonies and their peoples, writers like Léopold Sédar Senghor nevertheless embraced the language as one of liberty. Senghor, in his appreciation for French, argued for its universality: "We express ourselves in French since French has a universal vocation and since our message is also addressed to French people and others. In our languages the halo that surrounds the words is by nature merely that of sap and blood; French words send out thousands of rays like diamonds" (quoted in Ngũgĩ, 19). This position is explicit in the opening movements when Djebar posits it as the language of freedom and love in the "Three Cloistered Girls" chapter.

These girls are imprisoned by a patriarchal culture that defines a man's honor in terms of the perceived purity of the women in his household, by the veils they wear, and by Islamic culture and tradition. The girls are, however, "released" from their prison when they write: "these girls, though confined to their house, were writing; were writing letters to men; to men in the four corners of the world; of the Arab world naturally" (11). Having attended primary school, the girls were proficient enough in French not only to proofread their father's invoices but to write their pen pals. French afforded them a measure of freedom, if not physically, then imaginatively, as they built an alternate world/reality that was counter to their everyday lives. The letters delivered by the postman became their lovers, as the youngest sister and Djebar, curled up in bed together, "imagined [the] written words whirling furtively around, about to twine invisible snares around [our] adolescent bodies" (13). For the two young women, French opened up a world of beauty and a world of ideas that was fundamentally opposed to the stifling heat, for women at least, of Arabic. Arabic not only veils women, it separates those who speak it from the outside world. It weighs women with its secrets and its demands, whereas French allows the "body [to] travel far in subversive space, in spite of the neighbours and suspicious matrons; it would not need much [for the body] to take wing and fly away" (184). Thus, if the thrust of Arabic was/is to veil the senses, desires, feelings, and emotions, and to segregate, then French, within the context of *Fantasia*, is the channel through which these girls and Djebar could dream and explore their sexualities—French did not desire them to veil themselves.

But if French is the language of love, freedom, and the imagination, it is also the language of brutality and domination. It is the language, as Aimé Césaire has observed, of "howling savagery" (15). In *Fantasia*, this savagery is evident in the manner in which the French armada arrives in Algiers. On the lookout is "Amable Matterer [who] is at his post in the first squadron which glides slowly westward; he gazes at the city which returns his gaze. The same day he writes of the confrontation, dispassionately, objectively" (7). How objective was Matterer? Did he report that accompanying the armada were pleasure boats that had been hired by Parisians to view the bombardment of Algiers? Or that, along with the pleasure boats, "there were four painters, five draughtsmen and a dozen engravers on board" the royal armada (8)? The invasion of a people and the destruction of a culture is, in the eyes of the French, a spectacle, a performance that will affirm their innate humanism. Their victims, the savages, deserve their fate as they lack the fundamental tenets of humanity. Matterer and his crew are the first colonizers, as they observe—Matterer records that he was "the first to catch sight of the city of Algiers, a tiny triangle on a mountain slope" (6)—and report on what they see. Their position as witnesses also excludes them from the realities of the observed, and they perform what Mary Louise Pratt has termed "the monarch-of-all-I-survey scene" (201). The writer, the painters, and the engravers are necessary to the military occupation in Algeria, as they will simultaneously inventory the land and people and subordinate the observed to the power of their "superior" culture.

This idea of the writer, the painters, and the engravers as the first colonizers is significant to the development of both *Fantasia* and the historical Algerian invasion, given the role that the language of representation played in the actual process of colonial expansion (de Certeau 1988, xxv–xxvii). Without doubt, the solidification of political power is virtually indistinguishable from the structures of writing and language. The artist colonizes that part of discourse that will render the weak and the powerless to the margins of history. Djebar acknowledges the power of language and representation when she writes, "I, in my turn, write, using his language" (7). In using Matterer's language, she will work to dismantle the "institutions, traditions, conventions, agreed upon codes of understanding" (Said, 22) that supported political systems of dominance.

These systems can be seen in the representations, both visual and written, that proliferated in the nineteenth century. The general sentiment of the period was that the Arab was a barbarian who, because of his religion—Islam—could never successfully engage the egalitarian principles of the French Republic. These conversations about race and ethnicity continually animated the discussions regarding the different ethnic groups in Algeria. The prevailing sentiments of the period are reflected in Eugène Fromentin's remarks on the Arab people: "They are wild, uncultured, and ignorant. They embrace the two extremes of the human mind, the childlike and the genial. . . . They hold on to these attributes with invincible resistance or inertia" (16). This type of categorization, as Patricia Lorcin has demonstrated in her book *Imperial Identities: Stereotyping, Prejudice, and Race in Colonial Algeria,* enabled the Kabyle Myth to flourish. According to the myth, the Berbers had resisted the Arab invasion and the spread of Islam by moving to the mountains of Kabylia and the Aures. In these regions, they developed a system of government that was similar to European systems, as opposed to the Arabs, who had not progressed either intellectually or socially. Thus, the Berbers were above the Arabs in the chain of being, but below Europeans. As Edward Said observed in *Orientalism*, the Arabs were generally viewed as morally lax, irrational, and lazy, "much given to 'fulsome flattery,' intrigue, cunning, and unkindness to animals . . . their disordered minds fail to understand what the clever European grasps immediately, that roads and pavements are made for walking . . . they are 'lethargic and suspicious,' and in everything oppose the clarity, directness, and nobility of the Anglo-Saxon race" (38–39). This prevailing view of the "indigenous" population of Algeria was further complicated by the legal system that was introduced there. Gustave de Beaumont, in his report to the French National Assembly in 1842, declared that "a legislation of exception will be necessary [in Algeria]; and it is not just public safety which requires it thus; the differences in climate, the variety of peoples, different customs, different needs call for different laws. . . . Thus, there are in Africa effectively two societies that are distinct from each other which are becoming progressively more separate and each of which has its own system and laws" (quoted in Le Cour Grandmaison, 41). What this meant for the Algerians, in general, was one set of laws that governed the "natives" and another that governed the settlers. The differences created a system whereby "the French with the status of citizens may be compared to nobles and lords; they alone are judged by their peers; they alone, at least in principle, bear arms. And the natives, who are simply subjects, occupy a situation similar to that of commoners or serfs" (ibid., 44). Muslims were obliged to carry internal passports (ibid., 43) that identified their affiliations, and, to complicate matters even further, the Muslims were allowed to adjudicate problems among themselves according to the Sharia. This allowance created a system whereby Muslims were French "subjects" but not French "citizens." The Jewish minority were considered French citizens, but, seventy-five years after the conquest of Algeria, only twenty-five hundred Muslims had gained French citizenship. To do so, Muslims had to renounce Islam—a mandatory condition. Meanwhile, the Berber Kabyles, whom the French had deemed above the Arabs, were forced to accept Islamic law (Horne, 35–36).

The oppositions that existed in the political, social, and legal spheres in colonial Algeria were entirely dependent on conceptions of language. Language is viewed as the seat of culture. When another language is presented as mere babble, those who speak it and do not speak the language of the civilized are seen as animals. Djebar gives us an indication of this fact in the first of her two epigraphs: "Our sentinels were gaining in experience: they were learning to distinguish the footsteps and voices of the Arabs from the sounds made by the wild beast that prowled around the camp in the dark." In this quotation from Baron Barchou de Penhoen's *Expedition to Africa* (1835), not only are the Arabs incoherent, but their lack of a civilized language—they are more beasts than humans—legitimizes French colonial rule in Algeria.

The sounds that the Arabs make in Barchou's renderings of them are not far removed from Rousseau's concept of the primordial "cry of nature" (122). According to Rousseau, in the *Second Discourse*, the development of language "was no small effort of genius," one that allowed men "to establish social bonds" (123, 126) that differentiated them from animals. It stands to reason, then, that if the Arabs could only make sounds that resembled those of animals, then they had not advanced beyond the primitive, or the state of Rousseau's "natural man." It must be noted that Rousseau, as much as he valorized the idea of the primitive man, still assumed that civilized language, science, writing, and understanding were developed in Europe.

Rousseau's assertion that civilized language and knowledge developed in Europe provides a context for the representations of non-Western peoples as essentially *lacking* language. While Western languages are deemed coherent and rational, non-Western languages are incoherent and irrational. As such, they do not rise to the level of true "language." This view of non-Western languages leads to corresponding oppression in the political and social spheres. As always, the "other" would be judged according to European standards and would be found lacking. These standards, created by language, represented a form of violence that, as Jacques Derrida has remarked, "marks an episode of what may be called anthropological warfare," which warfare escalates into "missionary and colonial oppression" (107). If the Arabs were so incoherent, then it was necessary to institute the language of reason. To that extent, French became the national language in Algeria.

The imposition and domination of foreign languages was, as Ngũgĩ wa Thiong'o argued in *Decolonizing the Mind*, a form of "psychological violence" (9) that led to an alienation from the "natural and social environment" (17) of colonized peoples. Thus, "the domination of a people's language by the languages of the colonizing nations was crucial to the domination of the mental universe of the colonized" (16). Abdel Kateb Yacine describes his colonial education as entering into "the jaws of a wolf" (quoted in Mortimer, 102). The same ambivalence would be captured by Mohammed Dib in his short story, "Encounters," when he wrote, "There is another encounter, but I was not yet aware that I had already experienced it and which, subsequently, was to reveal itself as a determining factor while changing my life with the force of a necessity or a destiny, in a sense" (112). Captured in this brief summary is Dib's anxiety regarding a language that could be simultaneously liberating and oppressive. Underlying his anxiety is his belief that his use of French symbolically represents the continued colonization of Algeria, and, by extension, a continued act of conquest.

Fundamentally, language is a masculine construct because its registers, when applied to women, confine them, as Dennis Baron has observed, to the "home and hearth" (1), where men routinely practice the subjugation of women. Language then becomes the battlefield upon which the war for identity and sovereignty is waged in this postcolonial age. Female writers, including Djebar, are at once celebrated and reviled—celebrated by the Western world they challenge and by their people in private, but reviled in public by the societies they resurrect from various footnotes in history. As Deniz Kandiyoti has argued, this problem is common for women because they operate within very narrow confines of nationalist agendas that consider them "to be the custodians of cultural particularisms by virtue of being less assimilated, both culturally and linguistically" (382). The lack of linguistic assimilation is necessary because it assures a patriarchal society that its women will be tied to its "indigenous" customs, thus reproducing the boundaries of ethnicity and difference. The assimilated woman, on the other hand, comes with a hybrid perspective that is, at best, critical, and, at worst, lacking in all the "cultural particularisms" of the unassimilated woman. If language is the tool of men, and yet both Yacine and Dib experience such severe unease at the continued use of French, then what does it mean for a *woman* to use the language of the oppressor as her medium?

Djebar continues to deal with the fact of using French as a mode of expression in all of her literary productions.[1] She was soundly criticized for writing in French when the postindependence nation declared, "Arabic [is] our language." This precipitated a crisis for Djebar, who was symbolically and effectively barred from participating in the national agenda, as she could not speak Arabic. It is no surprise, then, that in 1970 Djebar began to study classical Arabic. This study coincided with a ten-year literary silence, partly due to her recognition that Arabic could not become her literary medium.[2] This position was ultimately a critique of the postindependence Algerian government, which had started a slow push toward the Islamization and Arabization of Algeria. For Djebar, the call to write in the national/mother tongue was in itself conflicted. What was the mother tongue? For Djebar, it was Berber, not Arabic, yet the language, with the exception of the Tifinag script used by the Tuareg, did not have a standard written form.[3] Furthermore, the movement towards Arabization meant the suppression of the Berber language and the imposition of Arabic as the national and implied mother tongue. Djebar's conflict is fully captured in her declaration that after "ten years [of silence] I finally felt myself fully a writer of the French language, while remaining deeply Algerian" (1992, 168).

The question of language and its ability to disorient and disempower are repeatedly explored by Assia Djebar in *Fantasia: An Algerian Cavalcade* (originally published in 1985 as *L'Amour, la fantasia*). In the novel, Djebar dealt with the French occupation of Algeria in 1830 and France's 132-year subjugation of the country. *Fantasia* is a polyphonic text with episodic chapters. The first part ranges from the annexation of Algiers in 1830 to the eve of the 1954–62 war for independence. In the section that deals with the capture of Algiers, Djebar relied on archival materials and letters by officers to families and friends. She also drew on travel journals and artistic representations of the capture of Algiers. The second sequence—covering the war of independence—relies on testimonials by the women who participated in the struggle. In reproducing the voices of women, Djebar inscribes these women into the history of modern Algeria—and in the last section she dialogues with the women whose voices she has already reproduced. In this manner, the author is able to weave the voices of the modern Algerian women into history. The different periods that Djebar covers correspond to movements she makes between languages—between French and Arabic and between French and Berber, which, for her, is the mother tongue. Thus, in transcribing the words of the women she interviewed, Djebar encounters her culture and ultimately her identity. This confrontation disorients the French-trained Algerian woman, as she is removed from herself and her society:

> I write and speak French outside: the words I use convey no
> flesh-and-blood reality. I learn the names of birds I've never
> seen. . . . In this respect, all vocabulary expresses what is
> missing in my life. . . . Settings and episodes in children's
> books are nothing but theoretical concepts. . . . My conscious
> mind is here, huddled against my mother's knees, in the darkest
> corners of the flat which she never leaves. . . . I do not realize,
> no-one around me realizes, that, in the conflict between these
> two worlds, lies an incipient vertigo. (185)

The "vertigo" that the young Djebar experiences is the battle between
two worlds and two very different languages. French is alienating, as
the words do not have any referents in Algeria; the native language,
on the other hand, is the language of the mother and confers identity. The mother tongue, silenced for so long, now aims to reclaim a
lost child. It is only by reclaiming that child that the mother will feel
complete. The alienation felt by the subject is acute because she cannot communicate with her culture, identity, and history. The memory
by which a woman can communicate the boundary markers of her
ethnicity and identity is lost. Thus, the alienated body becomes adrift
with no connection to the past. At the same time, she cannot claim the
French language because of the history of French depravity toward
her people. Here, we find that the mother tongue is neither barbaric
nor lacking in history and culture, but the French language is barbaric in purpose. The subject, torn between two languages and two
cultures, becomes traumatized as she attempts to negotiate and reconcile both histories. However, the histories and cultures are irrecon-
cilable, as one is marked by the blood of slaughtered Algerians.

    This conflict that exists between Arabic and French is one of the
problems of *Fantasia*. While many writers have seen the text as primarily feminist and believe that French serves to liberate women from
the darkness of the veil and of the Arabic language, I argue that Djebar uses French not only to give voice to silenced women, but as the
medium through which she challenges the history of the conquest of
Algeria as written by France and the French reporters, painters, and
generals who chronicled the fall of Algiers. If Djebar, as the historian, is to respond and write the truth of the Algerian conquest, she
must write it in French, as that is the only way she can retell the story.
This position is announced early on in *Fantasia* when Djebar gazes at
"Amable Matterer at his post in the first squadron which glides slowly

westward." Matterer is the recognized historian and his "knowledge" of the conquest and the people of Algiers will rely on an already established structure that separates his people from those who will be conquered. Thus, "he gazes at the city which returns his gaze." As Matterer gazes at the city, his history of the conquest is already written; the story that he tells will depend on the age-old binary of savage/enlightened. Djebar, as Matterer's modern-day counterpart, will in turn "write using his language but more than one hundred and fifty years later" (6–7) to revise Matterer's history.

The narrative structure of Matterer's history cannot be objective as it utilizes already established literary devices that have been developed by a language that sought to conquer those that did not fit into its lexical paradigms. The production of this history will construct the "other" as part of an experiment whose end result is the civilization of the natives. Hence, Matterer's account "fabricate[s]" the experience of the conquest to satisfy his audience. This fabrication is evident when Matterer recounts the massacre at the Staouel plateau: "one battalion's fire brought down [the] rabble and two thousand of them will never see the light of day again" (18). The emphasis in this account is not on the number of corpses but on the word "rabble." Even though the French soldiers defied the wishes of their superior officers, they were correct in shooting the two thousand prisoners, since these prisoners—the "rabble"—dared to defy the French, who were superior. Matterer's satisfaction at the massacre is evident as "the next day he placidly wanders among the corpses and the booty" (18). For him, the dead bodies are a mere footnote in history and the deaths a supplement to the tale of the heroic French soldiers who gunned them down. For Djebar, however, their voices cannot be silenced in the void created by French accounts of the conquest. The prisoners were defenseless and gunned down unarmed, and, as such, the retelling of their story not only gives them voice, but redefines the term "heroic."

If Djebar is then redefining terms and revising the history of the conquest, she cannot do it in Arabic: it does not contain the lexical codes and registers necessary to expose/unveil France's actions in Algeria. Therefore, across the sands of time, the language becomes the battlefield upon which the fight for the true history of the conquest will be waged. The power of language to articulate and fabricate the self and the other is quite evident in *Fantasia*, as the "natives" fail to create a contrapuntal relationship with their French overseers. In the novel, the journalist and playwright Jean-Touissant Merle relates an event in which the linguistic differences in Arabic are explored: "at the hospital a wounded man has not been amputated because his father withholds his permission! But our author does not tell what we are given to understand from other sources: namely that the host of military interpreters, brought along by the French army from the Middle East, prove incapable of translating these first exchanges— could the local Arab dialect be so unintelligible?" (32–33)

The French see Algerian Arabic as a production of unintelligible sounds. The father is incapable of entering into a rational discussion regarding the care of his son, and is in fact presented as irrational because he "withholds his permission." In other words, if he were civilized, he would immediately understand what is required of him. However, the criticism that is aimed at the man is a reflection of the ignorance of the colonizers. The local dialect is "unintelligible" to the French and their cadres of interpreters because the Arabic spoken in Algeria had been influenced by several different tribes.[4]

The roots of differences in the linguistic register can be found in the influences that existed in the Maghreb before the spread of Islam under the early Umayyad dynasty. The language that was/is spoken in the Maghreb is a combination of classical Arabic, the Berber language, and the language of the Corsairs, while the Middle Eastern translators spoke mostly classical Arabic. Words and pronunciations are quite different: thus, an Algerian speaking Arabic to an Arab from a Middle Eastern country would get nowhere, as the differences in colloquial usages become quite evident the farther one is removed from the Eastern Mediterranean. This lack of linguistic fluidity between and among ethnic groups becomes part of the arsenal for justification of colonialism. If these Arabs cannot understand the "other" Arabs, then colonization will usher in an age of enlightenment. Thus, it is imperative that Djebar utilize the so-called language of civilization to show the actuality of the conquest.

More important, however, is the impact of Islam on the development of Arabic. Because Islam is predicated upon the idea that all men are equal under one God, there are certain terms with pejorative meanings that exist in English and French that do not exist in Arabic. Thus, when the messengers "inform Pelissier [that] the fumigation has wiped out the entire Ouled Riah tribe . . . 1,500 men, some of them elderly, women, children, flocks" (72), the term "fumigation" would not have had the impact in Arabic that it did when written in French. Fumigation, within the context of the sentence, presents the fifteen hundred Ouled Riah as mere pests lacking in humanity. If the Algerians are pests and thus inhabit the lower reaches of the chain of existence, then their fumigation is necessary for the advancement of civilization and culture.[5] If the "other" is significantly dehumanized, then it becomes acceptable to perform acts of savagery on his body. This formulation is very apparent in *Fantasia* as Djebar has the dead human bodies inhabit the same space as "the carcasses of the animals already in a state of putrefaction"; "the corpses [according to the Spanish speleologists] are naked in attitudes which indicated the convulsions they have experienced before they expired." The speleologists would further observe that "the refugees in these hidden depths have been totally exterminated" (72). The juxtaposition of the terms "fumigate" and "exterminate" indicates the attitudes of the French toward the Ouled Riah tribe. These men, women, and children share the same space as the animals because they are no more than animals to the French.

Both terms have strong racial connotations that are not supported by the lexicon of the Qur'an. This is not to say that Islamic society does not have its social stratifications, but the racial overtones of such terminology run counter to the prophet's own preaching against the abuse of prisoners. In Suras 2:191 and 5:9, the Qur'an (as translated by Mohammad Zafrulla Khan) has the following edicts:

> Fight in the cause of Allah against those who fight against you, but transgress not. Once they start fighting, kill them wherever you meet them, and drive them out from where they have driven you out. . . . Fight them until all aggression ceases and religion is professed for the pleasure of Allah alone. If they desist, then be mindful that no retaliation is permissible except against the aggressors. (2:191)

> Let not a people's enmity towards you incite you to act contrary to justice; be always just, that is closest to righteousness. (5:9)

The Ouled Riah, having desisted by hiding in the caves, were surely expecting a cease-fire. The French army, rather than retreat in victory, celebrates a horrible fantasia—the reference here is not musical: rather, it is to a common Arab cultural celebration, in which men galloping on horseback wave their sabers or fire their guns to show off their equestrian skills—a fantasia in which the dead bodies become the actors in a macabre scene that pollutes the air. The Spanish speleologists write that the Ouled Riah displayed "barbaric courage" at the moment of their execution/massacre. But the question that Djebar asks is, Who is the barbarian, the savage? In leaving the dead to rot in the countryside, deprived of their rites of passage, are the French not the barbarians?

The fumigation indeed becomes a controlled fantasia in which Aimable Pelissier will exorcise the "demons" within the empire. But he does not succeed in completely wiping out the Ouled Riah, because they haunt him through the pages of his own narrative: "his verbose reports, which arrive in Paris, are read at a parliamentary session" (75). Pelissier, according to François Canrobert, "made only one mistake: as he had a talent for writing, and was aware of this, he gave in his report an eloquent and realistic—much too realistic—description of the Arabs' suffering" (75). Language, which had doomed the Ouled Riah, becomes their instrument of vengeance, as they return within Pelissier's report to expose his inhumanity. Thus, language becomes the medium through which the Ouled Riah will demonstrate the fabrication of history. Paradoxically, the language that was meant to silence them "resurrects" them for the revision of the history of the French in Algeria.

Pelissier, in an attempt to justify his actions, claims "that by a providential chance, the most obdurate among the Sharif's party succumbed" to the extermination. It is quite fascinating that providential order, that is, the hand of God, is credited with the massacre of the Ouled Riah. The massacred members of the Sharif's party inhabit a space that is itself devoid of any divine influence; as such, they do not occupy the human sphere, and hence their "extermination," a term that is normally used only in reference to the most despised creatures. The dead become objects to be gazed at and written about, but they, in turn, gaze at their murderers. This mutual attraction or horrified fascination with the "Other" as object leads Pelissier to "resurrect [for the historian] those Ouled Riah who die in their caves on the night of 19–20 June 1845" (75). Thus, language is simultaneously the tool of the conqueror and that of the liberator. It is language that dooms the Ouled Riah to extinction—orders from Marshal Bugeaud were to "smoke them out like foxes" (70)—and it is language and writing that will reinstate them and "preserve [them] from oblivion by the words of his routine report" (75). With these words, Djebar acknowledges the power of language to inscribe and describe people and cultures in and from history.

This power is clearly delineated in Armand Leroy de Saint Arnaud's actions two months after Pelissier had fumigated the Ouled Riah. After asphyxiating "at least eight hundred Sbeahs" (76), Saint Arnaud simply chose to remain silent. Unlike Pelissier, Saint Arnaud's report will not be forwarded to Paris and neither will it raise a firestorm of criticism from those Parisians who do not support the incursion into Algeria. Instead, the report is "burned in Algiers." This act is symbolic of the power that writing and language hold over the imagination. Yet, even Saint Arnaud cannot escape exposing his murderous deeds. Even though there is no official record of the "extermination" of the Sbeahs, a letter to his brother is a testament to his brutality: "I have all the exits hermetically sealed and create a vast cemetery. The bodies of these fanatics will be buried in the earth forever! . . . No one has been down into the cave! . . . I sent a confidential report to the Field Marshall, stating everything simply, without any terrible poetry, nor any imagery" (76). Several things occur simultaneously in Saint Arnaud's letter. In categorizing the Sbeahs as fanatics, he replicates the age-old discourse that posits the "other" as a diseased entity. The word "fanatic" does not, in Saint Arnaud's use, denote possession by God, but by a demon. He also implicitly indicts Pelissier for resurrecting, through his "terrible poetry [and] imagery," the Ouled Riah—"terrible" here does not mean bad, but powerful. But his letter also reveals an anxiety: he is the fanatic and thus the demon that is possessed by darkness. This unspoken anxiety forces him to claim, "Brother, no one is more prone to goodness by nature and disposition than I! . . . From 8–12 August, I have been ill, but my conscience does not trouble me. I have done my duty as a leader and tomorrow I shall do the same again, but I have developed a distaste for Africa!" (76). This claim renders him blameless; instead, the Sbeahs are to blame for their deaths. If only they had not been such fanatics, then they would not have met such a gruesome end. Scapegoating the Sbeahs protects Saint Arnaud from recognizing that his actions are debased and that he has become the very thing that he loathes: the savage. Saint Arnaud's letter to his brother confines the Sbeahs "through the merciless language of non-madness" (Foucault, ix). Or, in other words, since Europe has determined that its language, customs, and culture are essentially rational, then those who fail to fit within the standards are deemed irrational and thus to be confined. This idea that the "other" is diseased or mad unveils a fundamental truth that the European body, which is determined to be rational, is essentially diseased (Foucault, 30). In a sense, Saint Arnaud's letter performs the very function it was determined to silence. It becomes a form of evocation, which Lacan has argued is the function of language (Lacan, 86).

If Saint Arnaud's letter evokes the irrationality of the European, Djebar's report is also an evocation, because her aim is to recuperate, in the memories of the Algerians, the brutality of the conquest. To this end, she focuses on the body of "the dead woman lying beneath the body of the man who was protecting her from the bellowing ox. Because of his remorse, Pelissier keeps his corpse from drying in the sun, and these Islamic dead, deprived of ritual ceremonies, are preserved from oblivion by the words of his routine report. A century of silence has frozen them" (75). The rewriting of this scene evokes for the reader the terrifying ordeal of the Ouled Riah as they realized that their hiding place had become their graveyard. This type of "official report" is not available on the "fumigation" of the Sbeahs, so Djebar relies on oral accounts gathered from survivors of Saint Arnaud's massacre. Her guides to this history "are words in the French language—reports, accounts, evidence from the past" (78). These guides will give voice to the dead and will reinstate the Sbeahs in history. Djebar's use of French in re-envisioning the massacres follows a dialogic model that relies on the original accounts of the invasion to construct a history of the conquest and "weave a pattern of French words" (78) around the dead. This weaving of French words is an explicit acknowledgment of the power of language. It is also an acknowledgement that a challenge in any other language would not be successful, as Djebar "accept[s] this palimpsest on which [she will] now inscribe the charred passion of [her] ancestors" (79).

This is not to say, however, that Djebar is comfortable with the French language. It is as if the language, in this postcolonial moment, performs the same acts as those carried out by Pélissier and Saint Arnaud. The language strips her of her identity and mutilates her:

> To attempt an autobiography using French words alone is to lend oneself to the vivisector's scalpel, revealing what lies beneath the skin. The flesh flakes off and with it, seemingly, the last shreds of the unwritten language of my childhood. Wounds are reopened, veins weep, one's own blood flows and that of others, which has never dried. . . .

Speaking of oneself in a language other than that of the elders is indeed to unveil oneself, not only to emerge from childhood but to leave it, never to return. Such incidental unveiling is tantamount to stripping oneself naked as the demotic Arabic dialect emphasizes.

But this stripping naked, when expressed in the language of the former conqueror ... this stripping naked takes us back oddly enough to the plundering of the preceding century. (156–57)

The unveiling is a necessary act of transgression. A new scriptural relation to the conquest will be created and this new creation will become the "truth." She thus creates a breach, an opening, however painful, in the palimpsest that reinstates, in a much more concrete form, the contact of bodies and history. The "I" that relives the cries of the elders and represents them within the language that suppressed them signifies a rupture: the act of retelling will not be submissive, as it designates a rebirth. It is through the voice of the "other" that the obscene will be made visible. In respect to *Fantasia*, there is already a gap between the original and the revision, and between what was written and the revision of those originary documents. There is also a distinction made between the ethnocentric representation/definition of the "savage" and the redefined terminology—the "savage" in *Fantasia* is no longer the non-Western, the non-European. The act of silencing itself produces an endless discourse that will lay bare the truth.

This "truth" is discovered early on, when the myth of the civilizing mission is dispelled, to be replaced by the fundamental truth of the conquest:

For this conquest is no longer seen as the discovery of a strange new world, not even as a new crusade by a West aspiring to relive its past as if it were an opera. This invasion has become an enterprise of rapine: after the army come the merchants and soon their employees are hard at work; their machinery for liquidation and execution is already in place.

And words themselves become a decoration, flaunted by officers like the carnation they wear in their buttonholes; words will become their most effective weapons. Hordes of interpreters, geographers, ethnographers, linguists, botanists, diverse scholars and professional scribblers will swoop down on their new prey. The supererogatory protuberances of their publications will form a pyramid to hide the initial violence from view. (45)

The horde of interpreters who will descend on Algeria will fabricate a history that will not only "hide the initial violence" but will distort the reasons behind the incursion. In one swift stroke, then, Djebar questions Charles X's decision to invade Algeria. If it was not to discover and civilize a strange new world—after all, de Tocqueville would testify to the French National Assembly that "the Muslim Society in North Africa was not uncivilized; it only had a backward and imperfect civilization. . . . We have rendered Muslim society much more miserable and much more barbaric than it was before it became acquainted with us" (quoted in Horne, 29)—then why did Charles support the invasion?[6]

Rather than the inevitable project of the civilizing mission, Djebar posits another truth—that of colonization for economic purposes. Djebar's position is supported by Bugeaud's testimony before the National Assembly in 1840: "wherever there is fresh water and fertile lands, there one must locate *colons*, without concerning oneself to whom these lands belong" (quoted in Horne, 30). The fundamental reason for the invasion was economic, as the unemployed, unwanted, and disenfranchised from France, Spain, Italy, and Malta moved to Algeria and began farming lands that had been forcefully taken from the indigenous peoples. By 1870, forty years after the invasion, there were over two hundred thousand *pieds noirs* in Algeria (Horne, 29–31). The native Algerians became settlers in their own lands. Their story, however, was not available to the French public. What were available were accounts of the savagery of the Algerians and the heroism of the French army and settlers. The reports were full of "descriptive, seductive, and captivating stories of the numerous bloody, 'yet glorious,' raids carried out by the French army" (Fromentin, xx). Since the reports sent to Paris were full of titillating accounts, and thus were gross distortions, Djebar, in writing her story, had to contend with and revise these accounts. To destroy the existing "truths" as posited by the historians who chronicled the defeat of Algiers, Djebar had to utilize the very language in which they had first been recorded. Fundamentally, she recognized the power dynamics inherent in language: it is through language that civilizations are created and destroyed.

Thus, it is imperative for the historian, in this moment, to contend with the language that would deny the existence of her people. The French language becomes the battlefield upon which she will reinstate and reinscribe her people into history. *Fantasia: An Algerian Cavalcade* is the alternative history to that of the colonial representation of the French in Algeria. In using the language of the oppressors, Djebar uses, metaphorically, their voices to expose their brutality and their inhumanity. This writing becomes a journey at the end of which she will lovingly exhume the "buried cries, those of yesterday as well as those of a hundred years ago" (63). Djebar's journey has come full circle: in 2005, she was elected to the Académie Française as one of its forty "immortals." This position "authorizes" her to continue her examination of the French language and its role in shaping the modern perception of her people.

Notes

1. For Djebar, there is "a gap" between French and Arabic "that mirrors the yawning gap between two societies that still go on functioning side by side, but keep their backs stiffly to each other" (1992, 172). This gap made it impossible for her to write, so she would focus on producing movies/documentaries in which the tensions would not appear. The film *La Nouba des femmes du Mont-Chenoua* takes its title from the "Nouba," a traditional song composed of five movements. Because the film deals with women's personal and cultural histories, it is firmly located within the oral tradition, so she was not confronted with, as she has argued, the imperative "to write a Western narrative [from where she] must speak subjectively" (1992, 172). She raises these issues in this film and in *Women of Algiers*, originally intended as a sequel to *La Nouba*, which ushered in a new type of writing for Djebar, one in which she would not speak subjectively. For a thorough discussion of this idea, see Michel de Certeau's *The History of Writing*.

2. See the interview with Clarisse Zimra that is appended to the 1992 translation of *Women of Algiers in Their Apartment*. In a response to the question, "Were you still plagued by the old language question?" Djebar stated that she "had to wait until *L'amour, la fantasia* to be able to take charge of my writing, to be able to inscribe my innermost self in my work" (171).

3. McCarus (1995) gives a brief introduction to the different dialects and languages that fall within the term "Berber."

4. Classical Arabic, based on the Qur'an, is the same everywhere. Non-Arab Muslims recite the Qur'an without necessarily speaking the language.

Colloquial Arabic, on the other hand, varies within and among countries in the Arab world. In Lebanon the word for cherries is *karaz*, whereas the same word in Tunisia means a whale's testicles. *Hout*, in Tunisian Arabic, means fish (the equivalent of whale in classical Arabic), whereas in Lebanese Arabic fish is *samak*. In Tunisia, Morocco, and Algeria—all part of the Maghreb—local dialects are closely related. For a thorough examination, see Hannoum. As Hannoum has observed, the term "'Arab' refers to the Oriental of Orientalism whose image is all too familiar to the European reader; they are one and the same. They do not change, nor do they disappear. They are always dominant, and their domination brings destruction. In addition, the term 'Berber' . . . refers to newcomers in the field of Orientalism. They did not exist prior to the conquest of Algiers, or rather they were the Arabs, the Moors, the Saracens. The Berbers now exist in the French imaginary, but they join a category of people who have also been familiar to the European since the beginning of the nineteenth century: they are the primitives who represent the past of Europeans" (78).

5. In the context of *Fantasia*, "fumigate" is akin to terms like "gooks" and "Japs" used during World War II and the Vietnam conflict. These terms desensitize soldiers and the public to the brutality that is occurring, while dehumanizing the people who are being brutalized. The Algerians, in Djebar's scene, are indistinguishable from the animals on their farms.

6. The pretext for the invasion was ingenuous. According to the king's government, they were avenging an insult done to their consul in Algiers in 1827. The Dey of Algiers, according to the story, lost his temper and struck the French consul in the face with a fly whisk and called him a "wicked, faithless, idol-worshipping rascal" (Horne, 29). The real reason for invasion, however, was Charles's prior attempt, through Prime Minister Jules Armand Polignac, to reinstate the idea of the divine right of kings and the power of the nobility through a coup d'état. The French public would have none of this, and, to divert attention away from the king's unpopular regime, Polignac initiated a series of military engagements that ended with the invasion of Algeria. This tactic was initially successful, and the invasion became a public spectacle for those who could afford to travel to witness the bombardment. The incursion "was accompanied by a touch of the *fête galante*, with elegant ladies booking accommodation aboard pleasure boats to observe the naval bombardment of Algiers" (Horne, 29).

Works Cited

Baron, Dennis. 1986. *Grammar and Gender.* New Haven, CT: Yale University Press.

Césaire, Aimé. 2000. *Discourse on Colonialism.* New York: New York University Press.

de Certeau, Michel. 1988. *The History of Writing.* Trans. Tom Conley. New York: Columbia University Press.

Derrida, Jacques. 1976. *Of Grammatology.* Trans. Gayatri Chakravorty Spivak. Baltimore: Johns Hopkins University Press.

Dib, Mohammed. 2001. "Encounters." In *An Algerian Childhood: A Collection of Autobiographical Narratives,* ed. Leïla Sebbar, trans. Marjolijn de Jager, with a foreword by Anne Donadey, 103–14. St. Paul, MN: Ruminator.

Djebar, Assia. 1992. *Women of Algiers in Their Apartment.* Trans. Marjolijn de Jager with an afterword by Clarisse Zimra. Charlottesville: University Press of Virginia.

———. 1993/1985. *Fantasia: An Algerian Cavalcade.* Trans. Dorothy S. Blair. Portsmouth, NH: Heinemann.

———. 1996. "The Eyes of Language." Trans. Pamela A. Genova. *World Literature Today* 70 (4).

Fanon, Frantz. 1968. *The Wretched of the Earth.* Trans. Constance Farrington, with a preface by Jean-Paul Sartre. New York: Grove.

Foucault, Michel. 1988/1961. *Madness and Civilization: A History of Insanity in the Age of Reason.* New York: Vintage.

Fromentin, Eugène. 1999/1859. *Between Sea and Sahara: An Algerian Journal.* Trans. Blake Robinson, with an intro. by Valérie Orlando. Athens: Ohio University Press.

Hannoum, Abdelmajid. 2003. "Translation and the Colonial Imaginary: Ibn Kaldûn Orientalist." *History and Theory* 42 (1): 61–81.

Horne, Alistair. 1977. *A Savage War of Peace: Algeria 1954–1962.* New York: Viking.

Kandiyoti, Deniz. 1994. "Identity and Its Discontents: Women and the Nation." In *Colonial Discourse and Post-Colonial Theory,* ed. Patrick Williams and Laura Chrisman, 376–91. New York: Columbia University Press.

Lacan, Jacques. 1977/1966. *Écrits: A Selection.* Trans. Alan Sheridan. New York: W. W. Norton.

Le Cour Grandmaison, Olivier. 2006. "The Exception and the Rule: On French Colonial Law." *Diogenes* (International Council for Philosophy and Humanistic Studies) 53 (4): 34–53.

Lorcin, Patricia M. E. 1995. *Imperial Identities: Stereotyping, Prejudice, and Race in Colonial Algeria.* London: I. B. Tauris.

McCarus, Ernest N. 1995. "Berber: Linguistic 'Substratum' of North African Arabic." *Washington Report on Middle East Affairs* 13 (5): 31.

Mortimer, Mildred. 2000. "Assia Djebar's *Algerian Quartet:* A Study in Fragmented Autobiography." *Research in African Literatures* 28 (2): 102–17.

Ngũgĩ wa Thiong'o. 1986. *Decolonising the Mind: The Politics of Language in African Literature.* London: James Currey.

Pratt, Mary Louise. 1992. *Imperial Eyes: Travel Writing and Transculturation.* New York: Routledge.

Rousseau, Jean-Jacques. 1964. *The First and Second Discourses.* Trans. Roger D. and Judith R. Masters, ed. Roger D. Masters. New York: St. Martin's.

Said, Edward. 1979. *Orientalism.* New York: Vintage.

Part 2

WAVES OF RESISTANCE

The Casualties of Difference

3

Nawal El Saadawi's *Woman at Point Zero* within the Context of Arab Feminist Discourse

Amira Nowaira

Woman at Point Zero, published in the mid-1970s, has been generally hailed as a brave, groundbreaking work promoting a feminist agenda that is still trying to establish itself in third-world societies. It was described, for example, by a *Sunday Times* (London) commentator as "perhaps one of the most potent anti-patriarchy novels of our time" (Mahabane). Within the context of Arab feminist discourse, it clearly occupies a very distinctive position. Although it shares with the preceding discourse the general sense of indignation at the plight of women in Egypt and presumably the larger Arab world as well, it seems to challenge, and possibly subvert, some of the basic assumptions on which the whole movement towards women's liberation was built. What I will try to show here is that *Woman at Point Zero* represents a very different discourse from the one established and propagated by almost a century of advocacy for women's liberation.

The discourse produced by the early feminists was largely, although one has to admit not exclusively, an upper-class phenomenon. It generally reflected the preoccupations, views, and assumptions of this particular class and was by necessity constrained by them. The pioneers of the women's liberation movement in Egypt, such as Malak Hefni Nassef, Huda Sha'rawi, Esther Wissa, and others, were women who belonged to the upper, privileged strata of society. There were admittedly others from the middle class, such as Nabawiya Musa, who also played a leading role in the movement for women's education and was involved throughout her life in establishing schools for girls and attempting to improve their lot through education. But the discourses of these two classes were generally united in their principles and objectives, postulating that an upper/middle-class, Arab/Muslim woman needed education in order to be better equipped to participate fully in the life of society and shoulder her responsibilities both as wife and mother. Such views had gained currency, if not wholehearted legitimacy, by way of Kassem Amin's seminal work, *The Liberation of Women*, published in 1898.

Kassem Amin, the pioneering voice for women's liberation in Egypt, argued for the necessity of educating women based on his view that men could not possibly fulfill their own emotional and psychological needs with partners who were obviously ignorant and backward. "Women lagged behind men in intellect and education in such an abysmal manner that it was difficult for both of them to find a topic on which to talk together in mutual joy, nor to agree on any issue."[1] This, according to him, "was the most serious cause of men's as well as women's misery" (39), since it prevented them from attaining the emotional and intellectual bonding that can only be achieved through the compatibility of their minds. "For Amin, the principal benefits of Egyptian women's becoming educated and exposed to the world seemed to be two: they would become better mothers, capable of bringing up the kinds of good citizens required by the modern nation; and they would become better marriage companions for the educated modern man, capable of truly loving and understanding him" (Abu-Lughod, 256).

The early feminists of the first half of the twentieth century saw in education a panacea for all the ills that plagued women and relegated them to an inferior position. At the same time, they raised their voices against many prevalent and widely accepted practices, such as forced marriages and polygamy, and were engaged in heated discussions over a number of controversial issues such as veiling and women's right to work. However, domestic violence, female circumcision, sexual harassment by male family members, as well as the various types of abuse that lower-class women were frequently subjected to, were generally glossed over or completely ignored and treated as nonexistent. Largely and conspicuously excluded from the focal point of their interest were not only the masses of uneducated women living in poverty-stricken rural and urban areas, but also the marginalized women of the subclasses, particularly those living in moral limbo, such as prostitutes. It is true that the early feminists called for outlawing prostitution.[2] The issue for them, however, was to a great extent linked to and interwoven with the nationalist cause of liberation from British colonial domination. Also at stake was the issue of foreign privileges, which included the protection and, consequently, the promotion of European prostitutes operating in Egypt.[3] Their fight was largely conducted in the international arena. It was high on the agenda of the international feminist conference in Rome in 1923 attended by the Egyptian Feminist Union.[4] But prostitution as a serious social phenomenon was not fully investigated, and the economic and political causes giving rise to it were never subjected to public scrutiny. The pioneering women were particularly keen on pushing the cause of women's liberation forward, and an emphasis on negative aspects was probably deemed inappropriate and unhelpful to their cause.

It was important for the feminists in the early part of the twentieth century, while vehemently advancing the nationalist cause of liberation, to be seen to be firmly upholding the precepts of Islam and prevalent social dictates and notions. It is hardly surprising, then, that women's writings in the early decades of the century were replete with some patriarchal notions that it might have been more reasonable for them to challenge than to endorse, foremost among which was the idea of female virtue. It is fairly common in these works to find that women who deviated from the prescribed paths, even if this was not of their own volition, were condemned and branded as immoral and "fallen."

Women's fiction[5] dealt with the theme of the "fallen woman" as early as 1927, when Zeinab Mohamed's novel *Falling into Vice* was published in Arabic. The novel uses the epistolary form and presents the main character, Fikreya, through the exchange of letters written by two male characters, who consistently refer to her as an evil and irredeemably "bad" woman. This is a view that the writer herself obviously endorses and shares. Fikreya's lapse into vice, as is made abundantly clear throughout the narrative, is nothing more than the logical and expected outcome of a warped mind and a deeply ingrained sense of anger, the causes of which are not fully explored by the writer. Fikreya's actions are presented as lamentably reprehensible and blameworthy, but there is no attempt at understanding the motivating forces behind them. Moreover, the distancing device used in presenting Fikreya through the eyes of the two male protagonists further alienates the reader from her predicament and virtually bars any potential identification with it.

Similarly, in Aisha Abdel Rahman's *The Lord of the Manor*, the protagonist, a young woman named Samira, is a servant whose main interest lies in trapping the young master, who is already involved with another servant. By getting him to notice her, she hopes to fulfill many of her material ambitions. To do that, she feels impelled to steal in order to buy the clothes necessary to draw his attention, and from this point forward the path downward begins. The author's treatment of her main character smacks of condescension and moral censure. Like Zeinab Mohamed, she does not try to delve deep into the causes of the servant girl's actions, or to extend any sympathy for her plight.

Another novel written from the same vantage point is Sophie Abdallah's *Domoo' Al Tawba (Tears of Repentance)*, which, as the title suggests, deals with the fallen state of a young woman whose infatuation with a flirtatious young man leads her to utter ruin. After having abused her, he abandons her, and she is left to confront the only options open to her: either to go down the route of prostitution or to commit suicide. By choosing the latter, she reveals to the reader Abdallah's moral stand concerning the problematic issue of women's relationship to their bodies and the view that the body is ultimately the source of all evil. For a woman to survive in this patriarchal society, she has to keep her body completely under control, otherwise utter destruction will be her destiny.

Woman at Point Zero is built on a very different set of assumptions. It seems to question and challenge not only the givens and dicta of society but also the compromises made by the early feminists in order to ensure acceptance by the dominant modes of thought. This novel is not apologetic about its endorsement of the prostitute as a human being, while condemning prostitution as a dehumanizing practice and lamenting the conditions leading women to this kind of existence. It elicits sympathy for the woman who finds herself in this situation rather than subjecting her to heartless and unjust censure, as El Saadawi's literary forerunners often did. It presents a discourse that does not pay lip service to prevalent modes of thought and treats the deprived classes with a great deal of sympathy and understanding.

The storyline is simple enough. A woman psychiatrist, probably the surrogate self of Nawal El Saadawi, is carrying out research on the psychological makeup of female convicts. In the course of her work she becomes intrigued by the case of a woman prisoner waiting on death row, ironically named Firdaus, or Paradise, who refuses to say a word to anyone about her life or the circumstances leading her to commit murder.

The opening of the novel establishes the antithesis as well as the uncanny bonding between the narrator/psychiatrist and the female convict, the educated woman, who visits the prison as a professional researcher, and the inmate. They are placed in predefined physical spaces that further situate them on the opposite sides of a huge gulf. These two women, perfect strangers that they are, confront as well as reach out to one another across huge chasms of class, education, social status, and even of life and death. Their encounter in fact forms the narrative axis of the novel and is therefore more central to the overall meaning of the narrative than may be apparent at first. This is how the narrator introduces Firdaus:

> This is a real woman, a woman of flesh and blood. I met her a few years ago in the Qanatir Prison in the course of my research into the personality of some women who were accused or convicted of various offences.
> The prison doctor told me that the woman had been sentenced to death for having murdered a man. She was, however, a very different kettle of fish from the other women inmates. I wasn't likely to meet anybody like her inside or outside the prison, for she refused to meet or respond to anyone. She ate very scantily and only slept at dawn.[6] (5)

From the very start, Firdaus is presented as a woman apart, a woman who is no figment of the imagination, a woman of flesh and blood who dwells in the realm of negativity and whose strength lies in her powers of sustained and uncompromising rejection. There is no mistaking where the weight of the narrative lies. Pitted against each other, it is the lower-class woman, paradoxically enough, who seems to be in total control, not only of her own destiny but of the other woman as well. On the eve of her execution, she is the one who takes the initiative in telling her life history to the narrator/psychiatrist, who in turn becomes the passive recipient of the narrative. In this manner, as pointed out by Nadje Sadig Al-Ali, El Saadawi "disrupts the conventional power relationship, which is based on the perception of the physician as an embodiment of science and wisdom" (29).

The central story nested within the narrative frame is narrated by Firdaus herself. It tells of a life of abuse and poverty, leading the young woman from her rural beginnings, through a disastrous marriage to a man at least forty years her senior and a couple of failed love relationships, to a life of prostitution on the streets of the metropolis. The story ends with Firdaus having to kill the pimp who tries to blackmail her into a life of bondage and subservience to him.

The novel thus places the lower-class woman at the focal point of the narrative and relegates, at least structurally, the middle-class/professional woman to the periphery. The lower-class woman, marginalized by earlier discourse, becomes the pivot around which the whole narrative revolves. It is Firdaus whose voice articulates the grievances of women, particularly those of the deprived, underprivileged classes, and their attempts to escape the nets flung at them by the entire society from the day they are born. The novel thus seems to question and to challenge the upper/middle-class sensibilities that the narrator/psychiatrist represents.

We are given very little information about the woman psychiatrist/narrator. In contrast to Firdaus, who is endowed with self-expression, she is shrouded in silence, at least as far as her own personal experiences are concerned. Her frustrations and fears are only hinted at and vicariously expressed through her unusual interest in Firdaus. This interest seems initially to be part of her job at a women's prison, but with the progress of the narrative a more profound involvement becomes apparent. Fedwa Malti-Douglas finds that the encounter between the two women is presented in terms of a meeting of lovers, and argues that the relationship has lesbian overtones: "In her reaction to the prisoner's refusal and then willingness to see her, the psychiatrist has delineated an important bond between them: that of lovers. This is not a case of mere fascination on the doctor's part. The entire episode has sexual overtones. The gender of the lover in her comparisons is clearly identified: it is male" (48–49). But the psychiatrist/narrator's response to Firdaus's story, though described in terms that may be termed amorous or sexual, is explained in the final part of the novel. Perhaps for the first time, and without evasions or delusions, the educated woman comes into a headlong confrontation with herself and her life. Faced with truths that she has probably been evading throughout her life, her overriding feeling is one of shame: shame at the phoniness of her life, at the lies and the fears she is living with: "I was ashamed of myself, my life, my lies and my fears. I saw people rushing down the streets toward their hypocrisy and lies. I saw the newspapers pinned high at newsstands, filled with headlines all made up of lies. The flags of deception soared high. I pressed hard on the accelerator as though to trample on the whole world with my feet. As I suddenly stopped the car before it came into collision with the world, I realized that Firdaus was far more courageous than myself" (115). The psychiatrist clearly feels that she lacks the power of rejection, of refusal, of deciding against acquiescing, in spite of and perhaps because of the powers granted her by virtue of her position as part of the patriarchal system, the very system that gave rise to such situations as the one Firdaus finds herself in confrontation with. The muted anger and the frustration of the narrator thus stand in sharp contrast with the effusive self-expressiveness of Firdaus, whose very act of speech becomes her triumph over all the adverse circumstances of her life.

It is Firdaus's rejection of and contempt for the political power network and all the oppression it exercises that set her apart and above the professional classes represented by the psychiatrist. In her death, she feels that she will attain not only a state of liberation that she could not find in real life, but also a status equal to those who wield the reins of power: "I am waiting for them now. In a little while, they will come to take me away, and in the morning, I will not be here. I will not be in any place known to people. This journey to a place no one on earth knows about, including kings, princes, and rulers, fills me with pride. I have always been trying to find something to fill me with pride, something to make my head tower above the heads of all others, including kings, princes, and rulers" (112).

In *Woman at Point Zero*, the socially acceptable roles of some characters seem to undergo significant revision and redefinition. The prison warden, for example, is noticeably sympathetic to Firdaus. Contrary to the expected image of the prison warden as gatekeeper, this unnamed woman displays a keen sense of confederacy with the soon-to-be-executed prisoner. When the psychiatrist/narrator approaches her for permission to interview Firdaus, the warden is outspokenly indignant and snaps at the physician in a manner that is clearly unacceptable, both on social and hierarchical levels:

> "They're going to hang her in a few days. What would she want to do with you or with anybody else? Just leave her alone."

The warden's tone was indignant and she looked at me with eyes full of anger, as though I was the one who was going to hang her in a few days.

"I'm not in charge of anything, here or outside," I said.

"They all say that," she said angrily.

"Why are you so mad? Do you think Firdaus is innocent and does not deserve hanging?" I asked her.

"Whether she killed or didn't doesn't matter one bit. She's innocent and doesn't deserve hanging. They are the ones that should be hanged." (7–8)

The warden seems to identify closely with her incarcerated charge. Throughout the negotiations over the psychiatrist's meeting with Firdaus, the warden demonstrates a protectiveness that can only stem from a deep sense of identification with the prisoner, as a member of the oppressed classes, and resentment against the psychiatrist, as a member of the oppressor classes. Her use of the ambiguous pronoun "they" can easily refer to the whole society, the upper/middle classes to which the psychiatrist presumably belongs, or to men in general, who, perhaps in the warden's view, are ultimately responsible for Firdaus's predicament.

The paternal role likewise comes under El Saadawi's critical gaze. The novel is blatantly irreverent in its presentation of paternal figures such as Firdaus's father and uncle. Unlike earlier feminist discourse, this work is unapologetic about its censure of prevalent social and religious attitudes. In early feminist discourse, the authority of the father figure is frequently presented in a positive light. To cite just one example, Aisha Taymur, born in 1840 to an affluent aristocratic family, writes about her great infatuation at an early age with learning and education, and her rejection of traditionally assigned feminine roles. She notes that it was her father, rather than her mother, who was instrumental in allowing her to proceed with her intellectual pursuits and who encouraged her along the path of pursuing a literary career.[7] In Nabawiya Musa's memoirs, it is her brother who helps her, though rather reluctantly, along the path of education. He is the benign patriarch who is presented nonetheless as ineffectual and no match for his strong-headed sister (22–25). The father figure in *Woman at Point Zero*, on the other hand, is neither glorified nor romanticized. Firdaus's father is presented as selfish and brutish: "My father was a poor farmer who could neither read nor write. All he knew of life was how

to work on the land, how to sell the diseased cow before it died, how
to sell his virgin daughter before she became too old, how to steal the
produce of his neighbor before getting robbed by him, how to bend
down as though to kiss the mayor's hand but not actually to do it, and
how to beat up his wife every night until she licked the floor" (16).
Firdaus's father, it is made abundantly clear, is not a unique case. His
ignorance and brutality, like those of his peers, are compounded by a
total disregard for the ethical and religious codes that these men seem
to uphold on the surface. The sarcasm with which their hypocrisies
are exposed is hard to miss:

> Every Friday, he would wear a clean gown and go
> to Friday prayers at the mosque. Afterwards, I would see him
> walk with other men, talking of the Friday sermon. They
> would extol the Imam's masterful and extraordinary powers
> of oratory. Stealing was wrong, poisoning cattle was wrong,
> violating women was wrong, injustice was wrong, and beat-
> ing was wrong. Obedience was a duty, and so was the love of
> the homeland. To love the ruler was like loving God. May
> God preserve the king or the president and keep him for the
> country, the Arab nation, and the whole of humanity. (16–17)

The men of the village only pay lip service to the duties assigned to
them, not only by Islamic precepts but also by social and ethical mores.
When it comes to their day-to-day dealings with their families, ego-
ism motivates their actions: "No matter what happened, my father
would never sleep without his supper. Whenever there was no food
in the house, we all went without supper except for him. My mother
used to hide his supper from our eyes by placing it in the opening of
the oven. He would then sit alone to enjoy his meal while we looked at
him. I tried once to reach into his plate, but he hit me on the hand" (23).

Both Fatima Mernissi, the Moroccan feminist writer advocating a
reinterpretation of Islamic teachings, and Nawal El Saadawi seem to
start from the same premise and arrive at more or less similar conclu-
sions.[8] If men have tended to abuse women in Arab/Muslim societies
and refused to grant them their rights, it is because of neither the
Qur'an nor the Prophet, nor the Islamic tradition in general. However, while Mernissi adopts a theoretical approach to the problem,
El Saddawi offers the lived experience of women subjected to such
gross misinterpretations of Islamic teachings. In fact, the discrepancies

between the original religious teachings and the abusive practices are not presented within a theoretical framework in El Saadawi's novel. She seems to be relying largely on the reader's recognition of such disparities rather than trying to formulate a clear-cut theoretical position regarding this ongoing debate.

The Azharite uncle in *Woman at Point Zero* is a clear example of the tacit collaboration between the religious establishment and masculinity. He offers a rather blatant example of the abuse that the young Firdaus is subjected to, in this case by a close member of the family who is supposed to fulfill the role of guardian. The religious education he receives through the sacrifices of his mother, as we later learn, sets him apart socially from Firdaus's father, who spends all his life in the countryside working as a farmer.[9] This education empowers him both socially and religiously, but makes him at the same time more open to blame and censure. When he molests his young, inexperienced niece, his action cannot be divorced from the perception of him as a man of religion, and is therefore doubly shocking. Furthermore, his abuse of the sanctified role of uncle is particularly poignant, since Islam sets great store by the avuncular role. Equally shocking is the manner in which he, now married, disposes of his nineteen-year-old niece through marrying her off to an ugly old man in order to get rid of the financial burden she represents. The dowry offered to the uncle by the elderly bridegroom is a mouth-watering incentive that blinds him to the manifest disadvantages of such an arrangement. The Islamic injunction against marrying a woman through coercion is conveniently bypassed, and so is the Islamic plea for tenderness and sympathy in dealing with one's blood relatives, particularly women.

Firdaus's marriage is presented as the first step on the road to prostitution. The stinginess of the husband, his physical abuse of her, as well as his off-putting physical characteristics push the young woman to the streets to learn to fend for herself. While still married, the young Firdaus is beaten up by her husband and returns to her uncle for sanctuary against this abuse. But the uncle is completely unsympathetic. A husband, he tells her, may beat his wife to ensure her obedience. The uncle's wife, ironically enough, agrees with his view. She tells Firdaus that her husband, Firdaus's uncle, beats her as part of his prerogative as a husband. Firdaus has not witnessed such an event herself, so it is impossible for her to verify this statement, which may have been motivated by the wife's wish to keep Firdaus away from her family by getting her to accept her situation and stay with her husband at any price. In this instance, as in many others in the novel, Nawal El Saadawi is clearly confrontational about the abuse perpetrated in the name of Islamic precepts and presented as part of a heritage that should never be challenged or even questioned.

It is significant that Firdaus gets an education and receives her secondary school degree with flying colors. She seems to embody the fulfillment of the dream of many feminists who saw education as the cornerstone not only of women's personal fulfillment but also of the reform of the whole society. Firdaus's degree, however, is shown to be so superfluous that it is almost a laughing matter. It is only when she becomes a successful prostitute that she has her own library and has the free time to spend alone with her books. Her degree is placed in a prominent position in her apartment as ironic, perhaps defiant testimony to an ambition that was never fulfilled. Robbed of its authentic meaning as a gateway to a respectable life, the degree becomes a vacuous emblem decorating the walls. To attain the higher pleasures of the mind, a woman needs to stoop to selling her body to the highest bidder.

Even sincerity in love is no guarantee of entry into a more socially acceptable existence for women like Firdaus. Her love affair with a leftist revolutionary ends in disaster when he leaves her for a more socially and materially advantageous marriage. Firdaus's bitterness at the situation is expressed clearly and forcefully.

> In all my life, I hadn't known such excruciating pain. As a prostitute, the pain I felt was far less acute. It was a pain that was more unreal than real. As a prostitute, I was not myself, and my feelings were not mine. Nothing has hurt me as much as the pain I'm feeling now, and nothing has humiliated me as much. Perhaps because as a prostitute I had been overly humiliated, and no further humiliations were possible. Or perhaps because the prostitute's life is on the streets, there isn't much one expects there. But in love, I expected something. In love, I dreamt of becoming a human being. Perhaps as a prostitute I gave nothing for free, while in love I gave away myself, my body, my mind, and my efforts for free. I gave love all I had. I gave away myself without any weapons or defenses. As a prostitute, I was in a permanent state of self-defense, protecting myself by withdrawing into myself, giving men a passive, unfeeling body. I defended myself through my withdrawal and passivity, and passivity is a form of resistance,

telling men that they could take my body, but they would never be able to get me to reciprocate, get excited or feel even pain. (95–96)

"One is not born, but rather becomes, a woman," declared Simone de Beauvoir in *The Second Sex* in 1949. In *Woman at Point Zero*, Nawal El Saadawi argues that a woman is not born, but becomes, a prostitute, by tracing the process whereby it happens. She demonstrates how the forces contributing to the transformation of Firdaus from one state to another are tragic in the true sense of the word. They are tragic because the ultimate message seems to be that women have to surrender life in order to attain their full freedom. Firdaus's narration of her life story is the final expression of her ability to exercise her free will to the full. Death therefore becomes the fulfillment of an ultimate liberation that is not attainable in this life.

Woman at Point Zero presents a discourse that is confrontational, a discourse of rebellion "that is directed against patriarchy and all other forms of oppression" (Al-Ali, 33). It is a discourse that is also uncompromising in its handling of roles, issues, and ideas. In this sense, it challenges and puts in perspective the compromising feminist discourse that preceded it.

Notes

1. All excerpts are my translations from Amin 1898.
2. Prostitution was made legal in Egypt in 1905 by the British colonial power, with the proviso that it be conducted in specific places licensed for the purpose, that minors were not involved in the practice, and that prostitutes underwent weekly medical examinations. It was, however, outlawed by military edict No. 76 in 1949, which enforced the shutdown of brothels, Law No. 78, passed in 1951, and Law No. 10 in 1961.
3. For a comprehensive discussion of this issue, see Badran, chap. 10.
4. The fight against prostitution appears as item 9 on the social agenda of the Feminist Union Program drawn up and published in 1924. See Sobki.
5. Sawsan Nagui offers a detailed and interesting analysis of women's fiction in Egypt from 1888 to 1985.
6. This and all subsequent texts from the novel are my translations.
7. For a discussion and an analysis of the meaning of the paternal and maternal roles in Aisha Taymur's upbringing, see Hatem, 75–80.

8. See Fatima Mernissi, *The Veil and the Male Elite,* where she expounds her view that the manipulation of the sacred texts by men is a structural characteristic of the practice of power in Muslim societies.

9. Studying at the renowned Islamic university, Al Azhar, has always been regarded as a great privilege that bestows lifelong respect on those lucky enough to have been the recipients of this form of education.

Works Cited

Abdallah, Sophie. 1959. *Domoo' Al Tawba (Tears of Repentance).* Cairo: Arab Company of Publishing.

Abdel Rahman, Aisha. 1942. *Sayed Al-Ezba (The Lord of the Manor).* Cairo: Dar El Ma'aref.

Abu-Lughod, Lila, ed. 1998. *Remaking Women: Feminism and Modernity in the Middle East.* Cairo: American University in Cairo Press.

Ali, Nadje Sadig Al-. 1998. *Gender Writing/Writing Gender: The Representation of Women in a Selection of Modern Egyptian Literature.* Cairo: American University in Cairo Press.

Amin, Kassem. 1898. *The Liberation of Women.* Cairo: n.p.

Badran, Margot. 1995. *Feminism, Islam and Nation: Gender and the Making of Modern Egypt.* Princeton, NJ: Princeton University Press.

Hatem, Mervat. 1998. "Aisha Taymur's Tears and the Critique of the Modernist and Feminist Discourses on Nineteenth-Century Egypt." In *Remaking Women: Feminism and Modernity in the Middle East,* ed. Lila Abu-Lughod, 75–80. Cairo: American University in Cairo Press.

Mahabane, Itumeleng. 2000. "A Journey through Patriarchy and Beyond." *Sunday Times* (London), April 23.

Malti-Douglas, Fedwa. 1995. *Men, Women, and God(s): Nawal El Saadawi and Arab Feminist Poetics.* Berkeley: University of California Press.

Mernissi, Fatima. 1987. *The Veil and the Male Elite: A Feminist Interpretation of Women's Rights in Islam.* Trans. Mary Jo Lakeland. New York: Addison-Wesley.

Mohamed, Zeinab. 1927. *Al-Saqita Fi Ahdan Al-Radhila (Falling into Vice).* Cairo: Indian-Egyptian Press.

Musa, Nabawiya. 1999. *My History (Tarikhi bi qalam).* Cairo: Women and Memory Forum.

Nagui, Sawsan. 1989. *Al Mar'a Fi Al Mir'aa (Woman in the Mirror): A Critical Study of Feminist Fiction in Egypt, 1888–1985.* Cairo: Al Arabi Lilnashr.

Saadawi, Nawal El. 2002/1975. *Imraa Inda Nuktat Al Sifr (Woman at Point Zero)*. 6th ed. Cairo: Dar Al Mostaqbal.

Sobki, Amal El. 1986. *The Feminist Movement in Egypt between the Two Revolutions of 1919 and 1952*. Cairo: General Book Organization.

4

Nadine Gordimer's *Burger's Daughter*

Consciousness, Identity, and Autonomy

Nobantu L. Rasebotsa

> Art cannot change the world, but it can conribute to changing the consciousness and drives of the men and women who could change the world.
>
> —Herbert Marcuse, *The Aesthetic Dimension*

Nadine Gordimer's achievement as South Africa's premier novelist, short-story writer, critic, and Nobel Prize winner has been acclaimed as arising from her ability "to give the world a reckoning of the terrible cost of racism in her country that goes beyond what journalism can relate" (Prescott, 40).[1] In one of her interviews, calling attention to the world of racism and the paradoxical existence of blacks and whites in South Africa, she notes that "blacks and whites have been kept apart in some ways, but locked together in many others" and declares that the fact that these racial groups "have worked alongside each other, observing each other, absorbing each other's 'vibes'" inspires her writing. She asserts, for example, that "we know a great deal that is never spoken and this is a whole area rich in material for any novelist" (Elgrably, 28). Her experience and perception of the effects of South Africa's racial laws thus motivate her to sensitize her privileged, white society toward recognizing the need for interaction and transformation of their own consciousness.

In *Burger's Daughter*, as in most of her works, Gordimer's objective is to "change the consciousness" of the white South African people by addressing the inflexible and imperceptive views that, for a long time, kept South African political structures unchanged. "We whites [in South Africa] have been brought up on so many lies . . . [that] whites have developed a totally unreal idea of how they ought to live, of their right to go on living in that country. Consequently, they must undergo a long process of shedding illusions in order to fully understand the basis of staying in South Africa" (Blaise, 13). Rosa, the protagonist in *Burger's Daughter*, is Gordimer's example of someone who is trapped in this racial category and who must "undergo a long process of shedding illusions," not only to "fully understand the basis of staying in South Africa" but in order to create for herself a unique identity.

Critics, while addressing issues of racism, domination, oppression, and liberation, have analyzed *Burger's Daughter* from different perspectives, including historical, psychological, modernist, and feminist approaches. My own interest is to comprehend how the consciousness of an individual's life, whatever the experience, be it social or political, private or public, gets transformed and tested in this novel. I employ Paulo Freire's philosophy of "domination and transformation of consciousness" and Bibi Bakare-Yusuf's application of Existential Phenomenology to demonstrate how Gordimer attempts to find ways to "define the whole question of being and existence."[2]

Freire's statement that "every relationship of domination, of exploitation, of oppression, is by definition violent" (1973, 10) highlights his concern regarding the destructive nature of the dominant classes. Domination, he argues, is an attempt to create a "culture of silence" in which the dominated "are prohibited from creatively taking part in the transformations of their society and therefore prohibited from being" (1985, 50). Nonetheless, he is convinced that "the normal role of human beings in and with the world is not a passive one" (1973, 4). A person is able to move from "a naive state of consciousness to the level of critical consciousness" (1985, 87), and this results in a "critical capacity to make choices and tranform that reality" (1973, 4). This level of critical consciousness also builds one's capacity to reject the "prescriptions" of others (4). For her part, Bakare-Yusuf contributes tremendously to a greater understanding of oppressive power relations by encouraging a critical approach that "stresses transformation and productive forms of contestation" (11). According to her, "identity, agency and experience are not fixed or *given in advance*. Rather, they are . . . continuously being re-constituted and open to changing contexts" (18; emphasis mine).

In addition, I interrogate other critics' observations either to underscore my point of departure or to clarify how Rosa's "lived experience" transforms her consciousness, how she defines her identity, and how she achieves autonomy within the exceedingly oppressive environment of then-apartheid South Africa. Robert Boyers, for example, raises issues that are significant to what I suggest is Gordimer's central vision: the individual's transformation that emerges from his or her own critical consciousness of the reality of both "lived experience" and values, be they intrinsic or extrinsic.

> One may say that it [*Burger's Daughter*] is a novel of consciousness, but the statement must be modified to include the fact that *the* central consciousness is very largely preoccupied with public issues. . . . The dominant mode of *Burger's Daughter* is finally progressive rather than retrospective. In its movement toward reconciliation and affirmation it is a novel of growth, with that growth conceived as the achievement of a combined personal and political maturity. (1984b, 67)

A combination of personal and political consciousness has always been a condition of paramount importance to Gordimer in her depiction of those protagonists who are willing to involve themselves in and commit themselves to an authentic change in the political structure of their country.

Yet, as Rowland Smith observes, Rosa is "brought up to believe instinctively in the primacy of the political rather than the personal" (164). He concludes, in fact, that "the political failures, personal tragedies and endless suffering recorded in the novel have *hardly altered her appearance*" except that "she is livelier and less reserved" (173; emphasis mine). Smith appears to regard Rosa's consciousness as simply the product of submission to an overwhelming inherited tradition. Thus he oversimplifies the implications of Rosa's critical thinking, or "'internal' verbal discourse" (Althusser, 169), and views her critical assessment of her life as a way of remembering her past simply to "honor those aspects of the past that live on in oneself" (Boyers 1985, 144).

My point of departure is the role of the individual's reflective consciousness in an attempt to resolve certain pressures, imposed or inherited. In *Burger's Daughter* this consciousness is tied very specifically to the historical realities that affect Rosa's sense of place, purpose, and existence. Stylistically, the novel is rich in symbolism and irony. The epigraph, the title, and the structure are intertwined and organized around the binaries of dominator and dominated, black and white, father and daughter, private and public, internal and external world, repressed consciousness and critical consciousness. This dualism and integration is consistent with Gordimer's fundamental belief in the inseparability and paradoxical relation of the self and Other.

The novel's epigraph (from Claude Lévi-Strauss), "I am the place in which something has occurred," announces the existence of the whole political terrain in which Rosa's "being and existence" and "transformation" manifest themselves. Structurally, much is made of the symbolic importance of Rosa's journey from South Africa to France and England and back to South Africa, the country of her origin. At one level the journey symbolizes Rosa's progression toward authentic political consciousness.[3] At another level it signals the complex nature of the challenges Rosa faces on her arduous road to self-identity and self-autonomy. Gordimer's account of this journey confirms Bakare-Yusuf's notion that "identity, agency and experience are not fixed or given in advance. Rather, they are part of [one's] lived situation, continuously being re-constituted and open to changing contexts" (18).

In the opening paragraphs of the novel, the reader's attention is immediately drawn to the essential features and pressures of the insensitive white South African government: "Imagine, a schoolgirl," now turned frequent prison visitor because she has "somebody inside" (9). "Her hair was not freshly washed" and "she probably had not slept well the previous night and had not had time to eat between hurrying home from school and coming to the prison" (10–11). Prison life in South Africa, as anywhere else in the world, creates limitations, but Rosa's being outside prison does not in any way make her own life any more secure. Her frequent visits and constant link with those already condemned to prison, and those who will later die in prison, all hint at Rosa's own lack of protection from the life-threatening forces within South Africa and the insecurities of living in the prison-like country. She, like her imprisoned parents and associates, still experiences a very constricted life, and her sense of belonging is defined in relation to those whose political activities have been curtailed and whose voices have been silenced. According to Gordimer, this sense of imprisonment in South Africa, be it inside or outside actual prison, has to be recognized as equally challenging.

The tension exemplified through Rosa's separation from and connection to her imprisoned parents highlights the type of "lived experience" that raises the complex questions of existence that Gordimer continues to grapple with. Gordimer has explained, for example, that her "actual writing comes from the tension of being involved and yet standing apart," and, as stated earlier, her chief interest in writing is in finding "words to define the whole question of being and existence"[4] given the tension and the contradictions of her country's political situation. Thus, Rosa's consciousness regarding her being and existence as Burger's daughter gains particular significance through the title of the novel. Her early stages of existence have to be understood largely within the context of the history of her parents' political resistance.

Rosa's "being," or indeed the transformation of her consciousness, is defined in terms of her interaction with others at the prison. For example, visiting the prison, "The school girl pressed forward with the rest, turning her head with the *bold* encouragement with which glances were linking everyone" (9; emphasis mine). It is through interaction with other people going through similar experiences that she learns to be "bold," to "press forward"—and, as we will see, to forge ahead in life. Her experience as a prison visitor and her "remarkable maturity" (11) will further encourage her to independently devise the unconventional idea of using a hot-water bottle to communicate messages to her imprisoned mother: "The hot-water bottle is my own idea. My mother never used one" (16). Her growing consciousness of the world around her and her maturity are translated into creative thinking and action.

Karen Halil, in her insightful article on *Burger's Daughter*, recognizes Rosa's "subjectivity as a shifting process" (32). Her approach, however, differs from that of Bakare-Yusuf who, taking a cue from Merleau-Ponty and de Beauvoir, insists that "any account of existence must be approached from a variety of angles simultaneously" (16). In other words, while "lived experience," at least according to Bakare-Yusuf, underlies the "simultaneous" but "continuous" learning process (19), Halil's approach first "fixes" Rosa's experience regarding her parents' political dominance: "As a young girl, conscripted by her father's ideology, Rosa is a *static* subject who has not yet learned to travel. She is an *absolutely political* subject who has no private life, whose focus of lived experience is consumed by dominant discourses" (34; emphasis mine). Halil's argument locates "lived experience" with its transformative effects only in the possibilities presented by Rosa's departure from South Africa. That is why for her, Rosa, "who has not yet learned to travel," remains "static" until she travels to France. Halil's assertion that Rosa is already "an absolutely political subject" highlights the extent to which, under repressive governments, children such as Rosa, herself at the tender age of fourteen years, get politicized. If Rosa is denied any sense of individuality, as implied in Halil's conclusion that she "has no access to language except through another ideology" (35–36), and if, also according to Halil's judgment, Rosa's "father's word is law and Rosa has no word, no voice" (35), then it is crucial and worthwhile to gauge Rosa's growing consciousness and the extent of her political commitment through her own responses to the political, social, and cultural challenges she has to confront. One such response has already been demonstrated through Rosa's strategic use of the hot-water bottle during her prison visits, as her way of dealing with repressive structures. Rosa's strategic approach hints at the uniqueness of her identity as one who is likely to face the struggle successfully and probably remain unharmed by the violence of South Africa's political forces.

The crucial question of identity and its meaning in South Africa's prison context is brought to the fore in the first few pages of the novel, and in just one line to which a whole page is devoted. At the prison, Rosa reflects upon what people's perception of her role might be: "When they saw me outside the prison, what did they see?" (13). She recognizes that she will "never know. It's all *concocted*" (14; emphasis mine). In other words, her identity, created through the eyes of the public, remains a socially constructed representation. It is this "concoction" that Rosa, throughout the novel, reflects upon, challenges, defies, and then reconstructs.

In tracing Rosa's growing consciousness and her redefinition of identity, I find Bakare-Yusuf's approach useful. She notes that "the continuous interaction between world and embodied being suggests that through lived experience, a woman is always involved in the process of determining her project: discovering who she is, and what she will become" (19). Accordingly, then, what constitutes Rosa's identity is based on the "context of [her] existence" (16), which is multilayered. Such identity, Bakare-Yusuf believes, by way of Merleau-Ponty and de Beauvoir, should "be approached from a variety of angles *simultaneously*" (16; emphasis mine).

Yet Halil's reading of Rosa's experience of menstruation, described in the novel as the "monthly crisis of destruction, the purging, tearing, draining of my own structure" (16), seems to ignore this simultaneity. She instead interprets the "monthly crisis" as loss of "access to her body and her agency" (Halil, 35). Hence Halil's conclusion, quoting Meese, that it "signals the destructive machinery of apartheid" (35). Rosa's experience of menstruation, however, if approached in the sense that Bakare-Yusuf suggests, could instead signal an "awakening consciousness of [Rosa's] body"[5] (Wilson-Tagoe, 33), as she simultaneously tries to negotiate and contain the same destructive machinery of apartheid symbolized through her parents' deaths in a South African prison. The extent of Rosa's growing consciousness, the degree to which she experiences her body, the level of her self-reflection and the nature of her identity will all, according to Bakare-Yusuf's model, be "modulated by her specific situation and the value that the world places on that body."[6] And Rosa's "body" is highly valued, as a link between the world of the detainees and that of the activists outside the prison.

My own interest is in how Rosa, at the prison, responds to her menstruation and simultaneously, to borrow Bakare-Yusuf's phrase, "negotiates the world" (17). As if confirming this simultaneity, Rosa says, "As I am alternately submerged below and thrust over the threshold of pain I am aware of the moulded rubber loop by which the hot-water bottle hangs from my finger" (16). Rosa's experience of her menstrual pain, combined with her awareness of the responsibilities she has to fulfill as she confronts the world, hint at the existence of such polarities as the "biological factors, historical forces . . . [and] ethical considerations . . . that impinge" (Bakare-Yusuf, 16) on her consciousness. Thus, "in the context of [her] existence" (16), diverse forces influence her perspective at any given time—including both before and after her father, Lionel's, death.

After Lionel's death, Rosa's contemplative question sets the tone for her readiness to explore, analyze, and verify the connection between her past, present, and future: "Now you are free. . . . What does one do with such knowledge?" (62). Before her father's death, Rosa feels a sense of imprisonment, as her identity, that of living in her own father's identity as "Burger's daughter," denies her various aspects of freedom. She lacks freedom of movement ("I have no passport because I am my father's daughter" [62]), freedom of association ("People who associate with me must be prepared to be suspect because I am my father's daughter" [62–3]), and freedom of choice ("what I wanted was to take a law degree, but . . . [as] my father's daughter . . . I had to do something else instead" [63]). This lived experience, this denial of the right to think and act freely, creates inner tension and ambiguous feeling once her father dies: "I knew I must have wished him to die; that to exult and to sorrow were the same thing for me" (63). In order to grow, Rosa confronts these mixed emotions through self-reflection.

Rosa's relation with Conrad, a young man who is "neither a radical nor a radical sympathiser" (Boyers 1984b, 72), serves as a "catalyst" for a thorough demonstration of both their consciousnesses as reflective beings. They are critical and curious; to quote Denis Collins in his discussion of Paulo Freire, they seek "causal relationships in their perception of the world and of consciousness itself" (80). Conrad tells her, "You didn't cry when your father was sentenced. I saw. People said how brave. Some people say, a cold fish. But it's conditioning, brain-washing: more like a trained seal, maybe" (52). It is through such discourses about herself that Rosa's critical perception is stimulated. In her effort to explain her behavior and define her personal growth, she reflects, "If Lionel and my mother . . . if the concepts of our life, our relationships, we children accepted from them were those of Marx and Lenin, they'd already become natural and personal by the time they reached me" (50; ellipsis in original). It is her own critical comprehension of how her relationship with the political world evolved that helps her overcome the "naive state of consciousness" which, according to Freire, usually engages solely in action that is devoid of reflection, like that of a "trained seal."

Clearly, Rosa is aware of her inherited ideology. Her liberationist philosophy is consistent with that of Freire, who insists that such an inherited ideology, when "merely transmitted," is itself an "ideological myth, even if it were transmitted with the intention of liberating men" (1985, 86). In order to authenticate her beliefs, she must destroy the myth and retain only those ideas which validate her own view of the world. Rosa's grasp of her father's ideology is revealed not only through her own reflection on his ideals and ideological position but also through her constant attempts at clarification of the relationship between Lionel Burger and Conrad. She says to Conrad, "Lionel Burger probably saw in you the closed circuit of self; for him, such a life must be in need of a conduit towards meaning, which posited: outside self. That's where the tension that makes it possible to live lay, for him; between self and others; between the present and creation of something called the future" (86). Yet for Rosa the immediate future, after her father's death in prison, lay in her attempts to lead a private life largely divorced from the Burgers' politics and suffering. As a way of following her feelings, she resolves to leave South Africa to live in France. "The real reason" (196) for her departure, she says, was a donkey's suffering. Seeing a cart driver whip his donkey, Rosa has a vision of an entire history of "torture without the torturer, rampage, pure cruelty gone beyond control of the humans who have spent thousands of years devising it" (208). "After the donkey I couldn't stop myself. I don't know how to live in Lionel's country" (210). The forces of injustice in South Africa overwhelm her and drive her out of the country. Instead of confronting South Africa's problems, she would rather deny any connection with the country. To her, it is "Lionel's country," not hers.

Her decision to leave South Africa throws into contrast Lionel's conviction to continue fighting for political change in the country. Standing accused in court, Lionel had declared, "I acted according to my conscience on all counts. I would be guilty only if I were innocent of working to destroy racism in my country" (27). Yet Rosa would rather leave the country than fight, an action which, for somebody like Lionel, is tantamount to being guilty in every conceivable way.

Commenting on Rosa's simple stated reason for traveling abroad—"I want to go somewhere else" (184)—Brandt Vermeulen, a supporter of South Africa's apartheid policies who Rosa sees as being given a chance to prove, by furthering her passport application, that he is what he thinks himself to be, "an individualist . . . committed to the volk without sacrificing 'broad sympathies' and 'wide understanding'" (193), says that the word he heard was "'*know*' instead of 'go'" (185, emphasis mine). But Vermeulen's mistake is perhaps no mistake at all. In other words, Rosa's real purpose is not to travel for the sake of it; rather, it is to gain knowledge and grow in consciousness. After all, Rosa has admitted that she does not "know how to live in Lionel's country," implicitly not her own. She wants to "free" herself from Lionel's experience, but she recognizes that "To be free is to become almost a stranger to oneself" (81). She will come to know that, when she left South Africa in the name of freedom, it was that complete stranger in her—that lack of inner awareness and of a particular kind of experience—that pushed her toward disengagement from her origins.

This depth of awareness hints at Rosa's recognition of the conflicting notions of freedom and, once again, at Gordimer's own recognition of the contradictions and complexities of "being and existence." In Bakare-Yusuf's terms, these contradictions and complexities could be summarized as "certain forms of . . . personal and collective connections

and disconnections, capacities and limitations that confront [an indi-
vidual] and work through [her]" (16). Rosa confirms the existence
of these underlying forces.

> Lionel—my mother and father—people in that house,
> had a connection with blacks that was completely personal. . . .
> The connection was something no other whites ever had in
> quite the same way. A connection without reservations on
> the part of blacks or whites. The political activities and at-
> titudes of that house came from the inside outwards, and blacks
> in that house where there was no God felt this embrace be-
> fore the Cross. . . . [I]t was a human conspiracy, above all
> other kinds.
> I have lost connection. It's only the memory of child-
> hood warmth for me. (172)

In France and England, away from "Lionel's country," Rosa's
subsequent discovery of a vital connection between herself and the
South African people creates a shift in perception that forces her to reflect upon her role as a white South African. Earlier, a hint regarding
possibilities of a shift in consciousness is captured in her own words
after witnessing the donkey's suffering: "These are the things that
move me now—when I say 'move' I don't mean tears or anger. I mean
a sudden shift, a tumultuous upheaval, an uncontrollable displacement. . . . I don't know what metaphors to use to describe the process
by which I'm making my own metaphors for suffering" (196). This is
an indication of her move toward her own independent perception
and articulation of a future life in South Africa. It is this rigorous
self-scrutiny that finally motivates her toward a return to South Africa, determined to participate fully by committing herself to the oppressed Soweto children. Going to France, then, becomes a symbolic
journey of discovery, which translates not only into self-discovery
but also self-authentication, self-identity, and autonomy.

In France, her first contact, Katya Bagnelli, Lionel Burger's first
wife, becomes the catalyst through whom Rosa begins to "know" and
gradually appreciate the value of staying connected rather than disen-
gaged[7] Katya, a former communist, had herself abandoned Lionel
for "another life," just as Rosa now attempts to find a different life
"outside what he [Lionel] lived for": "I didn't come on some pilgrimage . . . to learn about my father. . . . I wanted to know how to defect

from him" (264). Rosa, however, admits that "It is not so easy to shut oneself off from them—these people. . . . [Lionel's] friends, associates—comrades" (113). Defection and isolation are not shown as valid options for Rosa, because interaction and interconnectedness are important aspects of Gordimer's concept of being and existence. Clearly, Gordimer, through Rosa, is critical of a life of isolation and disengagement.

Highlighting what she calls the "dangers of exclusion," Christine Sizemore (72) draws on Carol Gilligan's view that "psychological health and *development* . . . are grounded in one's relationship with self and others. Too great a loss of relationship poses a serious threat to healthy development" (Taylor, Gilligan, and Sullivan, 45). The process of Rosa's developing consciousness, therefore, can only be enriched through her relationship with Katya, who plays multiple roles: she is Rosa's host, surrogate mother, her father's first wife and friend. It is Katya's lived experience that Rosa could benefit from and identify with, as she confirms: "You tell me anecdotes of your youth that could transform my own" (263).

Indeed, Rosa's social and political consciousness is enriched as she meets Katya's associates and involves herself in various activities of the French world of entertainment: "I am beginning to understand that there is a certain range of possibilities that can occur within the orbit of a particular order of life; they recur in gossip, in close conversations . . . in noisy discussions" (238). Despite her high degree of involvement, Rosa still feels "an ass, among them. . . . Out of place" (235). Neither her disengagement from South Africa nor her involvement in France is complete. There is a sense in which Rosa feels the meaninglessness of life in France when she admits to herself that she really does not fit: "they assume my life is theirs, they've taken me in. But the manner of my coming—it doesn't fit necessity or reality, here" (235).

Rosa's awareness that she is a misfit implies not only her confrontation with reality but also her continuously growing consciousness as she recognizes the impracticality and the unrealistic nature of her decision to leave South Africa. France is a "whole world" that is "outside what [Lionel] lived for" (264), one that Rosa now "knows" but resists being overwhelmed by. Her own sensibility and perception seem to have reached the level that Gayatri Spivak has famously delineated: "One cannot of course 'choose' to step out of ideology. The most responsible 'choice' seems to be to *know* it as best one can, recognize it as best one can, and, through one's necessarily inadequate interpretation, to work to change it" (120; emphasis mine). Although Halil usefully quotes this passage from Spivak in her analysis of the novel, I would disagree with her related interpretation that, when Rosa moves from South Africa to France, she "moves from sexual passivity to sexual initiation" (39). France is not the "beginning of her exploration of her sexuality." After all, in South Africa she had a sexual relationship with Conrad, just as in France she had one with Bernard Chabalier. These are the two men with whom she had a "sexual tryst," to use Halil's term. The only difference is that in South Africa, as Rosa says, she and Conrad "had stopped making love together months before I left, aware that it had become incest" (70). The implication is that, in South Africa, Rosa suppresses her sexuality, even as she is trapped by political and racial repression. In France, she confronts her sexual drives and finds sexual liberation in the "arms of a surrogate mother, Lionel's first wife, who placed erotic freedom before the needs of the party" (Newman, 80).

It is true that, in France, Rosa lives the personal and private life that her parents had denied her. We should, however, recognize that, for Gordimer, it is not only living a long-wished-for private life free from South Africa's restrictions: most importantly, it is living a very personal *choice*, a response which is a consequence of Rosa's critical perception and recognition that hers has been, to use Freire's term, a "dominated consciousness." It is this mere imposition or transference of ideas that Rosa seeks to verify. Her success at validating her beliefs as authentically hers in the Freirean sense depends on her critical reflection and action upon the reality of what she has perhaps "internalized" (Freire 47–48).

For Rosa, to know and to "keep in touch with the personal and the political dimensions of her being" (Halil, 43) implies an exercise in comparison and contrast of lived experiences both inside and outside South Africa. She moves from South Africa to France, and then between France and England. As her physical space broadens, Rosa's lived experiences, in these different countries with different people, converge, allowing her to reach a complete recognition and acceptance of, in Bakare-Yusuf's formulation, "a complex web of . . . historical and cultural strands that invite continuation, adaptation or transformation" (22).

Through time, such challenging exposure creates mixed emotions. Inconsistencies manifest themselves in Rosa's conflicting responses to reality. In South Africa, she is secretly in love with a revolutionary,

Noel de Witt, but whenever she visits the prison, a symbol of extreme repression, she poses as his fiancée. Yet, in France, where "freedom" exists and "nobody expects you to be more than you are" (250), she is secretly in love with Bernard Chabalier but denies any connection with him: "Bernard Chabalier's mistress isn't Lionel Burger's daughter; she's certainly not accountable to the Future" (304). Similarly, in South Africa as well as in England, she naively claims Baasie, her childhood black friend, as her "brother" and believes they have both "defected." Yet, in England, when Baasie rejects any connection with her on the basis of her whiteness—"I'm not your Baasie, just don't go on thinking about that little kid who lived with you, don't think of that black 'brother,' that's all" (321)—Rosa begins to understand too well the complexities of the South African historical and political situation. Hence, as she concedes, "to couple his kind of defection with mine" (330) would be inappropriate. Such are the manifestations of Rosa's rigorous critique of the reality of her lived experience.

Rosa's stay in France, therefore, is not only a denunciation of paternalistic manipulation and domination, as John Cooke suggests, but also a declaration of her verification and validation of her political convictions.[8] In her conversation with Robert Boyers, Gordimer says, "It was necessary to have Rosa leave South Africa in order to show how impossible it was for her to stay away" (Boyers 1984a, 5–6). In other words, in South Africa she had felt the oppressive domination, but because the "dominated consciousness does not have sufficient distance from reality to objectify it in order to know it in a critical way" (Freire 1985, 75), she had to leave the country. Her perception of life in France in turn intensifies her political commitment to South Africa because, "for Rosa," says Gordimer, "these [French] people seem as if they're from another planet" (Boyers 1984a, 6).

Rowland Smith believes that Rosa returns to South Africa as a result of the the shock from Baasie's confrontation with her (102), but Rosa, through her monologue, ironically shares the truth with her now dead father: "It isn't Baasie . . . who sent me back here." The "idea" to return to South Africa can be traced back to "You [Lionel] and my mother and the faithful [who] never limited yourselves to being like anyone else" (332)—that is, categorized and dismissed as white. Her identification with Lionel signals her move toward self-acceptance as Burger's daughter, an identity she had previously attempted to reject because at the time it reduced her personal identity to merely being like her father and not herself.

The extent of Rosa's changing consciousness is not obvious to Bernard Chabalier, her French lover. Even as "Rosa came to awareness of her own being like the rising tick of a clock in an empty room" (272), he misinterprets her social involvements in France as an indication of her political indifference to the violence of South Africa's racial politics. Hence, he thinks he can dissuade her from her political intentions: "you can't enter someone else's cause or salvation. . . . the blacks—their freedom. . . . It's not open to you" (297). Even as he reassures her, "There's plenty you can do, Rosa. In Paris, in London. . . . Enough for a lifetime" (297), Rosa's own awareness of the impossibility of erasing her past is played out in her thoughts: "If you live in Europe . . . things change . . . but continuity never seems to break. You don't have to throw the past away" (249; first ellipsis in original).

While her past and sense of belonging now draw her closer to South Africa than Europe, her vision of the future South Africa remains uncertain. She wonders, "how will they fit in, white people?" Her prediction is that "When they lose power, it'll be cut. Just like that! . . . Africans will take up their own kind of past the whites [herself included] never belonged to" (249). Rosa's ability to perceive the complexities and uncertainties of the future calls attention to her ever-shifting consciousness as she struggles with purposeful reflection on those aspects of her existence that could bring meaning to her political identity. In a way, Rosa's image of herself as both an alienated and a committed South African confirms Gordimer's belief that "life is aleatory in itself; being is constantly pulled and shaped this way and that by circumstances and different levels of consciousness" (1992, 6).

As a result, when Rosa finally returns to South Africa, certainly mature beyond her twenty-seven years when she went to "Europe for the first time" (231), we are convinced that her growth in consciousness, her acceptance of her own identity as Burger's daughter, and her ultimate personal choice to do "everything . . . in the name of future generations" (328) have been a continuous process from childhood to adulthood. Indeed, when the reader first meets her at the age of fourteen outside the prison, Rosa is symbolically playing a marginal role. In adulthood, she, like her parents in prison, is now at the core of South Africa's political activities, reaching for and achieving higher and larger goals. She now actively negotiates her identity as one who fights a common cause with blacks. After all, she, too, has gone through a very painful experience, losing both her parents soon after their own experience of the violence of the white South African government. It seems clear that Rosa's resolve to assist in healing the black children's physical and emotional pain is also a way of confronting her own internal pain. Her actions and attitude fit Linda Klouzal's definition of a resourceful woman: "A woman who can confront her internal pain is able to seek creative solutions to her considerable external difficulties and take action" (258).

Action is also key to Gordimer's philosophy, as she signals by quoting the Ming-era Chinese philosopher Wang Yangming in her epigraph to the second section of the novel: "To know and not to act is not to know" (213). Thus, Rosa translates what she knows into action, rather than allowing herself to be overwhelmed by black people's suffering. She boldly embraces what Klouzal poses as the "existential question: how do people deal with suffering?" (257). Rosa's response is to work among Soweto children and assist them in the slow but sure walk to freedom, expressed metaphorically in her words, "I am teaching them to walk again, at Baragwanath Hospital. They put one foot before the other" (332). Through her newly assumed role, Rosa expresses positive feelings about the future of the children, while simultaneously conveying a sense of self-fulfillment through her contribution to history and the black community. Rosa's resourcefulness, her participation in the struggle for the autonomy of the self and that of the blacks, "heightens her level of awareness of her own agency" (Klouzal, 256).

Having gained insight into the black children's lives, having become convinced that the future is now in their hands, Rosa draws a parallel between them and Lionel: "you were a bit like the black children—you had the elation" (349). Her ascription of similar qualities to both her father and the black children hints at the common identity Rosa wishes to establish between South Africa's racial groups. Such a perception is clearly rooted in her own social and political experience; as Klouzal puts it, "A woman's experience contains her definition of the situation" (256).

Although there are differences in Rosa's and Lionel's experiences, the uniqueness of her identity as Burger's daughter cannot be denied. "Womanist theorists," according to Tuzyline Allan, would explain this seeming contradiction by the concept that "difference also contains sameness" (119). Like Lionel, who "knew that his schoolgirl daughter could be counted on" (12) in the struggle for liberation, Rosa, too, later leans heavily on her father's inspiration: "when people are dead one imputes omnipotence to them" (349). It is now Rosa who invites her father's participation, spiritually. Even if this is an indulgence in fantasy, the reality is that she feels herself to be part of a larger community comprising multiple identities.

Although the novel's structure is cyclical, allowing the protagonist to come literally full circle to her original place, it is tempting to regard this kind of progression as a dead end. But critics who do so lose sight of the fact that learning starts with experience, and one experience feeds into the next. A continuous learning process enriches, through reflection and action, the earlier experience. Initially, in South Africa, Rosa operates within conditions created largely by her father's consciousness, not her own. Then, her stay in France and her visit to London push her to confront a reality that she has to reflect upon, even to the extent of conceptualizing it in an abstract manner through the monologues. Back in South Africa, she returns confidently to an experience that she can define for herself and actively participate in. The warmth, sincerity, and frankness of the monologues (see, especially, 328–32 and 348–52) highlight Rosa's increased depth of perception. Her shift in attitude is also recognizable in her remembrance and redefinition of her relationship with her father. Hers is a transformed consciousness, as indeed it reflects a progression from the previous, alienated self, who did not "know how to live in Lionel's country," to the now-committed self with a very strong conviction that "No one can defect" from Lionel's country (332).

The importance of Rosa's complex and expanding consciousness, her growth through an integrated lived experience, her multiple sense of identity, and her sense of autonomy and self-determination are expressed both symbolically and literally throughout the novel. Consequently, when Rosa finally goes back to South Africa, it is not simply to "come to terms with [her]self . . . [or] to confront without illusion the circumstances . . . in which [she] must live" (Boyers 1984b, 67), as if her action is inevitable. It is, rather, a conscious decision of a now-autonomous individual who takes risks on her own account. She can now join those who attempt to "re-order society in such a way as to do away with as much suffering as possible" (Boyers 1984a, 6). And we are satisfied that Rosa is now "conscientized" and can act in the "fullness of conviction"—because "conscientization," according to Freire, "is not a purely mental process that simply makes men aware of their situation in history, for simple awareness without action leaves political structures untouched" (quoted in Collins, 79). Gordimer's philosophy,

like Freire's, is that thought and action go together and that underlying every action are knowledge and a transformed consciousness.
Having gone through various shifts in consciousness, Rosa has also
examined and formed her own identity, a process that in turn has allowed her a high degree of autonomy.

Rosa's detention in a South African prison shows, especially, the
heightened degree of her commitment. In prison, she is the self-fulfilled
woman who, as her friend Flora reports, "hadn't changed much" (360).
Rosa's resistance to apartheid and her connection to the black prisoners find expression in the therapeutic laughter she shares with Marisa
during their physical therapy sessions, and "the female warders . . .
could not prevent messages . . . from being exchanged between the
races" (354). This ineffectiveness of prison laws in keeping racial
groups separate signals the collapse of apartheid; meanwhile, "the State
may have to drop charges" against Rosa (360). Rosa has sustained the
struggle for liberation in South Africa, maintained her commitment
as a political activist, and established her unique identity as Burger's
daughter. Not only is she, in Flora's words, "all right" and in "good
shape," she has also sustained herself and literally kept her youthful-
ness: "She looked like a little girl" (360).

Discussing the essence and nature of "well-being" despite the accompanying challenges of the struggle, Klouzal outlines the "sustaining qualities" and the "therapeutic" nature of women's activism and
struggle for liberation. She maintains, "The first [characteristic] is
a sense of one's place in history, an awareness of a legacy of struggle and suffering similar to one's own. The second is the importance
of community and secure relational ties. The third is the memory,
through stories, of empowering acts" (259). These features also lie at
the heart of *Burger's Daughter.* Its underlying mix of concrete lived
experience, abstract learning, critical thinking, and active participation, represented through Rosa's experience of consciousness, identity,
and autonomy, all integrated, certainly make this novel an enduring
piece of work.

Gordimer's own commitment to investigate and understand the
complexities of South African white domination and her interest
in the reeducation of her white community have also allowed her,
through interaction with blacks, to educate herself in the attitudes of
the dominated section of apartheid South Africa. Acknowledging her
ever-changing consciousness, a consequence of her constant reflection
on and reexamination of the reality of her country's situation, Gordimer

says, "My own consciousness has changed. . . . And, no doubt, if I keep my wits about me for a few more years, it'll keep on changing" (Gray, 270).

Notes

1. Describing the impact of this novel, Judie Newman says white "society saw itself very clearly as the target of *Burger's Daughter,* as the banning of the novel, the reaction of the South African censors, and the ensuing international furore, bore witness" (68).

2. Gordimer addresses the question of "being and existence" in much the same way as Bibi Bakare-Yusuf would like us to understand existential phenomenology: that it "teaches us to focus on existence rather than predetermined essence" (Bakare-Yusuf, 21). This approach analyzes "existence and lived experience" by "avoiding making prior assumptions regarding a subject and an object" (16).

3. Clingman examines *Burger's Daughter* as a "fictional way of working out the . . . problem" of constructing an authentic "white consciousness" (see 176). Rosa could be read as a representation of a truly heightened consciousness.

4. This statement paraphrases part of Gordimer's Nobel Prize lecture in 1991. For her, "being and existence" are two terms, inextricably intertwined, and their dualism has to be recognized and explored. The quotations are from an interview excerpted by Esther B. Fein in a *New York Times* article, "Isolation and Connection in Gordimer's Art," October 10, 1991 (accessed at http://query.nytimes.com/gst/fullpage.html?res=9D0CE1DE1F3EF933A 25753C1A967958260&sec=&spon=&pagewanted=all).

5. This experience calls to mind Bakare-Yusuf's emphasis on the importance of a woman's "experiencing her body," her ability to communicate with or to listen to her own body.

6. As Bakare-Yusuf explains, "existential phenomenologists argue that they see the body as being fundamental to experiencing the world, but recognise that it only acquires significance when placed in a bio-cultural and historical context" (17).

7. Leewenburg describes Katya as one of Rosa's "model[s] for female behaviour"(29).

8. In fact, most critics agree that when Rosa leaves South Africa she does so in an attempt to cut her links with the past, represented by her manipulative father, and the oppressive apartheid system.

Works Cited

Allan, Tuzyline Jita. 1995. *Womanist and Feminist Aesthetics: A Comparative Review.* Athens: Ohio University Press.

Althusser, Louis. 1971. "Ideology and Ideological State Apparatuses." In *Lenin and Philosophy and Other Essays,* trans. Ben Brewster. New York: Monthly Review Press.

Bakare-Yusuf, Bibi. 2003. "Beyond Determinism: The Phenomenology of African Female Existence." *Feminist Africa: Changing Cultures,* no. 2 (October–November): 8–24.

Blaise, Clark. 1984. "A Conversation with Nadine Gordimer." *Salmagundi* 62 (Winter): 9–13, 16.

Boyers, Robert. 1984a. "A Conversation with Nadine Gordimer." *Salmagundi* 62 (Winter): 3–8, 13–15.

———. 1984b. "Public and Private: On *Burger's Daughter.*" *Salmagundi* 62 (Winter): 62–92.

———. 1985. *Attrocity and Amnesia: The Political Novel since 1945.* New York: Oxford University Press.

Clingman, Stephen. 1986. *The Novels of Nadine Gordimer: History from the Inside.* Amherst: University of Massachusetts Press.

Collins, Denis E. 1977. *Paulo Freire: His Life, Works and Thought.* New York: Paulist Press.

Cooke, John. 2003. "Leaving the Mother's House." In *Nadine Gordimer's Burger's Daughter: A Casebook,* ed. Judie Newman, 81–97. Oxford: Oxford University Press.

Elgrably, Jordan. 1984. "A Conversation with Nadine Gordimer." *Salmagundi* 62 (Winter): 20–31.

Fein, Esther B. 1991. "Isolation and Connection in Gordimer's Art." *New York Times,* October 10.

Freire, Paulo. 1970. *Pedagogy of the Oppressed.* New York: Herder and Herder.

———. 1985. *The Politics of Education: Culture, Power and Liberation.* South Hadley, MA: Bergin and Garvey.

———. 2005/1973. *Education for Critical Consciousness.* New York: Continuum.

Gordimer, Nadine. 1979. *Burger's Daughter.* New York: Viking.

———. 1992. "Writing and Being." *Staffrider* (Johannesburg) 10 (2): 5–10.

Gray, Stephen. 1981. "An Interview with Nadine Gordimer." *Contemporary Literature* 22 (3): 263–71.

Halil, Karen. 1994. "Travelling the 'World Round as Your Navel': Subjectivity in Nadine Gordimer's *Burger's Daughter.*" *Ariel: A Review of International English Literature* (Calgary) 25 (2): 31–45.

Klouzal, Linda. 2003. "The Subjective Side of Development: Sources of Well-being, Resources for Struggle." In *Feminist Futures: Re-imagining Women, Culture and Development,* ed. Kum-Kum Bhavnani, John Foran, and Priya Kurian, 256–62. London: Zed.

Lazar, Karen. 1992. *"Jump and Other Stories:* Gordimer's Leap into the 1990s: Gender and Politics in Her Latest Short Fiction." *Journal of Southern African Studies* 18 (4): 783–802.

Leewenburg, Rina. 1985. "Nadine Gordimer's *Burger's Daughter:* Why Does Rosa Go Back?" *New Literature Review* (Armidale, NSW) 14:23–31.

Newman, Judie. 1988. *Nadine Gordimer.* London: Routledge.

Prescott, Peter S. 1991. "Two Sides of Nadine Gordimer." *Newsweek,* October 14.

Sizemore, Christine W. 1997. "Negotiating between Ideologies: The Search for Identity in Tsitsi Dangarembga's *Nervous Conditions* and Margaret Atwood's *Cat's Eye.*" In "Teaching African Literatures in a Global Literacy Economy," special issue, *Women's Studies Quarterly* 25 (3–4): 68–82.

Smith, Rowland. 1980. "Living for the Future." *World Literature Written in English* 19:163–73.

Spivak, Gayatri. 1988. "The Politics of Interpretations." In *In Other Worlds: Essays in Cultural Politics,* 118–33. New York: Routledge.

Taylor, Jill McLean, Carol Gilligan, and Amy M. Sullivan. 1995. *Between Voice and Silence: Women and Girls, Race and Relationship.* Cambridge: Harvard University Press.

Wilson-Tagoe, Nana. 2003. "Representing Culture and Identity: African Women Writers and National Cultures." *Feminist Africa: Changing Cultures* 2:25–41.

5

Dreams of (Dis)order

Competing Visions of Colonial Nigeria in Buchi Emecheta's *The Joys of Motherhood*

Tuzyline Jita Allan

> History does not belong only to its narrators, professional
> or amateur. While some of us debate what history is or was,
> others take it in their own hands.
>
> —Michel-Rolph Trouillot, *Silencing the Past*

> Whenever people say something bad about places that I love I
> always come out with a shocking statement. My way of telling
> people to shut up is to shock them. So to answer Braziller's
> question and to stop him from repeating the fact that Africa
> was no longer fashionable in terms of literature, I said that I
> was going to write a saga. That my books about Africa would
> take the form of a saga.
>
> —Buchi Emecheta, *Head above Water*

Literary appreciation of Buchi Emecheta has grown in tandem with the rise of critical interest in African women's writings during the last three decades. Her work embodies the collective confidence of African women's personal, political, and artistic responses to ideologies of power and domination, and she shares with the other writers in this book a symbolic victory in opening up new vistas for understanding the intricacies of African cultural life and the female culture embedded within it. Yet while placing her within this circle of defiant camaraderie, it is also necessary to ensure that her distinctiveness is not lost. She has succeeded, for example, in taking ready advantage of her ambiguous location "between" Nigeria, her birthplace, and London, where she has resided since 1962. Emecheta repositioned herself in the space between borders when she embarked upon an artistic career a decade after she arrived in England, seeing the rupture as a chance for closer scrutiny of her different but intersecting worlds. The themes growing out of her divided sense of belonging are gender-weighted, but they also call up aspects of colonial history to enlarge postcolonial perspectives on Africa. In her dual critique of the excesses of the British Empire and indigenous African patriarchy, Emecheta has established a tone of rebuttal befitting her location between cultures, in a border site which, according to Azade Seyhan, is characterized by "perpetual motion, confrontation, and translation. In writing and re-collection, the concepts of home and border become transportable, carried around in the form of political commitment and critical vision" (115).

Writing from the border site as someone who is also passionate about her African identity, Emecheta frequently draws on and challenges the colonial history of Nigeria. Her disputes with unchecked power have earned her a reputation as "the prototype of the palava woman," committed to addressing and redefining the problems of postcolonial Nigeria. Chikwenye Okonjo Ogunyemi elaborates on the cumulative power of Emecheta's resisting impulse: "in an unprecedented fashion, she holds up for scrutiny different forms and loci of oppression: motherhood; child power and child abuse; rape, incest, and sexual harassment; militarism; sexism; slavery; imperialism; (post) colonialism; classism; elitism; ethnicism, and more" (224). If there is a common thread among these thematic areas of interest, it is a pervasive sense of history. A denizen of the border, Emecheta is aware of how easy it is to get lost in a fog of misconceptions arising from the dominant delineations of history. Hence, as John Hope Franklin cautions, "[i]n discussing the history of a people one must distinguish between what has *actually* happened and what those who have written the history have *said* has happened" (41; italics in the original) With her past imprinted on her second-class citizenship in postimperial Britain, Emecheta firmly believes in Franklin's recommendation. Conscious of the fact that the disparagement of Africa and Africans is rooted in much of the history of European colonialism of Africa, she has taken it into her own hands to challenge the dominant narratives of the event, as Michel-Rolph Trouillot, the distinguished scholar of reconstructive Haitian history, suggests in the first epigraph to this essay.

The Joys of Motherhood provides a concrete example of Emecheta's method of developing an oppositional narrative of colonial history. The novel belongs to a subgenre she described in her autobiography as "my type of documentary novels" (1986, 228). She seemed then to be referring specifically to the early works—*In the Ditch* (1972), *Second-Class Citizen* (1974), *The Bride Price* (1976), and *The Slave Girl* (1977)—but her fifth novel, *The Joys of Motherhood* (1979), also links up with this category. Emecheta expressed great pride in these books, and they are indeed the extraordinary creations of a splendid mind. "My domain may be the empire of things," she wrote, "but there I am queen" (1986, 228). Her "empire of things," unlike Britain's ideological empire (the comparison is undoubtedly intentional), focuses on the "little happenings of everyday life" (1988, 175), mainly survival stories about women. It is also likely that in addition to suggesting the range of her subject matter, the phrase "empire of things" points to the fact that the other empire was very much on her mind during this early phase of her literary career. In a 1990 interview with Adeola James, Emecheta would call for a change of subject in African literature. "Everything coming out of Africa, in literature," she declared, "is still concerned with colonialism, what the Englishman has done to us. . . . It is about time we started writing about ourselves now" (James, 39). But since her own writing is an important part of the African literary intervention in colonial history, British colonialism will likely remain a powerful subtext in her fiction.

The subject receives particular attention in her documentary novels as part of a broader critique of ideological systems of oppression. The effect sought by Emecheta in engaging the subgenre is evident in Barbara Foley's definition: "the documentary novel aspires to tell the truth, and it associates this truth with claims to empirical validation. . . . [It] is distinguished by its insistence that it contains some kind of specific and verifiable link to the historical world" (393–94). The truth *The Joys of Motherhood* aspires to tell comes against the backdrop of the British colonial policy of indirect rule in Africa. "Lugard's bourgeois dream of order" (34), as the historian Barbara Bush aptly describes the policy, serves as a potent symbol of Britain's effort to entrench its power in its African colonies; I will turn to Lugard below. The novel explores the destabilizing impact of indirect rule on colonial Nigerian society through a gendered prism that allows for the reworking of the imperial-dream metaphor into a compelling account of coercive maternal desire. The protagonist's nightmarish dreams, in which she is taunted by her *chi* (personal spirit) with the gift of a mud-covered baby boy, at once mimic British fantasies of establishing order and stability in colonial Nigeria and point to a parallel state of social disorder, with disproportionately damaging effects on women. While this maddening power in the novel is largely fueled by sexual politics, part of the narrative intent is to challenge the assumptions and practices of colonial rule, particularly the prominence assigned to the policy of indirect rule. To articulate her critique of this policy, Emecheta seems to draw on the Igbo sense of duality, cryptically described by Chinua Achebe: "Wherever Something stands, Something Else will stand beside it. Nothing is absolute" (68). Thus the novel poignantly invokes as subtext British-inspired fantasies of colonial rule in Nigeria to crystallize an alternative and unidealized narrative of life lived under a punishing colonial order. To understand Emecheta's critique of the long-held view of indirect rule as a cure-all administrative policy in colonial Africa, it is necessary to address briefly the context of that rule's unsettling impact in Nigeria during the period that provides the historical backdrop to *The Joys of Motherhood*.

Indirect Rule, Colonial Nigeria, and Gender Disorder

As the colonial model for administering law and order in Nigeria in the 1900s, indirect rule bore the dual mission of enforcement and pacification. Both goals were to be realized through the powers of traditional chiefs who would serve as surrogates for the British colonial administration. The mix of ideology, pragmatism, and militarism, in the view of advocates of indirect rule, made for an effective administrative strategy that would be less vulnerable to the vagaries of African life than its predecessor, direct rule, which basically was "a single legal order, defined by the 'civilized' laws of Europe" (Mamdani, 16). Lord Frederick Lugard, the imperial soldier and administrator who devised and implemented the policy in Uganda and Nigeria, made the case for British rule through native authorities in his book

The Dual Mandate in British Tropical Africa, underscoring the importance of "decentralization" and "continuity" in strengthening Britain's
advantage in the colonial field. The former entailed delegating authority to native chiefs in the implementation of the rule of law and
order, while the latter aimed at improving the quality and practices
of British administrative personnel, especially the district commis-
sioners and officers, to ensure effective operations on the ground. To
put indirect rule on a firm footing, Lugard envisioned a native administration financially supported by a native treasury and capable of
maintaining social order through native courts. This "ensemble of
powers merged in the office of the chief," whose role included "making rules" (Mamdani, 53).

After experimenting with elements of indirect rule in southern
Uganda in the late 1890s, Lugard put the policy into full gear in
northern Nigeria during his tenure as high commissioner between
1900 and 1906. To establish order, he sought "a more authoritarian
administration and he realised that the Fulbe emirs and their relatively sophisticated institutions could serve his purpose" (Iliffe, 200).
But the program faced higher hurdles in the south, where the "non-
monarchical order" of Igboland (Mamdani, 41) and the problem of
warring interior states, such as Yorubaland, led to an adjustment of
indirect rule to allow for the invention of "tribes," where necessary,
and the attendant appointment of chiefs with a mandate to maintain order, collect taxes, and administer social justice. "British control
over the interior," Robert July writes, "slowly tightened until by 1914,
when the northern and southern provinces and Lagos were amalgam-
ated as the Colony and Protectorate of Nigeria, all pretence of independent native authority was dropped" (354). Degenerating into
an "anti-democratic 'direct rule'" (Bush, 113) and "a law-and-order
administration" (Mamdani, 109), indirect rule bred a host of abuses,
including the widespread use of military and police force, mandatory taxation and labor laws, and the subversion of indigenous laws
and institutions. Lugard's double tenure as governor of southern and
northern Nigeria (1912–13) and governor general of the whole of
Nigeria (1914–19) set the stage for a deeper push by the colonial administration into Nigerian life, fueling discontent and resistance.

Women felt the burden of indirect rule in their personal and social
lives as the protective elements within African traditions eroded. In
Yorubaland, for example, "[t]he loss of the traditional powers of chiefs,
kingmakers, Ogboni, and priests also meant the loss of the powers

of the female chiefs (Iyalode and Erelu) and priestesses" (Johnson-Odim and Mba, 11). Kamene Okonjo paints a more dire picture for Igbo women. In her view, "under colonialism women in southeastern Nigeria suffered the greatest loss of power. . . . In many ways the Women's War of 1929—the so-called 'Aba Riots'—can be seen as Igbo women's demonstration for the right to be consulted on matters that affected them" (55). Moreover, critics commonly make the connection between women's loss of power and colonial racism: "This diminution of women's status and power was reinforced by the prejudices and assumptions of the British colonial administration officers who worked for a government in which there were scarcely any women and who therefore did not expect—or wish—to find women involved in Southern Nigeria's government" (Johnson-Odim and Mba, 11). Indeed, the colonial construction of African gender identities failed to account for women's multiple roles in the society or their ability to straddle a range of conflicting worlds—urban and rural, traditional and modern, personal and public. Yet, as recent studies of African women's colonial histories show, while colonialism eroded women's advantage in the social domain, resistance to indigenous and colonial patriarchies remained a core female strength.[1]

The Women's War of 1929, for example, has become an enduring symbol of Nigerian women's anticolonial protest despite and, perhaps, because of the British effort to weaken the power of the event and women's agency by renaming it the "Aba Riots." The broad historical consensus is that the revolt, championed by Igbo women, was sparked by concern that the taxation system imposed on men under indirect rule would be extended to include women. Facing the threat of taxation and a host of other oppressive actions by warrant chiefs, the women, mostly market traders, coalesced into small armies of protesters to send a message to the British administration and its handpicked subordinates that underestimating women could prove costly. In late November 1929, after a period of protracted unrest, thousands of women descended upon the British colonial headquarters, armed with songs of rebuke and the force of their bodies.[2] It was a show of vast discontent that left more than fifty women dead and fifty others wounded, but it also offered compelling evidence of heroism, cohesiveness, and effective leadership. "We will continue fighting until all the Chiefs have been got rid of, but until then the matter will not be settled," a spokeswoman asserted before a postwar Commission of Enquiry (quoted in Bastian, 264). Another declared, "Our grievances are that the land is changed—we are all dying" (quoted in Bastian, 268).

The sentiment expressed in the second statement resonates powerfully in the subversive anti-colonial subtext of *The Joys of Motherhood*, which points to ways in which the land had changed under Lugard's policy through the troubled eyes of the main character and her continuing struggle to become a mother. Nnu Ego's unbending faith in the traditions of her culture, particularly as they relate to marriage and motherhood, is shown to be an alienating desire. Indeed, Nnu Ego's displacement in Lagos correlates with an image of herself as a misfit in a changing landscape of beliefs, attitudes, and relationships. Change as leitmotif runs throughout the novel, shattering the dreams and lives of some characters and raising the hopes of others. Social instability is exemplified by Nnu Ego's crisis-ridden family, but at the same time the forces of change help give life to the aspirations of Nnu Ego's oldest boys, who end up studying abroad, and her co-wife, Adaku, a symbol of the new woman.

Emecheta's view of the changes in African societies brought about by colonialism is hardly monolithic, but judging from the moral tone of *The Joys of Motherhood* she seems to envision it in terms of excess. The protagonist's travels from Ibuza, her hometown, to Lagos and back represent stages in the coarsening of her life that eventually leads to her death. This riveting drama of lost innocence stands with great poignancy against the backdrop of the destabilizing campaign of indirect rule. The omniscient narrator portrays Nnu Ego as having social status in Ibuza, and losing this power to poverty and chaos in Lagos as she struggles to preserve the hope and optimism of the maternal dream. In the end, her otherworldly message is expressed as a generalized rage against women's desire to become mothers at all costs, including the hostile social and political environment of colonial rule. Given the grim cost of her own maternal aspirations, Nnu Ego's rejection of other women's desperate pleas to mother thus translates doubly as a textual critique of the romanticization of motherhood and colonial dreams of conquest.

Dueling Dreams of Motherhood and Colonial Desire

While Emecheta allows her heroine mythic transcendence in the end, she keeps a firm grip throughout the novel on the naturalistic details of the clash between maternal and colonial desire, as dramatized in Nnu Ego's descent from agrarian nobility to citified destitution. The opening scene puts Nnu Ego, the twenty-five-year-old protagonist, on the streets of Lagos on a dewy morning in 1934, running barefoot from the "servants' quarters" of the (colonial) "master's bungalow" (7) toward a bridge, to end her life in the waters below. As we learn how she got to this point in the chapters immediately following this episode, we get the picture of a woman caught in the flux of events she was not prepared for by her previous life in her hometown of Ibuza. The "love child" (24) of Nwokocha Agbadi, a "wealthy local chief" (10) and his "priceless jewel" (11), the beautiful and proud Ona, Nnu Ego, whose name means "twenty bags of cowries" (26), is of aristocratic lineage and as such inherits a tradition-centered, patriarchal culture with rigidly defined gender roles. Reeling from the implications of her failure to bear children in her first marriage, Nnu Ego arrives in Lagos with great expectations of fulfilling the cultural mandate of motherhood in her second marriage.

She is hugely disappointed with the new domestic environment, where the colonial "master" is neither charming nor benevolent like her father, and her second husband, Nnaife, pale-skinned and potbellied, suffers terribly by comparison with her first. To add cultural insult to personal injury, Nnaife is employed in the colonial couple's home as a washer man, and his job description includes washing the undergarments of the colonial administrator's wife. The initial determinants of Nnu Ego's estrangement in Lagos thus derive from the degenerating threat of the colonial presence in the city. There are harder realities in store. Her firstborn son (the cherished emblem of her culture) dies; the Meers family returns to England in the wake of the looming Second World War; and, unemployed, Nnaife finds seasonal work at sea and in the battlefields of the war. Meanwhile, Nnu Ego's crisis escalates, even though, with frequent pregnancies and childbirths, some aspects of her dream of motherhood have been realized.

Faced with a brutal colonial economy and an expanding family to support by herself, Nnu Ego's life gradually spirals out of control. She manages to eke out a substandard living from petty trading during Nnaife's extended absences, but she is overwhelmed by events as the demands of childrearing increase and her weakened body and spirit impede her ability to cope both physically and emotionally. Nnu Ego's co-wife, Adaku, strikes out defiantly on her own to raise the odds of her own survival in the city. Her own choices repudiated by Adaku's example, Nnu Ego nonetheless continues to affirm the cultural values of maternity and womanhood that have been the hallmark of her life. In this frame of mind, she is caught flat-footed by the colonial system during Nnaife's trial, when her testimony helps convict her husband, who is sent to jail for five years. Filtered through an interpreter, her words sound a discordant note with the all-European jury, reinforcing the portrait of her precarious existence within the paternalistic colonial system. This is by no means the final blow to Nnu Ego's pride as the mother of nine children. After a protracted struggle to affirm her culture's ideal of motherhood, she dies alone "by the roadside" (224) in her hometown. Her sons—Adim is studying in Canada and Oshia, in America, is said to have married "a white woman" (224)—return to give her an expensive funeral. The shrine built in her honor comes to be frequented by barren women longing for the joys of motherhood. Their pleas, ironically, go unanswered.

The title of the final chapter in *The Joys of Motherhood,* "The Canonised Mother," offers clues for reading the text as a revisionist narrative of colonial rule in Nigeria. While critics have generally noted the title's significance as a critique of gender ideology, it also opens up the novel's anticolonial subtext for inspection. The narrative facts point to "canonized mother" as a trope linking the imperialist and patriarchal strains of canonized discourses that undergird Emecheta's reconstruction of the master narrative of colonial conquest. Lugard's grand dreams of creating order out of the chaos of colonial Nigeria draw on what Martin Green calls "the energizing myth of English imperialism . . . the story England told itself when it went to sleep at night; and, in the form of its dreams, . . . [convinced itself] to go out into the world and explore, conquer, and rule" (3). In her book on H. Rider Haggard's African romances, Lindy Stiebel underlines the sexualization of this myth and the adventure narratives that emerged from it by noting that the idea of "Africa as land found its most demonised yet desirable form in the metaphor of the sexual lover/mother/murderess" (20). Then, as Sander L. Gilman points out, there is "Freud's intent to explore [the] hidden 'dark continent' and reveal the hidden truths about female sexuality, just as the anthropologist-explorers [and writers, it may be said] were revealing the hidden truths about the nature of the black" (257). Robert Young has also noted that an obsessive "crossing and invasion of identities: whether of class and gender . . . or culture and race" constitutes "*the* dominant motif of much English fiction" (emphasis in original). This fiction, he believes, projecting the English sense of "uncertainty and differ-ence outwards," is "concerned with meeting and incorporating the culture of the other" and "often fantasize[s] crossing into it, though rarely . . . completely." He calls this tendency "colonial desire, whose attractions and tendencies were no doubt complicit with colonialism itself" (2–3).

Emecheta's "canonized mother" thus carries a discursive subtext, an underlying story about the role of Africa and African women in canon formation, a process closely allied with the colonial project. The two Africa-related constructs merged in mid-nineteenth-century colonial discourse with "the personification of the continent as a woman" (Hammond and Jablow, 71). W. Winwood Reade, British traveler and writer, initiated this literary tradition and its colonizing aesthetic when he declared, in a semifictional account of his travels to West Africa, "Look at the map of Africa. Does it not resemble a woman with a huge burden on the back?" (quoted in Hammond and Jablow, 72). The statement doubly inscribes the African woman as Other, the bearer of colonial and national burdens. The two burdens converge in Emecheta's representation of Nnu Ego as an overburdened subject and help to explain the irony implicit in the character's depiction as "the canonized mother." With her fate and the nation's inextricably linked, it is no surprise that Nnu Ego's disorientation and death are portrayed in the context of her society's unraveling. Emecheta takes the idea of the canonized mother a step further by suggesting that, while Nnu Ego's identity was fixed within the narrow confines of colonial ideology, in death she becomes an enigma, self-empowering and unpredictable. Aspiring mothers fail to comprehend her brutal rejection of their pleas for motherhood, but the act stands as an exer-cise of agency, underscoring the inadequacy of the colonial myth as an interpretive framework for understanding the lives of Africans and African women. It also frees up historical agency for the African woman-as-writer to reveal alternative truths about the burdens of colonial rule.

In *The Joys of Motherhood*, Emecheta organizes her critique of co-lonial rule in an alternative dream-text that mimics the colonial adventure narrative and its double vision of conquest and order. The imperial dream to control the sexualized (and therefore malleable) Af-rican landscape reconstitutes itself in the novel as Nnu Ego's night-marish longing for motherhood, which thrusts her into the rough and tumble of colonial Lagos, where she feels the full import of the unsettling effects of indirect rule. Her dreams of achieving a stable, orderly transition into old age through the power ascribed to mothers in her culture collide with the imperial fantasy of establishing order in Nigeria through control of native life in the country. Because Emecheta's intertwined themes of gender and colonial oppression do not allow for placing unqualified blame on the latter for Nnu Ego's tragedy, the text's dream symbolism serves to heighten narrative consciousness of how colonial fantasies of power helped create real-life suffering at the turn of the century, for most people generally and for women in particular. The figurative and the actual thus combine to create both thematic nuance and a richness of content.

In Nnu Ego's quest narrative, colonial Lagos is her destination, the place where she hopes to see her maternal dream fulfilled. The city, however, offers cold comfort. In *The Origins of Modern African Thought*, Robert July describes the political and social climate in Lagos under Lugard's governorship:

> Lagos during the First World War was a honeycomb of division within the native African community—between conflicting groups of Muslims, between warring Christian church factions, between nationalists of different degrees of intensity, between tribal groups and rival economic interests, between the educated and uneducated, and between factions within the body of westernized Africans. In addition, there was a mounting discontent with British rule which added its complication to the divisiveness within the city. During his administration, Lugard had managed to alienate substantial portions of the Lagos population, and antipathy towards him and his programme tended to become mingled with the factionalism already plaguing the community. (418)

"This is Lagos," as Flora Nwapa would later declare in the title of a short story about the impact of the city's dislocated sensibilities on her young female protagonist, herself a newcomer to the metropolis like Nnu Ego before her. It is in such a Lagos that we see Nnu Ego on that fateful morning, fleeing from the sight of her dead son to drown herself in a nearby river. Her alienation may be due in part to her failure to establish meaningful friendships with her peers, as Emecheta herself suggests,[3] but it is also true that Lagos proves too daunting a place for any dream to take hold, let alone her dreams of motherhood nurtured in a rural backwater. Robert July's account of the psychic division that characterized the city's educated elite during the turmoil of colonial rule sheds light on Nnu Ego's state of anxiety, dependence, and isolation: "Psychologically, . . . they had received a shock which tended to make them live in two dissociated worlds— the real workaday world in which material betterment and more effective government were gratefully accepted, and the fantasy world involving their traditional, social, religious and political affiliations and loyalties" (419).

While Nnu Ego's struggle for maternal fulfillment is far removed from the cares of the Lagos intelligentsia that are the subject of July's analysis, she, too, has to grapple with a gnawing sense of disjuncture. A prominent member of the village aristocracy in Ibuza, she becomes chronically poor in Lagos. Nnaife, her second husband and an Ibuza native himself, is regrettably reduced in Lagos to the domestic role of a washer man for the colonial administrator and his wife, in sharp contrast to the blissful models of masculinity that inspired Nnu Ego's youthful quest for motherhood—her father, "He who roars like a lion" (29), and her first husband, Amatokwu, who personifies her romantic ideal. She feels a palpable discomfort with Nnaife's shoddy appearance and more so with the fact that he feels no qualms about washing Mrs. Meers' undergarments. Raised by her father, steeped in respect for the rituals of manliness, Nnu Ego initially regards Nnaife as representing the antithesis of traditional Ibuza male culture. Significantly, in an argument the couple has over news of Nnu Ego's first pregnancy, she refers to Nnaife as "a shatterer of dreams" (49), a chilling remark that takes on prophetic overtones as Nnaife entangles himself further in the omnipresent structures of colonial rule. Her husband's chronic unemployment, long absences from home, and the humiliations of an emasculating colonial culture form a trail of psychic abuse with devastating consequences for Nnu Ego's search for maternal fulfillment.

Conceptually, the text links the coarsening of Nnu Ego's life in Lagos with the destabilizing impact of colonialism on the existing social system. What gives the narrative greater poignancy is Nnu Ego's ambivalence toward the dominant colonial and patriarchal social order. Despite her initial misgivings, for example, about Nnaife being manifestly unfit to help her live her dream, she is soon lulled into a false sense of security—until she is back in the pit with the death of her son. Her self-division mirrors the divided city July describes above, one caught in its own struggle against colonial dreams of conquest. In this context, Nnu Ego's private pain is emblematic of the riot of feelings that set the nation alight under colonial rule.

Nnu Ego's psychic split is textually inscribed in the surrogate identities she is assigned in the novel's section titles—"the mother," "a failed woman," "a good daughter," "a mother of clever children," and "the canonized mother." Like "good wife" (65) and "senior wife" (122), these terms are signifiers of a cultural value system that may have given meaning to the bucolic life of female paragons like her mother in her hometown of Ibuza, but which has been emptied of virtually all signs of vitality in the alienating environment of colonial Lagos. Nnu Ego uses every ounce of emotional reserve to leverage her past in reestablishing her life in the city, but her struggle becomes a searing revisitation of the challenges she faced in Ibuza. She fights particularly hard to control her identity as senior wife, and, tellingly, it is during this phase in her life that she finally admits to being resistant to change.

In a conversation with Adaku, Nnu Ego gets a bit of advice from her younger co-wife about relationships between husband and wife: "Oh, senior wife, I think you are sometimes more traditional than people at home in Ibuza. You worry too much to please our husband." Nnu Ego's latest worry comes on the heels of her giving birth to twin girls and thinking, rightly, that Nnaife will not be pleased. Faced with the shattering logic of her rival's remark, Nnu Ego becomes evasive. First, she blames her doting father for failing to let her know that, as Adaku puts it, "It's a man's world this." Then she tries to impugn the character of her co-wife's "low family." When her defensive reaction fails, she finally gains epiphanic insight: "You are right. The trouble with me is that I find it difficult to change" (127). This is clearly an unsustainable strategy in a city throbbing with change.

Nnu Ego is also compelled to struggle against the racial attitudes of British administrative officers and other personnel. Her husband's job is the primary source of the stinging humiliation she feels in this regard. One can only imagine how Nnu Ego's life would have turned out had she married the "old chief with a sense of the tried, traditional values" (36) that her father imagines for her as he contemplates the rapidly changing social environment and the rising threat of modernity. Meanwhile, she has to sit back and watch her husband take enough humiliating blows for both of them. Dr. Meers, we are told, "worked at the Forensic Science Laboratory in Yaba" (41); it is not clear whether or not he is the district officer. But that does not seem to matter in the broader scheme of things: the novel reflects a historical reality in which colonial officers across the spectrum fully endorsed Lugard's policy. Anthony Kirk-Greene's description of the district officer's duties reflects the impact of Lugard's ideas regarding the implementation of effective systems of colonial rule in Africa:

> Improving law and order or imposing it were under-standably the first preoccupations of the earliest of District Officers. . . . The diaries of the District Officers at the time were full of entries about installing a new chief as a break with the past, introducing a tax-gathering system, meting out what at least seemed to them to be justice, and settling fights and feuds. . . . After 1920 new needs called for new breeds. Now men were required who had brains in their heads as well as fire in their bellies. And from 1926 the Colonial Service reached a fresh level of professionalism, whereby every cadet underwent a year's post-graduate course at Oxford or Cambridge or later in London. (Kirk-Greene, xv)

The improvement in the education of colonial officers was an outcome of Lugard's "dual mandate." Meanwhile, divisions between the colonizer and the colonized remained. One description of the servant class, for example, has an interesting resonance in relation to *The Joys of Motherhood:*

> For a young man living on his own, servants played an extremely important role. They came to him by various means. Some were selected more or less at random from servants' parades held at headquarters, some were inherited from previous incumbents, some were brought in by other servants, some simply turned up on the verandah with their "books," the testimonials or "chits" from previous employers. . . . Here would be found such old colonial chestnuts as "I'm sure this boy will do you as well as he has done me," and "This cook leaves me on account of illness—mine, not his." Mocked though they were by employers, these "books" were held in high regard by their servants. (Allen, 72–73)

This picture of unembarrassed pleasure on the part of both the writers of these testimonial "books" and prospective employers speaks to the racial attitudes of colonial officers. The language of diminishment evokes the objectification of slaves during previous episodes in the tragic encounter between Africans and Europeans. In *The Joys of Motherhood*, Dr. and Mrs. Meers typify the colonial couple, self-representing as racially superior. The former, described as the "white master"(41), leaves much of the onus of interacting with the servants to his wife. In fact, Dr. Meers's only utterance in the text is his ideologically driven response to Nnaife's leave-taking at the end of the very day Nnu Ego arrives in Lagos to join her husband: "Good night, baboon" (41). The remark's denigrating impact is immediate, and Nnaife tries in vain to regain his compo-sure in the presence of his newly arrived bride. He "could tell that Nnu Ego did not approve of him. But he could not help the way he was made" (43), Emecheta writes, referring to Nnaife's sudden self-conscious awareness of his body image following Dr. Meers's racial insult. In this context, the colonial officer's "generous" reference letter promising reemployment for his "devoted servant" (85) car-ries a double irony: it trivializes Nnaife sufficiently to ensure that he is not rehired and it writes the trivialization into history. Nnu Ego intuitively reads between the lines and insists that her husband seek employment elsewhere.

The Second World War undermines Nnu Ego's dreams of ma-ternal fulfillment perhaps more than the racial attitudes of whites, whom she rarely encounters. Nnaife's absence for four years makes permanent her anguish over her impoverished state, at a time when her *chi* had been kind enough to give her real children rather than the images of baby boys she chased after in her dreams when she first came to Lagos. Ubani, a close family friend, sums up the impact of the war on Nnu Ego as he welcomes Nnaife from the battle-fields of Germany and Burma: "My friend, Nnu Ego behaved very well during your absence, you know. She fought the war too here in your family"(183). The remark conjures up an image of Nnu Ego, the embattled heroine, struggling to eke out an existence for herself and her children in her husband's absence amid the shambles of her life. But the war metaphor extends beyond her familiar "routine of scraping, saving, counting every penny" (190). It points to Nnu Ego's psychological battle over the terms of her maternal quest. The Euro-pean war and its aftermath clearly mark a turning point in Nnu Ego's adventure narrative. She goes through an early stage of anguished hope to a point where her dreams of motherhood are fulfilled, but she remains joyless. In the end, as her world falls apart, she sees a need for retrospection:

> Nnu Ego had allowed herself to wonder where it was
> she had gone wrong. She had been brought up to believe that
> children made a woman. She had had children, nine in all,
> and luckily seven were alive, much more than many women
> of that period could boast of. Most of her friends and col-
> leagues had buried more children than they had alive; but her
> god had been merciful to her. Still, how was she to know that
> by the time her children grew up the values of her country,
> her people and her tribe would have changed so drastically,
> to the extent where a woman with many children could face
> a lonely old age, and maybe a miserable death, all alone, just
> like a barren woman? (219)

As she ponders her painful enculturation into Lagosian society,
Nnu Ego finally grasps the truth about the nature of her struggle.
The European war may have been the tipping point in her material
condition, but her emotional vicissitudes amount to a raging internal
war of her own. Take, for example, her many culturally based ratio-
nalizations for desiring the "joys" of motherhood. As a mother of
boys she would enjoy privileges denied mothers of girls, like Adaku,
or barren women, for motherhood is after all a palliative that offers
relief from the pain of childbirth and the strain of child-rearing.
Then there is the fact that she has done the impossible—had a child
at forty years of age, although that child was stillborn. Finally, as a
mother of clever boys, she expects to bask in their glory.

Nnu Ego comes to realize that this traditional narrative is subject
to change within the heterogeneity of Lagos life. Her nation under
colonialism is a contested terrain, even for dreams. Her dream of
maternal glory is, in fact, a death wish, made even more certain by the
novel's journeying motif. "Going away on a journey stands in dreams
for dying," Freud asserts in *A General Introduction to Psychoanalysis*
(169). On the other hand, her son, Oshia, nearly dying from malnutri-
tion, had been awakened in time from "his beautiful dream" (103) by
Mama Abby. One of many dreamers in the novel, he later embarks on
his own journey, which takes him into the African diaspora, another
colonial outpost. For her part, as she nears the end of her journey,
the ever-prescient Nnu Ego predicts her own death, and in less than
a month she dies on the side of the road upon which she had set out
more than forty years earlier.

"Whose dream was it anyway?" Barbara Bush asks in setting the
tone for West African challenges to colonialism between 1929 and

1945 (101). The question resonates with Emecheta's poignant invocation of the dueling dreams of motherhood and colonial power in *The Joys of Motherhood*. Indeed, as another historian, Frederick Cooper, writes, "The difference between the dream and the nightmare would soon prove central to the collapse of the colonial project" because "[t]he will of colonized people kept intruding itself into the apparatus of control" (110). In its rewriting of the colonial dreams of power as nightmare, Emecheta's novel stands on a solid foundation of anticolonial resistance, with echoes of the women's rebellion in 1929 and the author's postcolonial artistic insurgency.

The novel illustrates how the colonial project, ostensibly messianic, was in reality a tortured journey inward into secret and hidden zones of desire, conflict, and hatred. Emecheta, a writer who typically takes on the puzzles of everyday life, allows Nnu Ego's tragedy to become emblematic of a subversive truth.

Notes

1. See, for example, Jean Allman, Susan Geiger, and Nakanyike Musisi, eds., *Women in African Colonial Histories* (Bloomington: Indiana University Press, 2002); Tabitha Kanogo, *African Womanhood in Colonial Kenya, 1900–1950* (Oxford: James Currey, 2005); Jean Allman and Victoria Tashjian, *"I Will Not Eat Stone": A Women's History of Colonial Asante* (Portsmouth, NH: Heinemann, 2000).

2. Judith Van Allen, in an early account of the event, provides the following description:

> In November of 1929, thousands of Igbo women from [Calabar and Owerri] provinces converged on the Native Administration centers—settlements that generally included the headquarters and residence of the British colonial officer for the district, a Native Court building and a jail, and a bank. . . . The women chanted, danced, sang songs of ridicule, and demanded the caps of office (the official insignia) of the Warrant Chiefs. . . . At a few locations the women broke into prisons and released prisoners. Sixteen Native Courts were attacked, and most of these were broken up or burned. . . . British District Officers called in police and troops, who fired on the women and left a total of more

than 50 dead and 50 wounded. No one on the other side was
seriously injured. (60)

3. See Emecheta 1988, 178.

Works Cited

Achebe, Chinua. 1998. "'Chi' in Igbo Cosmology." In *African Philosophy: An Anthology*, ed. Emmanuel Chukwudi Eze, 62–72. Oxford: Blackwell.
Allen, Charles, ed. 1979. *Tales from the Dark Continent: Images of British Colonial Africa in the Twentieth Century.* London: Andre Deutsch.
Bastian, Misty L. 2002. "'Vultures of the Marketplace': Southeastern Nigerian Women and Discourses of the *Ogu Umunwaanyi* (Women's War) of 1929." In *Women in African Colonial Histories*, ed. Jean Allman, Susan Geiger, and Nakanyike Musisi, 260–81. Bloomington: Indiana University Press.
Bush, Barbara. 1999. *Imperialism, Race and Resistance: Africa and Britain, 1919–1945.* London: Routledge.
Cooper, Frederick. 1996. *Decolonization and African Society: The Labor Question in French and British Africa.* Cambridge: Cambridge University Press.
Emecheta, Buchi. 1972 *In the Ditch.* London: Allison and Busby.
———. 1974. *Second-Class Citizen.* London: Allison and Busby.
———. 1976. *The Bride Price.* New York: George Braziller.
———. 1977. *The Slave Girl.* New York: George Braziller.
———. 1979. *The Joys of Motherhood.* New York: George Braziller.
———. 1986. *Head above Water.* London: Fontana.
———. 1988. "Feminism with a small 'f'!" In *Criticism and Ideology: Second African Writers' Conference*, ed. Kirsten Holst Petersen, 173–85. Uppsala: Scandinavian Institute of African Studies.
Foley, Barbara. 1996. "The Documentary Novel and the Problem of Borders." In *Essentials of the Theory of Fiction*, ed. Michael J. Hoffman and Patrick D. Murphy, 392–408. Durham, NC: Duke University Press.
Franklin, John Hope. 1989. *Race and History: Selected Essays, 1938–1988.* Baton Rouge: Louisiana State University Press.
Freud, Sigmund. 1924. *A General Introduction to Psychoanalysis.* New York: Washington Square.
Gilman, Sander L. 1986. "Black Bodies, White Bodies: Toward an Iconography of Female Sexuality in Late Nineteenth-Century Art, Medicine,

and Literature." In *"Race," Writing, and Difference*, ed. Henry Louis Gates Jr., 223–61. Chicago: University of Chicago Press.

Green, Martin. 1979. *Dreams of Adventure, Deeds of Empire.* New York: Basic.

Hammond, Dorothy, and Alta Jablow. 1970. *The Africa That Never Was: Four Centuries of British Writing about Africa.* Prospect Heights, IL: Waveland.

Iliffe, John. 1995. *Africans: The History of a Continent.* Cambridge: Cambridge University Press.

James, Adeola, ed. 1990. *In Their Own Voices: African Women Writers Talk.* Portsmouth, NH: Heinemann.

Johnson-Odim, Cheryl, and Nina Emma Mba. 1997. *For Women and the Nation: Funmilayo Ransome-Kuti of Nigeria.* Urbana: University of Illinois Press.

July, Robert W. 1967. *The Origins of Modern African Thought.* New York: Frederick A. Praeger.

Kirk-Greene, Anthony. 1979. Introduction to *Tales from the Dark Continent: Images of British Colonial Africa in the Twentieth Century*, ed. Charles Allen. London: Andre Deutsch.

Lugard, John Frederick. 2000. "Principles of Native Administration." In *Historical Problems of Imperial Africa*, ed. Robert O. Collins, 105–20. Princeton, NJ: Markus Wiener.

Mamdani, Mahmood. 1996. *Citizen and Subject: Contemporary Africa and the Legacy of Late Colonialism.* Princeton, NJ: Princeton University Press.

Nwapa, Flora. 1992. *This Is Lagos and Other Stories.* Trenton, NJ: Africa World Press.

Ogunyemi, Chikwenye Okonjo. 1996. *Africa Wo/Man Palava: The Nigerian Novel by Women.* Chicago: University of Chicago Press.

Okonjo, Kamene. 1976. "The Dual-Sex Political System in Operation: Igbo Women and Community Politics in Midwestern Nigeria." In *Women in Africa: Studies in Social and Economic Change*, ed. Nancy J. Hafkin and Edna G. Bay, 45–58. Stanford: Stanford University Press.

Seyhan, Azade. 2001. *Writing outside the Nation.* Princeton, NJ: Princeton University Press.

Stiebel, Lindy. 2001. *Imagining Africa: Landscape in H. Rider Haggard's African Romances.* Westport, CT: Greenwood.

Trouillot, Michel-Rolph. 1995. *Silencing the Past: Power and the Production of History.* Boston: Beacon.

Van Allen, Judith. 1976. "'Aba Riots' or Igbo 'Women's War'? Ideology, Stratification, and the Invisibility of Women." In *Women in Africa:*

Studies in Social and Economic Change, ed. Nancy J. Hafkin and Edna G. Bay, 59–85. Stanford: Stanford University Press.

Young, Robert J. C. 1995. *Colonial Desire: Hybridity in Theory, Culture and Race*. London: Routledge.

6

In the Pauses of the Historian's Narrative

Yvonne Vera's *Butterfly Burning*

V. M. (Sisi) Maqagi

Yvonne Vera is one of the most acclaimed writers in Zimbabwe. Before her passing in 2005 at the age of forty, she wrote six novels and edited a collection of short stories. Her novels are characterized by her unfailing eye for the details of the imagined ordinary and daily lives of the poor inhabitants of Zimbabwe townships. This focus probes and teases into the open some of the taboos of the patriarchal society whose aspirations were and are completely suppressed and marginalized by both the British colonial masters of their time and the masters of postwar Zimbabwe. Hidden and unspeakable acts and desires are central to her novels, in order to uncover the multiple traumas witnessed and experienced as a result of unequal power relations within the colonized society. Indeed, external sociopolitical forces impinge with devastating effect on the internal relations of the colonized society she portrays. Gender hostility, effaced masculinity, dysfunctional individuals and communities, fragmented histories and lives, varying levels of female self-assertion and self-annihilation are some of the concerns that Yvonne Vera raises with uncompromising frankness. She probes the silences that, because of its nature, historical discourse compels. It is these silences that this chapter seeks to examine. In *Butterfly Burning*, Vera explores the trauma and consequent hysteria of gender-role transformation, the emasculation resulting from land dispossession, and the vibrant, reconstructive role of Kwela music. Paramount in this exploration are narrative strategies that visualize and concretize past experiences.

Terence Ranger, a Zimbabwean historian to whom *Butterfly Burning* is dedicated, has stated that the novel is "written in the pauses of the historian's narrative" (697). Implicit in this formulation is Ranger's acknowledgement that history's masquerade as a totalizing metanarrative can be subverted by ideological, situational, spatial, or temporal interruptions that problematize notions of accuracy, objectivity, and the seamless translation of past events into the present written record of those events. When Ranger says that *Butterfly Burning* "will remain much more real and vivid than a historical reconstruction" (699), he affirms the contingency of readings and interpretations of past events. It is in these pauses or discontinuities that Vera inserts her own imaginative rendering of minutely depicted personal histories of those without power. She thus effectively foregrounds the validity of her own interpretation of what happened in the past and interrogates the truth-value of official historical discourse. This draws attention particularly to how women relate to the historical and social changes of their times, as agents rather than passive victims.

Vera has succinctly characterized her primary interventionist project, explaining that "I prefer to look at the particular because it makes me question the grand, the bigger, the larger thing which everybody might be saying" (Hunter, 80). Her questioning probes the lives of black people whose presence is erased, but whose ancestors' heroic spirits are a proud, if remote, reminder of what (it seems) they could never be—a reminder which, as such, remains a constant (unconscious) reproach. As she puts it in *Butterfly Burning*, living in Bulawayo "is to live within the cracks. Unnoticed and unnoticeable, offering every service but with the capacity to vanish when the task required is accomplished. So the black people learn how to move through the city with speed and due attention, to bow their heads down and slide past walls, to walk without making the shadow more pronounced than the body or the body clearer than the shadow. It means leaning against some masking reality—they lean on walls, on lies, on music" (3–4). Yvonne Vera assails the sustained violence of the British that was initiated with the quelling of the First Chimurenga in 1896. In this context, the passage just quoted describes the effect of the repressive strategies of colonialism. The colonized inhabit a world that Frantz Fanon describes as constrained, "strewn with prohibitions" and "divided into compartments" (29). It is a world that bears similarities to the apartheid world of South Africa, with the segregation policies of the nationalist government.

In a culture that actively promotes a language of indirection and a posture of subservience (especially in women), outspokenness about controversial, taboo subjects marks Vera's novels, many of which have been nominated for literary awards. Talking about this openness, she has stated: "Our forefathers crafted a language that made it difficult to address these contentious issues. In African culture, for example, to talk to my father, I bow. If I am announcing that somebody has died, I use a particular language, a particular tone . . . so as to convey the message. But for subjects like . . . rape . . . you are not allowed to mention it. Even to your mother, who must pantomime the news if she tells your aunt" (Soros).

In her quest to break the silence culturally imposed on women, Vera joins the ranks of black women writers such as Toni Morrison, Alice Walker, Tsitsi Dangarembga, Buchi Emecheta, Ama Ata Aidoo, Mariama Bâ, Lauretta Ngcobo, Flora Nwapa, Bessie Head, and a host of others. All these women articulate and interrogate oppressive practices in their own communities. They have painfully scrutinized the very fabric of their societies, the threads of which include so many impositions and limitations placed on women, exacerbated by the sociopolitical contexts of their lives and those of their men. Although Vera registers the steady resilience of women who bear the marks of men's wars and conflicts, especially in *The Stone Virgins* (2002), her novels also expose women's pain and their suffering.

Vera has said, "My tales are tragic, rather than sad, meaning they have a catastrophic force" (Soros). It is significant that Vera uses the word "tales," for it foregrounds the primacy of orality over textuality in the shaping of her novels. Eva Hunter records her as stating, "I always have to find the voice first, before I can tell the story. Once I find the voice, I could sit for forty, fifty hours and finish the book because it's just like I am swimming, once the voice is there" (85). There is a sense in which telling the story is grounded in "finding the voice" and the sensation of the speech act, quite apart from the ideological perspective and political tone of her subject matter. Meanwhile, the tragic or catastrophic force points to the fundamental dignity of the women characters at the center of her stories. The women are invariably confronted with questions of life and death in personal, social, political, and national spaces. However, they regenerate their inner courage as they transcend the forces that seek to keep them in line. It is the inner core of this resilience that Vera probes and foregrounds in her novels.

Her collection of short stories, *Why Don't You Carve Other Animals?* (1993), portrays women during Zimbabwe's war of liberation. Their stories reflect courage and hope sustained in spite of the fear that the war inspires in them. In *Nehanda* (1993), Vera rereads the historical facts regarding a woman who led a rebellion against British forces, turning the account into an exploration of "mythical consciousness." Nehanda's extraordinary courage inspires emulation as well as elevation to the realm of legend. The novel also examines the connection or interrelation between women and the land.

Under the Tongue (1996) is a painfully frank novel that portrays the unbearable trauma of incest, the first Zimbabwean novel to examine this taboo subject. Uncovering the unspeakable violence and the resultant anguish that are visited on Zhizha in her home, the novel also reflects the innate strength and innocence of the protagonist in some of the author's most lyrical and beautiful language. *Stone Virgins* (2002) has been described as "moving into more controversial and contentious territory than most writers, be they men or women, have dared to write about" as it probes the experiences of women, the ethnic and political violence of the 1980s, and the current political violence in Zimbabwe (Soros).

Butterfly Burning tells the story of a beautiful, young, naive girl, Phephelaphi, whose ever-undiminished ambition to be the first black nurse in Bulawayo ends in ashes. As a result of her mother's death, Phephelaphi stays with Zandile, her mother's friend, before moving in with her much older lover Fumbatha, a migrant worker whose sole intention is to protect her and provide her with shelter. However, with her growing ambition to become a nurse, his male ego is affronted by this challenge of female desire for independence and professionalism. Phephelaphi discovers that she is pregnant, but because the hospital forbids admission of pregnant women, she performs an abortion on herself. The description is long, detailed, and assumes the aura of ritual as she becomes the dual agent of death and birth. Fumbatha and Phephelaphi become estranged. In the anger that erupts, she is painfully disabused of her ignorance about her own personal history and that of Fumbatha. She discovers that her mother is, in fact, Zandile. Getrude, whom Phephelaphi believed to be her mother, took her from

Zandile, who had rejected the child at birth, and raised her as her own. Phephelaphi also finds out that Fumbatha's father was one of those who were hanged in 1896 during the first Chimurenga. When she becomes pregnant the second time, two weeks before she is admitted for training as a nurse, she burns herself to death.

The story unfolds in Bulawayo around 1948, in Makokoba, a "native" township characterized by poverty, squalor, and congestion. Completely forgotten by those in power, the inhabitants of Makokoba are overwhelmed by desolation and alienation, which they attempt to alleviate by losing themselves in Kwela dance, alcohol, and prostitution.

Yet, however much they may lean on music and other behaviors to mask the harshness of their reality, they cannot escape the barrenness of the landscape on which their lives unfold. Confronted by their bleak surroundings, the children escape into their imaginative world, where they "see rainbows" (14) even in the "pungent and decayed water" (15) of the ditches. The author conveys the infinite rage and sadness in the sharp irony of the children's innocent revelry and inquisitiveness in the face of the criminal negligence of the factory owners. Yet Vera's condemnation of unequal allocation of resources is not strident, but subtle. This subtlety is poignantly rendered through the children's curiosity and exuberance, as they remain unaware of the dangers of their environment. Vera describes the ditch with its black sediment as toxic, yet fascinating to young minds. Water and air pollution, as an aspect of the deliberate impoverishment of the landscape around townships, completely escape the attention of the children. In probing the cracks within which the blacks live, Vera exposes the malicious disregard for the safety of the township inhabitants that is displayed by the owners of industrial factories. Behind the huge profits brazenly exhibited by these white-owned factories is the devastation of the environment from their careless disposal of waste material and the consequent health hazards. The unequal economic power relations exacerbate the devalued status of the township inhabitants. Although this might make them unnoticeable, their very existence in the margins of the dominant society destabilizes its centrality. The boundary that marks the township as a marginal site is one of natural aridity, of rocks and thorn bushes and "land so empty and barren the soil simply slides and falls among a few stunted shrubs, scarcely living" (15).

The desolation of the environment is even more harshly rendered by the architecture of containment and poverty, which Frantz Fanon finds to be characteristic of the colonized world. "It is a world without spaciousness; men live there on top of each other. . . . The native town is a crouching village, a town on its knees, a town wallowing in the mire" (30). In describing the township of Makokoba, Vera confirms Fanon's findings along with similar indictments of colonial strategies in the slums of District Six, Sophiatown, in various books by South African writers. Even the names of the township, Makokoba (meaning "bent with fragility and walking with stealth"), and the street, Sidojiwe E2, seem to describe more the subservience and the rejection of the people who live there than the place itself.

For all the solidity of their brick walls, the houses in Makokoba are claustrophobic, hazardous, and too porous for privacy. They are huddled so close together that the inhabitants' intimate lives are unwillingly though abundantly shared with their neighbors. Congestion and penury make their private domestic space a public space in which "neighbours could not help but possess each other's secrets"—neighbors whose "precious words needed witnesses to gather them into a song" (41).

More than the loss of privacy, the crowding exposes the more fundamental loss, the dispossession of land. Discussing manifestations of violence in the colonial world, Frantz Fanon addresses the importance of the land: "For a colonized people the most essential value, because the most concrete, is first and foremost the land: the land which will bring them bread and, above all, dignity" (34). The loss of dignity in the world of *Butterfly Burning* was already sealed in the various land apportionment acts of earlier decades. A. J. Wills provides a useful account of the uneven distribution of land in colonial Rhodesia. The land rapidly passed into European hands, while the reserves could not hold the growing population. Thus, in describing the material reality of Makokoba township, Yvonne Vera draws attention to the specificity of black people's struggles as a result of macropolitical and macrohistorical disruptions in colonial Zimbabwe—including the severe curtailment of their movement even within their designated areas and the particular affinity between the straitened circumstances of individuals and their damaged environment.

In such circumstances, Kwela music and dance become much more than recreational activities; they function as an opium that temporarily enables the residents of Makokoba to escape their pain. Kwela epitomizes the ingenuity of the mechanics of survival. It transforms the very source of their oppression into an attempt to transcend restraint. Kwela music is like the African American blues music that articulates and therefore works through the pain of those who sing, play, and hear it. As described in *Butterfly Burning*, "It is a searing musical moment, swinging in and away, loud and small, lively, living. Within this music, they soar higher than clouds; sink deeper than stones in water. . . . Kwela means to climb into the waiting police Jeeps. This word alone has been fully adapted to do marvelous things. It can carry so much more than a word should be asked to carry; rejection, distaste, surrender, envy. And full desire" (3). The loaded and ambivalent quality of Kwela music, appealing to as much as reflecting highly opposed moods, mirrors the complexity of these people's lives. Improvised, drawing on a variety of musical instruments, this music reflects the contingent character of those lives. The bodies of the listeners become instruments of defiance as they transmute police brutality and control into their opposite: agency, and capacity for artistic expression. The deliberately conscious ambiguity inherent in Kwela proclaims the people of Makokoba's control, however fragile, over the meaning of words and their physical expression. In this way, the inhabitants attempt to wrest the power to name their reality, to structure and shape their own pain. They choose their own method of dealing with the existential predicament of the urban context: "Kwela seeks strand after strand of each harsh illusion and makes it new. Sidojiwe E2 (retrieved after being thrown away) . . . is fresh with all kinds of desperate wounds" (3).

Phephelaphi experiences the elucidatory power of Kwela music for the first time when she visits Deliwe's shebeen. The immediacy and power of the impact on her is dramatically rendered through Vera's use of the present tense. The music is persistent and urgent in drawing a response from her. The notes of the guitar punctuate Phephelaphi's keen observation of the room as well as an acute awareness of herself. It evokes her sensuality as it caresses her, thrills her, and pulses under her skin (see 55–56). The intense and rising emotional and psychological force within Phephelaphi is reflected in images of a felled tree and the progressive violence of a river in flood. The sound and effect of the trumpet player on the crowd are portrayed in natural images of a hurricane and a rainbow, an apposition that reflects complex levels of intensity. Ultimately, the therapeutic essence of Kwela music becomes paramount as it prizes open Phephelaphi's not-yet-healed wounds from her mother's death. She works through what has been a recurring memory of her mother's murder, metonymically figured in a falling hand: the music heals; it enables her "to cross the distance it asks her to cross and to touch, finally, before it reaches the ground, the hand falling down from the doorway, to keep it there" (57). A final reconciliation with her mother's death is achieved through the evocative sounds of the music.

In a later scene, Kwela music evokes the more positive or lighter side of the general misery of Sidojiwe E2. A walk by Fumbatha and Phephelaphi down the street becomes a rare occasion of solidarity and celebration, between themselves and with the community, as they hear "a song clear the night of all its troubles and set the heart free," and thus become "part of something that is unplanned, something free like night" (72). Despite this clearing and this freedom, however, the music elucidates their pain, revealing an unconscious disquiet as Fumbatha "holds tight to Phephelaphi," "holds her securely" (73) in the face of a gloomy metaphorical landscape and a wailing flute. Still, "[t]hey dance with a joy that is free, that has no other urgency but the sheer truth of living, the not-being-here of this here-place" (74). This paradox foregrounds their perpetual desire to transcend both the spatial and the sociopolitical constraints of their township environment.

However, the other dancers' more energetic and sensuous movements, unrestrained by spatial limits or existential pain, overtake the sedate dance of Fumbatha and Phephelaphi. The agile female dancers are completely possessed by Kwela as they abandon their bodies to the music. Their dance is described in images of physical exertion, of the unrelenting force of their bodily presence, of the fullness of self-expression despite a political dispensation that condemns them to invisibility and silence. In a particularly incisive examination of the significance of music in *Butterfly Burning*, Lizzy Attree perceives Kwela music as the metalanguage of resistance, healing, and freedom: "Kwela is a metaphor for the transformative power of language, which is capable of reproducing or redefining experience in limitless ways, facilitating transformation by making moments of life bearable. Like metamorphosis, these transformations illustrate the agency of both the character and the reader; the role they each play in translating or detecting a change in meaning is pivotal" (73–74).

Butterfly Burning follows a complex narrative strategy through the adoption of modernist techniques involving both narrative structure and the language of narration. The arrangement of chapters is such that they build compellingly to the shock of abortion and self-immolation. However, they are not arranged in a predictably logical sequence, especially the first eight chapters. These are discrete, self-contained, visually and emotionally evocative vignettes, juxtaposed alongside each other in a cumulative but paradoxical depiction of utter desperation and joy. The pervasive Kwela music becomes the thread that holds these chapters together, as its reverberations are felt in the sounds and motions of different activities, as in cinema. In an interview with Jane Bryce, Yvonne Vera explains the influence that cinematography has on her writing: "I've always been visually oriented, and before I worked at National Gallery, perhaps my larger influence was film, and how images are prepared, constructed and made to move. I also have a strong leaning towards photography. When I'm writing . . . I start with a moment—visual, mental—that I can *see*, and I place it on my table, as though it were a photograph" (219). Capturing a succession of moments that uniquely unfold on the same canvas, through visual and mental significance, sets "into motion the forces that lie dormant in things and beings" (Minh-ha, 147).

There is a vivid image in the first chapter of laborers cutting grass in the sweltering heat. Stripped of any political power and consigned to invisibility, they rely on Kwela music to mask their unbearable reality. The second chapter breaks away from 1946, as it presents harrowing images of seventeen men hanged as a result of the rebellion, the first Chimurenga in 1896. However, rather than creating a discontinuity, this chapter goes back in time to establish the historical and political reasons for the characters' current defeat and humiliation. The laborers' rhythmic swaying movements in chapter 1 mimic the melancholy swaying of those seventeen bodies fifty years before. The pause with which the novel paradoxically begins introduces an ominous implication of dormant power, with the word "waits" positioned right at the end of the second chapter. The third chapter is another snapshot, this time of an environment made hazardous by industrialization. The picture of children in tattered clothes playing and being naturally inquisitive highlights the multiple loss and dispossession that filters down to the younger generations. Thus, in the course of three brief but highly charged images, the reader/spectator is left with a picture of desolation, deprivation, and a struggle for survival.

In these introductory chapters, Yvonne Vera sets the political tone of the whole novel by foregrounding the material conditions of the characters' lives in Makokoba Township and how these relate to the community. Training her narrative lens on the urban space, she shows it as one of male activity, which is nevertheless overtaken by female activity. These chapters form the backdrop against which the story unfolds.

The ensuing chapters show the positioning of each character and how the characters' connections with one another shape the perplexing, blazing picture at the end. Fumbatha's recollection of his first meeting with Phephelaphi in chapter 4 is one of two scenes in the whole novel that shimmer with the lightness of joy (the other being in chapter 12). Yet, even here, Fumbatha is positioned in an ambivalent space both physically and ideologically.

The characters' location in Bulawayo presents various levels of alienation from the land, their histories, and therefore their identities. While chapter 5 shows Zandile's own loss of identity, the juxtaposition with other chapters emphasizes the contrast in her manner of dealing with it. The next two chapters narrow their focus to the immediate surroundings: the street Sidojiwe E2 and the small, one-room house Phephelaphi and Fumbatha share, with no possibility of privacy. Chapter 8 is another imagistic one, reiterating the condition of exile that has befallen the inhabitants of Makokoba. Just as much as the station people are beings in transit, suspended between the rural areas and their destinations, so are the urban township inhabitants. They are all presented as having lost their moorings and therefore having no sense of direction.

Taken together, the subsequent three chapters signal a turning point in Phephelaphi's self-conception. She finds Deliwe—a self-assertive, domineering, and rebellious shebeen queen—exhilarating and worth emulating. As a shebeen queen, Deliwe illegally sells liquor to men in her house. Phephelaphi's own form of self-assertion is to resolve to become a nurse, a yearning that demolishes the core of Fumbatha's masculine being. When Phephelaphi goes to Deliwe's shebeen at night, she embarks on a journey of self-discovery and self-emancipation, acutely aware of the defiant nature of her action.

Chapter 12 offers a beautiful image of communal celebration and self-expression whose buoyancy is in distinct contrast to the gloom and despondency of the ensuing chapters. Zandile's flashback, for instance, in the following chapter, recounts a history of gender abuse, displacement of war returnees, and Zandile's own struggle against marginalization. Back in 1948, the opening up of new opportunities represented by Phephelaphi's imminent admission for training creates a strong juxtaposition of the generational differences in the choices available to mother and daughter. But Phephelaphi's discovery of her pregnancy in chapter 14 brings on a sense of hysteria that will find its full expression in chapter 16, where the dramatic quality of the first-person point of view contrasts the workings of a frenzied mind attempting to process a crisis with the desolate, excruciating trauma of her self-administered abortion. This is the longest chapter, with its deliberately detailed description of Phephelaphi's mental experience. The atmosphere of extreme tension and conflict builds over the following three chapters, leading to Fumbatha's betrayal of Phephelaphi. Their life together crumbles still further when their true histories are bitterly revealed, and when Phephelaphi discovers that she is pregnant once again, she is furious over Fumbatha's claim on her body. The narrative ends with Phephelaphi's suicide, a blazing, terrible image of her anger that confronts Fumbatha when he returns to their home. Through the cumulative force of her images, culminating in that of Phephelaphi's immolation, Vera makes an unmistakably powerful statement.

Adding human depth to the skillful use of cinematographic technique in structuring her narrative, Yvonne Vera's portrayal of her characters is deeply perceptive and searching. She places them, male and female, in a particular historical and sociopolitical context and probes their experiences and thoughts as they struggle to forge a viable life for themselves. The narrative voice often glides smoothly from the context or the environment into a character's mind, and vice versa, allowing her to present both subjective and objective perceptions of the character's predicament and his or her surroundings and sociopolitical context. All the characters have inner lives that are predicated on historical loss, suffering, and "the privacy and intensity of unarticulated pain" (Attree, 69), and the paucity of dialogue in the text both intensifies their subjective experiences and enables the narrative voice to probe the deeply embedded silence within them. In her interview with Eva Hunter, Vera has spoken of her technique of character development and presentation: "I . . . like to give a strong psychological profile to female characters, which is something I have not found in earlier literature. Yet we live so much of our lives internally and it is really important to explore that. It's an entire world which I find to be mesmerizing and it brings me closest to the character when I can enter her mental world" (81). Although she specifically mentions female characters, her remarks can be applied to her treatment of male characters as well. In a sociopolitical context that imposes silence, invisibility, and absolute subservience, both black males and females tend to live their lives internally. However, because of the unequal power relations within the patriarchal society that Vera portrays, the women are more reticent in externalizing their thoughts and perceptions. Yet, under the liberating influence of liquor in an urban setting, the women in *Butterfly Burning* "say whatever is on their minds . . . laugh, and fail to apologize. Apologies are unpleasant, and . . . involve bending the knees right down and coming back up; this, of course, they no longer have the strength for" (48).

The development of Fumbatha and Phephelaphi's relationship is such that it allows for an intimate portrayal of their mental world. When Fumbatha meets Phephelaphi for the first time, he immediately associates her with the elemental forces of nature—air, water, and the sun—and in his mind she assumes their life-giving qualities. The narrative voice foregrounds the transformative power of her presence: she "rose out of the river like a spirit. . . . her eyes glittering like jewels before him. . . . She rose out of the water like the sun. . . . She was water and air" (21). Phephelaphi's youthful energy and strength of character are apparent in her movement and in each word she utters. As the descriptive images progress from similes to metaphors, so will the intensity of Fumbatha's dependency on her later in the novel. Yet this dependency manifests itself in paradoxical terms: even at this first encounter, he already sees her as some form of possession. While he acknowledges her strength and courage, he also sees her as something that the river has given him: "It had given him this woman, spitting her onto the rock like a dream" (22). His mythologizing of Phephelaphi confers on this encounter an aura of mysticism for his own individual benefit. He subjects Phephelaphi to a male gaze that deprives her of the very agility and courage he seems to admire. Ann Kaplan defines such a gaze as a "one-way subjective vision" that involves "extreme anxiety—an attempt in a sense *not* to know, to deny, in fact" (xvi–xvii; emphasis in original). Fumbatha's gaze is reductionist in that, in the grip of his own fears and anxieties, he sees Phephelaphi as a compensation for his losses. Hence the paranoia that he might lose her. "He never wanted to let her go. . . . He could never free her. . . . He would remember her. He would hold her. Fumbatha had never wanted to possess anything before, except the land. He wanted her like the land beneath his feet from which birth had severed him. Perhaps if he had not been born the land would still belong to him. The death of his father had not heralded birth" (23).

Fumbatha's myopic vision does not go beyond what he wants. In equating Phephelaphi with the land, he idealizes and commodifies her, suppressing her own needs and perceptions as an individual. He makes her compensate, somehow, for the loss of the land as he becomes revitalized and rejuvenated in her presence. His extreme fear that he might lose her foreshadows the conflict that will be brought about by her yearning to train as a nurse. In a flashback in chapter ten, we are in Fumbatha's mind as he recalls his incredulity that Phephelaphi's application for nursing would ever be considered. He actively discourages her and demands her loyalty because "He mistrusts the city which does not understand the sort of triumph a man and woman can find and share in their solitude" (60). While his fear of the city is understandable, given the moral and social decline in Makokoba, the masculine ego that inscribes him as a provider would limit Phephelaphi to the privacy of the domestic sphere. Providing her shelter and protection validates his manhood, invests it with the dignity that is daily trampled upon in his life as a common laborer. He reverses the "unmistakable shame" of his work by assuming the authority to forbid her training. The anger and frustration that build up in him are not so much directed against Phephelaphi as they reflect the sense of his own futility. His cumulative political emasculation is exacerbated by the nullification of patriarchal control over Phephelaphi, a young woman whose determined drive for independence and self-direction resists his restraining influence. Ultimately, it is a test of wills: "Fumbatha wonders if she will apply. Phephelaphi wonders if he can stop her" (61). The implicit challenge and questioning of Fumbatha's ability to limit her yearning comes through clearly.

As the narrative voice weaves in and out of Phephelaphi's consciousness, we become aware of a growing assertiveness that seeks to transgress the physical limitations of the Makokoba location, to create a larger space for her own agency, and to fulfill her burning desire for transformation as well as for being at the forefront of development. Her pioneering spirit, which Fumbatha is attempting to stifle, is conveyed when we are told that "It is not the being a nurse which matters, but the movement forward—the entrance into something new and untried. Her heart rises in an agony of longing. She is going to be the first to train, if the occasion allows her" (60). Advancement, alertness to new opportunities, and a passion for self-fulfillment are only some of the personal traits that Fumbatha refuses to countenance. When they start living together, Phephelaphi keeps "all her thoughts at bay" and relies on "his every thought and attention" (26). She grows dependent on him. However, her meeting with Deliwe changes her perception of herself and her relationship with

Fumbatha. For her, Deliwe epitomizes life experience, independence, and self-assertion. Phephelaphi begins to question not just her own reliance on Fumbatha, but his excessive protectiveness. When she decides to visit Deliwe's shebeen alone at night, flouting Fumbatha's unspoken will, it is to exercise her own judgment.

Phephelaphi's visit to Deliwe's shebeen becomes a journey towards self-reclamation. Using something like a stream-of-consciousness technique, Vera sets the external commotion of the shebeen against Phephelaphi's processing and assessing of what is unfolding. The present tense conveys the urgency and immediacy of her project, which she undertakes within the relaxed setting. The contrast between the mental distance Phephelaphi experiences and the physical proximity of the men in the shebeen creates a space for interrogating their social stereotype of woman. Significantly, the metaphorical descriptions of Phephelaphi echo the expressions of Fumbatha's totalizing male gaze in an earlier chapter. Here, we see her ambivalence about being a woman in a strange place. Her initial feelings of inferiority are transformed, though, through a painful contemplation of Getrude's murder. Her intense awareness of herself in terms of gender foregrounds the woman-centeredness of her quest. We learn that "She is intensely aware of being a woman. A woman in a room. It is a simple fact. It is so new to her. . . . A precipice, and she is standing right on the lip of its fall. . . . The ground below is the solid rock of a woman. She can stand on it, so she lets herself fall as far as she can reach" (55). The metaphor of a precipice encapsulates the precarious position inherent in the relationship between men and women, a danger rooted in this society's construction of womanhood. As Teresa Ebert explains, "Woman is produced in social signification as the other on which the very existence of man and the asymmetrical relations of exploitation, power, and privilege in patriarchy depend. Woman, then, would not be in and of herself an oppositional presence to man and patriarchy, but would be revealed as simultaneously in a position of oppression in patriarchal capitalism and as one of the crucial supports of that system" (quoted in Davies, 70).

Far from supporting the tactics of other-ing inscribed in the patriarchal system, Phephelaphi's intense awareness of being a woman affirms her own reconstruction of womanhood. It is significant that she institutes her own process of revaluation in a woman-defined space. As shebeen queen, Deliwe is positioned as a transgressive female figure who consciously disrupts the very basis on which both patriarchal power and white colonialist dominance are founded. It is also within this space that Phephelaphi chooses to relive and re-experience the trauma of her mother's murder. Deliwe and Getrude exemplify different strategies of confronting social and economic marginalization within an urban area—which, through the migratory labor system, has become defined as a male space. Being excluded from jobs in the formal sectors, women are compelled to look for alternative, informal jobs. Beer brewing, prostitution, and domestic work are some available options, which, however, expose them to extreme gender violence.

Deliwe's defiant confrontations with the police repeatedly justify their brutality. Phephelaphi's introspection gives her the power to define another, truly liberating trajectory, which begins by her reconciling herself to her mother's violent death, then placing herself and her own project at the center. She might be in a position of inferiority according to the patriarchal system, but she is determined not to be one of the crucial supports of that system. Her quest to find herself is clearly expressed in the following passage:

> She wanted the sense of belonging before that kind of belonging which rested on another's wondrous claim, being herself because she was a flower blooming in her own green pool, to be able to pick the flower which was herself from the water before he reached out his own strong arm and did all that for her and made her feel empty and waited upon. . . . She had to find what she could here, from within her own land, from her body. (69)

Her feminist consciousness comes to the fore as she seeks her own power of self-determination by actively constructing her own identity. In defining her path, she appropriates Fumbatha's metaphoric description of her and thus defeats his objectification of her by investing her own agency and meaning in those descriptions.

The crisis that she experiences when she discovers her pregnancy at the same time that she is to be admitted for training as a nurse is literally one of life and death. Examining her body closely, she does not feel elated. She is "pained" not only by the changing shape of her body, but most of all by the fact that this pregnancy spells the end of the career path and the lifestyle that would make her unique: "She wanted an opportunity to be a different woman and 1948 was a year when hope opened like a bright sky and an educated black woman could do more. The offer was there and it made her breathless just to imagine being anything else other than what she was. It was nothing she knew but she wanted it, missed the future somehow. She was nothing now. . . . She wanted to be something with an outline . . . she wanted some respect, some dignity, some balance and power of her own." Pregnancy means that Fumbatha "had now intruded on her dream" (91). He has trespassed within her land—her own body—and has turned her dream of wholeness into the nightmare of disintegration. Her body has become a text on which this disruption is physically inscribed. Her body, "her own land," becomes a site on which Fumbatha has staked his claim, in which he has planted his seed, thus wresting from her control over her own future.

Her radically different view of pregnancy makes her occupy a deviant space within society. Instead of celebrating the fecundity of maternal creativity, she is filled with fury and desperation over the patriarchal disruption and domination, over the cancellation of the identity she is creating for herself. In such a position of emotional, psychological, and physical alienation, she sees, as if for the first time, the real condition as well as the significance of Sidojiwe E2 in particular, and Makokoba in general. The mental breakdown she suffers in Deliwe's house is symptomatic of the disintegration of her own identity. Her frenzy is reflected in the punctuation, a series of commas in a long paragraph that illustrate the effusions of unstructured meanings/communication.

Many critics have noted that madness or nervous breakdown has become a trope that frequently features in black women's writings. While Chikwenye Okonjo Ogunyemi sees it as sometimes "a temporary aberration preceding spiritual growth, healing, and integration" (74), for Carol Boyce Davies it is a deviant position that challenges culture but does not change its structures (see 77). Ogunyemi's perception of madness is grounded in the womanist project reflected in Bessie Head's *A Question of Power*, Mariama Bâ's *So Long a Letter*, and Toni Morrison's *The Bluest Eye*, all of which aspire to healing and positive, integrative endings. This ultimate wholeness is achieved, in spite of bitter awareness and experience of multiple marginalizations, within black patriarchal culture, operating under the more overwhelming, global, white domination. On the other hand, Davies locates madness in women's larger abrogation of society's intransigent expectations. The madwoman is a "resisting figure" (77) because, seeing beyond the limitations of patriarchal demands, she refuses to participate within them. Thus, in her novel *Nervous Conditions*, Tsitsi Dangarembga employs the trope of the madwoman to exemplify women's resistance against patriarchal and colonial entrapment, and to convey the toll this resistance takes on them, emotionally and intellectually.

In light of the foregoing discussion, Phephelaphi's panic is a temporary aberration undergone by a resisting woman. However, for Phephelaphi there is no healing nor any integration, for the structures do not change, though the last line of the novel, "at midnight" (130), gives the hope of a new dawn. When she returns from Deliwe's shebeen she collects her thoughts to consider the process of her resistance. In a prolonged moment of desperation, anger, and anxiety, in the lonely silence of the room, she makes an anguished decision about the child she is expecting. This moment of decision is preceded by a passage in which Phephelaphi attaches ponderous significance to every movement in the room, her mental state expressed in unhurried descriptions that mimic the cinematographic technique of slow motion. Earlier in the narrative one of the two people who were quarreling in the street threw a stone into her house and it broke the window. It is this stone that Phephelaphi imbues with dual significance. It becomes symbolic as it gathers into itself all the experiences connected with the shattering. It becomes an object that prevents the irretrievable loss of memory. It also adumbrates the abortion she performs in the following chapter.

In her heightened self-awareness, the silence and darkness become symbolic of her own existential alienation and extinction: "She denied her own existence and moved, like a shadow, back to the window. She heard nothing. No voice called. Nothing shouted. No one moved. . . . The emptiness had decided all there was to decide about her insignificance and her lack of wisdom and she was nothing but a shallow substance. There was evidence of her lack. She was nothing. . . . She was nothing under the sky" (94–95). Such abnegation of self is symptomatic of the psychic trauma Phephelaphi experiences. Her response to pregnancy interrogates the much-avowed naturalness of maternal feelings. Phephelaphi lights a candle, and the detailed description of her actions in doing so deflects attention from her internal turmoil. The narrative voice invests the flickering light of a candle in a tiny room in a black township with symbolic power.

> The darkness was whole. The light soft. Then the light grew whole, the darkness soft. In the whirring of the dark and in the ringlet of fear that rose above her she slipped to the floor

and crouched near the cup and the candle, her elbows hit the wall above which was the broken window, above which was the light, above those strange tall trees, the red roofs, the telegraph wires, above which was the moon and the stars, above which was her mounting sorrow, her desperate panic, and the child. (95)

The reverberation of a single, small action that implies the participation of the whole universe magnifies her predicament and intensifies the urgency of her need of a self-defined path, as much as does the overwhelming reality of the child. The intensity and enormity of her decision engulf the whole universe.

Chapter 16 is one of the most shocking and detailed treatments of a taboo subject in literature that I have ever read. In it, Vera focuses on the emotional and psychological trauma in Phephelaphi as well as on the act of abortion itself. As both the agent who performs and the witness who registers the effects of this "irreversible harm" (98), Phephelaphi is utterly alone, without support. Vera feelingly images this turmoil through her superbly crafted language and narrative style, exploring Phephelaphi's internal world through the character's perception of the landscape around her and her location in it. The connection between landscape and woman's psychic state calls into question the normalization of landscape and the urban environment as a male domain. It therefore locates Phephelaphi at the center of the struggle to be acknowledged as a legitimate inhabitant of the urban landscape. Landscape thus becomes the bearer of her own experience. Her physical and emotional isolation is reflected in the barrenness of the land. Her need for succor is emphasized by the bruising absence of a soothing and therapeutic natural environment. Her sensation of weightlessness is induced by the desire to escape the trauma of her experience.

Vera's employment of pathetic fallacy serves to externalize a whole range of her character's emotional and psychic disturbances. After the narration first draws attention to the natural objects constituting the physical landscape of Makokoba location, Phephelaphi uses recurring images of water, the river, the thorn bushes, the land, and the sky as symbols of her own agony. In the absence of community or a companion with whom to communicate her trauma, she projects her pain on the landscape—which, in seeming sympathy with her predicament, becomes an extension of her desolation in its aridity. In a pain-filled delirium, Phephelaphi sees red dots on the thorn bushes. These dots turn into birds, which fly away. They signify her guilt and her anguished desire for that guilt to be removed. Other images in the novel—of burning, of heat, light, and lightning—heighten its tension and foreshadow its terrifying ending, even as they project at the same time the mesmerizing paradox of sensuality, beauty, and pain.

However, it is not in symbolic images but in the graphic details of Phephelaphi's abortion—she uses a thorn—that Vera captures the essence of the excruciating pain that Phephelaphi administers, acknowledges, and owns. "It is herself, her own agony spilling over some fine limit of becoming which she has ceased suddenly to understand, too light and too heavy. It is she. She embraces it, braces for the tearing. . . . She has to accept her own pain in order to believe it, to live in it, to know its true and false nuances, for she desires desperately what is beyond the pain" (99). We are confronted with a resolute yet fearful young woman who both acknowledges the harm and bravely submits to the consequent agony. Both the process and the agony constitute a border psychic space in which a transition from one state to another occurs. The ambivalence characteristic of this space is found in the wavering of her mind between total collapse and self-awareness. She spares herself no pain. She exerts her own punishment on herself, reminding the reader of Mazvita, in Vera's *Without a Name* (1994), who is compelled to kill her child and then to carry it on her back as a burden that she must suffer. Finally, the only way that Phephelaphi can bear the unbearable is to lose consciousness: "not being part of anything at all, not her body. . . . [In] a quiet stretch of time where she is not. Not being" (100).

Stephanie A. Demetrakopoulos has commented on the complexity of the conflict between history/culture and maternal instincts. While the bond of mothering is a massive force, she argues, it has a dark and painful side: "maternal bonds can stunt or even obviate a woman's individuation or sense of self" (69). When Phephelaphi commits abortion on herself, it is a radical acknowledgement of the self and a projection of that self into the future. In a historical and sociopolitical context that is inimical to female progression, her act inevitably recalls her own rejection by her biological mother, Zandile. At that time, Zandile had felt that "A child was an agony. . . . She needed lightness . . . not the burden of becoming a mother" (124). The difference, though, is that while Zandile, newly emerged from the rural areas in the 1920s, was dazzled by city life, Phephelaphi, in 1948, yearned to create history.

When Phephelaphi performs the act of burial, she observes a sacred ritual, manifesting mourning as a process of self-healing. Through these actions, Vera uses the complex connection between Phephelaphi and the land to probe the silent endurance of abortion. In her interview with Bryce, Vera explains: "I also want to capture a history, but history is in a moment. A woman is in the forest, she's alone, the ground is bare. What is her relationship to this landscape, and who is she in this moment? She's endured all these other things, but at this moment, her mind is collapsing. How does she endure this moment?" (223) In her confusion and self-reproach, Phephelaphi imbues the land with ambivalent powers of forgiveness and rejection. As she digs with her hands, the soil is at once soft and pliant as well as hard and rocky. The terrestrial hardness is mirrored above: "the sky is a solid unforgiving blue all round" (106). She might be utterly alone and unnoticeable, but to the earth and sky her presence and her actions are known. She will later use this aloneness as a shield of alienation from Fumbatha. When he "returns into the hidden truth of her actions" (110) he immediately feels the emotional and psychological distance between them. His intense need of her is rebuffed by her feelings of guilt and fear: "He feels the pain of their separation as though she has rejected him with entire words" (111). Phephelaphi manifests the intensity of her experience through actions, not words, just as Fumbatha silently and intuitively admits to the failure of his dream that "only she could bear his children," and to the loss of her as a refuge (112). He needs Phephelaphi more than she now needs him.

Vera projects the abortion as an image of ambivalence, signifying two contradictory but related processes. On the one hand, abortion is a termination of potential life; on the other, it rekindles and revives, giving birth to a new sense of self in Phephelaphi. After descending into the abyss, she emerges with her strength renewed: "Each moment is hers and she recalls each detail with clarity even while she is still living it, living in it, part of it, and parting from it. Rising, she must remember" (107).

This strength is the validation of her conscious actions and experiences at a particular moment in history. Her acknowledgement of the consequences of her actions speaks of her courage, as she "seeks her own refuge" (128). The cradle of thorns that she weaves is evocative of this simultaneous process of termination and renewal. However, her suicide is a flaming manifestation of her rage and despair, her dissent against the subordinating patriarchal inscription on her body. The switch in point of view at this moment dramatizes the intensity of Phephelaphi's feelings. Dropping the mediating voice of the narrator, Vera has the "I" articulate directly Phephelaphi's own perceptions.

In tandem with Yvonne Vera's interrogative stance, she eschews a perfect closure of her story. Within the frame of the text, the fictive persona Phephelaphi writes herself out of history, while Vera the writer inscribes her, as a type, into history by writing the text. By her death and annihilation in the text, Phephelaphi seems to represent and speak for all black women who are silenced by repressive patriarchal and sociopolitical practices. However, the text also seems to raise questions about the boundaries of motherhood and the value of self-destruction.

Works Cited

Attree, Lizzy. 2002. "Language, Kwela Music and Modernity in *Butterfly Burning.*" In *Sign and Taboo: Perspectives on the Poetic Fiction of Yvonne Vera,* ed. Robert Muponde and Mandi Taruvinga, 63–82. Harare, Zimbabwe: Weaver.

Bryce, Jane. 2002. "Interview with Yvonne Vera." In *Sign and Taboo: Perspectives on the Poetic Fiction of Yvonne Vera,* ed. Robert Muponde and Mandi Taruvinga, 217–26. Harare, Zimbabwe: Weaver.

Davies, Carol Boyce. 1994. *Black Women, Writing and Identity: Migration of the Subject.* London: Routledge.

Demetrakopoulos, Stephanie A. 1999. "Maternal Bonds as Devourers of Women's Individuation in Toni Morrison's *Beloved.*" In *Toni Morrison's Beloved,* ed. Harold Bloom, 69–78. Broomall, PA: Chelsea House.

Fanon, Frantz. 1990. *The Wretched of the Earth.* 6th ed. Trans. Constance Farrington. London: Penguin.

Hunter, Eva. 1998. "'Shaping the Truth of the Struggle': An Interview with Yvonne Vera." *Current Writing* (Durban, South Africa) 10 (1): 75–86.

Kaplan, E. Ann. 1997. *Feminism, Film, and the Imperial Gaze.* New York: Routledge.

Minh-ha, Trinh T. 1989. *Woman, Native, Other: Writing Postcoloniality and Feminism.* Bloomington: Indiana University Press.

Muponde, Robert, and Mandi Taruvinga, eds. 2002. *Sign and Taboo: Perspectives on the Poetic Fiction of Yvonne Vera.* Harare, Zimbabwe: Weaver.

Ogunyemi, Chikwenye Okonjo. 1985. "Womanism: The Dynamics of the Contemporary Black Female Novel in English." *Signs* 11 (1): 63–80.

Primorac, Ranka. 2002. "Iron Butterflies: Notes on Yvonne Vera's *Butterfly Burning.*" In *Sign and Taboo: Perspectives on the Poetic Fiction of*

Yvonne Vera, ed. Robert Muponde and Mandi Taruvinga, 101–8. Harare, Zimbabwe: Weaver.

Ranger, Terence. 1999. "The Fruits of the Baobab: Irene Staunton and the Zimbabwean Novel." *Journal of Southern African Studies* 25 (4): 695–701.

Simpson, Paul. 1993. *Language, Ideology and Point of View*. London: Routledge.

Soros, Eugene. 2002. "Yvonne Vera: Breaking the Silence." *World Press Review Online*, September 23. Available at http://www.worldpress.org/Africa/736.cfm (accessed April 22, 2008).

Vera, Yvonne. 1993. *Nehanda*. Harare, Zimbabwe: Baobab.

———. 1993. *Why Don't You Carve Other Animals?* Harare, Zimbabwe: Baobab.

———. 1994. *Without a Name*. Harare, Zimbabwe: Baobab.

———. 1996. *Under the Tongue*. Harare, Zimbabwe: Baobab.

———. 1998. *Butterfly Burning*. Harare, Zimbabwe: Baobab.

———. 1999. *Opening Women's Spaces: An Anthology of Contemporary Women's Writing*. Harare, Zimbabwe: Baobab.

———. 2002. *Stone Virgins*. Harare, Zimbabwe: Weaver.

Wills, Alfred John. 1990. *An Introduction to the History of Central Africa: Zambia, Malawi and Zimbabwe*. 4th ed. Oxford: Oxford University Press.

Part 3

REGENERATION

Labor Pains and Tentative Steps toward Independence

7

Mapping a Female Mind

Bessie Head's *A Question of Power* and the Unscrambling of Africa

Chikwenye Okonjo Ogunyemi

"I work with my hands," she said, proudly. "I have always worked. I do any kind of work."

The small boy had been listening to the conversation with bright, intent eyes. Caught up in the rhythm of her statement, he unconsciously put his hands on the table and *mimicked:* "I work with my hands. I have always worked. I do any kind of work." . . .

Wickedly he *repeated:* "My God, this child is very bad."

Again, there it was, the pretty, crinkling smile of deep humour. It was so brief, so carefully parted with that all the power of her personality seemed to depend on severity and reserve. (Head, *A Question of Power,* 91; emphasis supplied)

In fact two mimetic movements are involved. One is the duplication in song [read: writing] of the spirits, detail by slow-moving detail. . . . The other mimetic movement depends upon this invocation of the spirits [read: hallucination] because,

since they duplicate the physical world, then to bring them
forth by means of song is to mimetically *gain control* over the
mirror-image of physical reality that they represent. (Taussig, 105; emphasis supplied)

A Question of Origins, Duplication, and Power

Bessie Head's third novel, *A Question of Power* (1974), by its makeup
as autobiografiction,[1] is mimetic. In this version of literature, the
South African–born Head (1937–1986) duplicates the lived and living
life, which encapsulates "mankind's history" (36) with its repetitive
patterns, accessing power through her text. As a single mother in exile
in Botswana, prone to mental breakdowns, she draws on the work
to control her mental health. As a biracial person with an unknown
black father and abandoned by the white side of her family, and as a
wife who ditched her husband, she utilizes the novel to "out" her trai-
torous family. Further, she employs the work to exercise intellectual
power by contributing to the discourse of postcolonialisms set up
since the European scramble for Africa in the nineteenth century. As a
descendant of both those who came to Africa as part of this frenzied
race and those who suffered because of the scramble, Head stands in
a strong position to speak to a world gone out of kilter.

Rereading this biomythography[2] by Head, who never got to return
"home" to a free South Africa, this reader finds her southern African world bizarre. However, it is notable that, in the postapartheid
era, South Africa's Truth and Reconciliation Committee effected a
certain freeing of the collective mind, similar to what Head displays
in the novel through the extraordinary disclosures that facilitate
the serenity of Elizabeth, her mentally ill protagonist. Now that
terrorists—individuals, gangs, governments of different religious
leanings—haunt and sometimes police the global precincts, wreaking
untold havoc that places us dangerously close to World War III, *A
Question of Power* stands as cautionary and philosophically civilizing,
as it depicts the horrific results of state-induced terrorism on a personal level. The terrorism unleashed on Africa and elsewhere by Europe, America, and the Middle East in the nineteenth and twentieth centuries has boomeranged, as Middle Eastern monotheisms proliferate
and destabilize the world. The work clarifies the intimate relationship

between good and evil, a complicated nexus that many religious fundamentalists in the twenty-first century seek to simplify by dividing the world into two categories and repudiating the evil Other.

Head carried an enormous baggage with her from South Africa: racism, errant sexuality, insanity, poverty, statelessness, and a need to reinvent her genealogy. She anguished over her burden, revisiting it in her novels *When Rain Clouds Gather* (1968), *Maru* (1971), and, especially, in her tour de force, *A Question of Power*, now posthumously recognized as one of the hundred best books from Africa in the twentieth century. This distinction acknowledges her expertise as a writer; as importantly, it publicly accepts her as a full-fledged African, a gesture that legitimizes her and would have tickled her to no end.

In a kaleidoscope of shifting, spiritual responses to leaders in the racially torn region of southern Africa, in *A Question of Power* the biracial Head[3] implicitly speaks to Prime Minister Seretse Khama of her adopted Botswana, to which she fled in 1964. Like her unknown father, who represents Africa's unwritten history, Khama had dared to associate with a white woman in spite of the laws against miscegenation in neighboring South Africa. Against the opposition of whites and many Batswana, he married the British Ruth Williams, producing children like the "Coloured" Head. To Head, therefore, Khama successfully transformed the sketchy, demonizing story of her origins, with an absent father whose identity remained undisclosed by Head's mother. In *A Question of Power*, Elizabeth's mentor, Sello, a monk in a brown suit, doubles as Khama, who doubles as a father figure for Head. Head also speaks to Khama's deputy, Quett Masire, about what she considers the African burden; he, represented as the womanizing Dan, epitomizes the men who had sexually harassed her in Botswana (MacKenzie, 24).

Distressed by what she perceived to be a hostile, exilic environment, Head, a single mother with a son, suffered nervous breakdowns. In a therapeutic move, in *A Question of Power* she wrote about the voices and hallucinations that led to this pass, representing herself as Elizabeth, a teacher, writer, and gardener. Elizabeth alienates her hosts in Motabeng during her breakdowns by mixing reality and illusion[4]; fortunately, the village rallies round her, she is hospitalized, and she later recovers by busying herself with gardening, an essential task in this desert country.

Head's painstaking biographer, Gillian Stead Eilersen, bemoans the fact that Head "would never know the identity of her mother, grandmother, brother, uncles or aunts" (8). Eilersen, having no information about the black father, attributes Head's "artistic bent" to her mother (see 7–8). Yet Head wished to tell all, while her mother was silent about the crucial issues of paternity and family, issues that would trouble Head for the rest of her life. She made artistic use of the story of her origins, a situation that members of her mother's tight-lipped family could not have relished. The familial silence left it to Head, as unfilial writer, to imagine the parental sexual relationship that produced her (see Eilersen, 75).

In our 1981 conversation during my visit to Serowe, Botswana, Bessie wondered about her physical features, family resemblances that, from photographic evidence, Eilersen rightly associates with her mother (see 17–18). Head also inherited her mental imbalance from her mother, who was institutionalized in a mental asylum when Bessie was born. In a letter to her friend Randolph Vigne, Head conjectures about her parents:

> A birth such as I had links me to her in a very deep way and makes her belong to that unending wail of the human heart. . . . Why? How do I know if she loved my father? She must have been as mad and impulsive as I. She must have loved going at a man and grabbing him around the neck and found white men too stiff for that game. You can only do that to a black man. He just loves it when you go at him and grab him around the neck. I am just like her. I like to do things to men and say all kinds of horrible things and be very provocative.
> (*Gesture*, 65)

Speculating about her parents' sexuality has psychological implications: her resemblance to her mother compromises her daughterly relationship with her imagined father, inadvertently turning him into a father-lover. She explores this delicate boundary confusion in *A Question of Power* with the paternal and ascetic Sello, who, in a mad moment, Elizabeth wrongly accuses of incest. Dan is the incorrigible womanizer of the story. She derives her criminalizing and pathologizing sexual attitude from her experience of apartheid South Africa.[5]

I wonder, as Bessie wondered in our conversation, if the father, who disappeared in reality and is seemingly absent textually, is the griot from whom she inherited her penchant for the autobiographical and the historical. Certainly, he left a genealogical gap, producing an obsession in Head, as griot, to retell stories that textually replace the missing parents. She recapitulates her genealogy through four generations (including her son, Howard), basing it on the maternal side of her family. Continuing the artistic fusion, she Africanizes her nervous breakdown by ascribing it to witchcraft. In a recuperative gesture, Elizabeth/Head, as her father's daughter, finally claims identification with Africa as a sign of being healed, defying the killing spirit of Europe's scramble.

In mapping this female mind in its movement from insanity to sanity, therefore, I would note that Head rights her white fathers' wrongs, replacing their fracturing of Africa with her/Elizabeth's healing as an African. In the intellectual process of unscrambling the scramble in *A Question of Power*, Head, intersubjectively or through conscious imitation, reproduces the grand theoretical responses of black men who established discourses on the scramble's twentieth-century fallout—W. E. B. Du Bois with his racial thrust, Frantz Fanon with his psychological excavation, and Walter Rodney with his socioeconomic take. In my mapping, Michael Taussig's treatment of mimesis (imitation; literary representation of reality) and alterity (otherness; the traumatizing experience of being considered different) illuminates her approach to mimicry better than does Kenneth Parker's limiting definition of "mimics [as] consumers of that which is not authentically ours" (66). Head's eclectic turn of mind enabled her to take something from all her heritage groups, thereby reproducing herself in the subjective position of a masculinized African single mother. As a griot with an encyclopedic technique, she represents people with assuredness. In a collaborative capacity, she uses agriculture to improve the lot of her community. And, as an iconoclast, she deconstructs religion's high ground to achieve peace of mind as a woman.

Unscrambling the Scramble

Named after her mother, Bessie Amelia Birch Emery, and identifying with the staunch Christian wife of Khama the Great, Elizabeta, who was called Mma Bessie (Nixon, 129), Bessie Emery Head, fatherless daughter without a fatherland, gradually invents a maternal line—white and black. Her life, then, is a political statement, interrogating the arrogant power displayed in the scramble for Africa, the product of the infamous Berlin Conference of 1885. Following the end of the international slave trade and, ostensibly, of slavery, the conference, one of the later outcomes of the European so-called Enlightenment that shortchanged people of color and women, by the twentieth century had produced weird national states and unhealthy states of mind. As Rob Nixon surmises, about Head,

> [D]enied the solidarities of family, race, and nation, Head generated a compensatory matrix of allegiances transnationally to the Southern African region, locally to a particular village, and within that, to a community of women. Head's haunting quest for alternative, improvised grounds for her identity generated an oeuvre that testifies, with singular intensity, to the inventedness of many of the most authoritative social categories—nation, family, race, and history. (107)

In his brilliant assessment, Nixon zeroes in on the fact that Head was not a nationalist but a continentalist, a freed temperament, a nomadic border crosser in the true pan-African spirit that countered the constricting, mean-spirited conference. That conference's cartographers, with pencils as weapons of mass destruction, their murky officialese replacing the clarity properly associated with mapping, in their frenzy of possession so scrambled Africa that it has not recovered from the act of terrorism. Homegrown terrorists have exacerbated the situation, taking advantage of the ensuing chaos.

Through her own fantasies in *A Question of Power*, Head interrogates this fantastic, conjured-up world and the arrogance of imperial fictional reality that continuously unravels—the story of the world. Writing about the hallucination that in turn conjures up people from the real world becomes an imitation of an imitation of life.[6] This mimesis of a mimesis, to follow Taussig, is a way to control power in the unstable worlds of ill health and exile.

To Head, Elizabeth's condition as an individual encapsulates the familial, the national, and the continental, tying all into what she perceives to be global—a sweeping view of history. As she comments in her address at a conference in Nigeria, she sees the universe through the lens of the individual.[7] She critiques being silent about evil and prophesies the evil uses of power. With an imperial gesture, tapping into the "power grid," she writes about and questions the postcolonial situation still colored by the premise of the nineteenth-century scramble: European superiority. As a typical refugee and stateless person/United Nations citizen, she buys into mid-twentieth-century ideas of equality, the need to address poverty, and the obligation to feed the world's peoples explicitly set forth in the United Nations charter. These issues are critical in a reading of *A Question of Power.*

To the various European redrawings of the map of Africa, from the Berlin Conference on downward, Head's granddaughterly response takes a political,[8] sociological, and psychological turn when she introduces a discussion of "incomprehensible"[9] Danish novels (*Question,* 79). As Jacqueline Rose has said in regard to *A Question of Power,* it seems that commentators like Lewis Nkosi run "the risk of sliding into imperial diagnosis of the type that has rushed to read derangement where legible political protest was in fact what was being expressed" (403; see also James Garrett's defense of Head, 122–23). The novel is undeniably political. Head explores her subjectivity by peopling her mental space with communities unimagined by her white grandfathers. Like them, she is not interested in the idea of the nation with its exclusions. However, she questions their right to produce intolerable conditions by drawing maps and employing legalese, and in her turn redraws the map of the continent through writing and accepting the beauty inherent in the power of its diversity.

Whereas European diplomats and cartographers carved up and recombined real territories and peoples, Head creates interconnections and intersections in abstract, topological spaces. These meeting points exuberantly make room for new formations. The future unfolds at the intersections of race (in Elizabeth) and ethnicity (in Shorty, with his Setswana). In Elizabeth's horticulture and agriculture, transplants reshape the new place as they struggle and eventually thrive in the new soil. In the sphere of religion, Elizabeth represents key figures, practices, and fundamental concepts in African Traditional Religions, Buddhism, Judaism, Christianity, and Islam. Her female mind, therefore, seems to unite the hitherto disparate, countering what Walter Rodney has described as imperial divide, conquer, and rule tactics that bolster underdevelopment (see 198). Elizabeth's spirituality and ethics are dialogic channels that make for meaningful communication in decolonizing the mind. The office of woman tackles invasions while interrogating the positional, especially woman's duties to the other, to the self, to the community, to the future generation, and to the formation of a new continent.

The conference that formally launched the scramble poses the question of power in a global context, which Head, as the unwitting product of that scramble, tries to unscramble in her works. The conference affirmed a set of power dynamics that has spanned three centuries: the imperialism of the waning years of the nineteenth century and its continuous reproduction of poverty; the rabid racism of the twentieth century, rooted in colonialism, and its most vicious expression, apartheid. Disquietingly, all these forces continue unabated in the twenty-first century.

The Grand Response

Grand theories and narratives from Africa and its diaspora have countered the scramble by addressing and transforming the issues raised by it. In *The Souls of Black Folk* (1903), the renowned, pioneering African American sociologist W. E. B. Du Bois (1868–1963) emphasizes the divisiveness of the color line in these memorable words that set off a global discourse on race: "Herein lie buried many things which if read with patience may show the strange meaning of being black here in the dawning of the Twentieth Century. This meaning is not without interest to you, . . . for the problem of the Twentieth Century is the problem of the color-line" (5). Du Bois's prophetic, prefatory remarks could have been the "forethought" for Bessie Head writing *A Question of Power*, seventy-one years later, about blacks far away in South Africa striving under a similar racist yoke.

The psychiatrist and influential theorist, Frantz Fanon, born in Martinique but operating from Algeria, shifts the discourse in *Les Damnés de la Terre* (1961; translated in 1963 as *The Wretched of the Earth*) to colonialism and the political, positioning the interacting participants on the psychic level by examining the mental health problems that plague the colonizer and the colonized. For the settlers, this "hostile world, ponderous and aggressive because it fends off the colonized masses with all the harshness it is capable of, represents not merely a hell from which the swiftest flight possible is desirable, but also a paradise close at hand which is guarded by terrible watchdogs" (52–53). This prolonged, mentally unhygienic cat-and-mouse relationship takes a heavy toll: "This is why any study of the colonial world should take into consideration the phenomena of the dance [read: football] and of possession. The native's relaxation takes precisely the form of a muscular orgy in which the most acute aggressivity and the most impelling violence are canalized, transformed, and conjured away. . . . This disintegrating of the personality . . . fulfills a primordial function in the organism of the colonial world"

(57–58). Head's mental life, as represented through Elizabeth, attests to Fanon's observation.

In *How Europe Underdeveloped Africa* (1972), Guyanese intellectual and political activist Walter Rodney explores the economic motivations leading Europe to the scramble. He traces the roots of African underdevelopment and impoverishment to the slave trade and slavery, colonialism, and capitalism. In her novel, Head's conception of the sources of African poverty is much the same, and it is clear that she would readily agree with Rodney's take on the question of power:

> The decisiveness of the short period of colonialism and its negative consequences for Africa spring mainly from the fact that Africa lost power. Power is the ultimate determinant in human society, being basic to the relations within any group and between groups. . . . In relations between peoples, the *question of power* determines maneuverability in bargaining, the extent to which one people respect the interests of another, and eventually the extent to which a people survive as a physical and cultural entity. When one society finds itself forced to relinquish power entirely to another society, that in itself is a form of underdevelopment. (224; emphasis supplied)

Head maneuvers and imposes her will on Africa and her readers through writing in her revised version of post-scramble history in *A Question of Power*, a mimesis of a mimesis with its spiritual and psychosexual thrusts. Thus, one can say she uses these men's theories to tackle the South African and African experiences: she echoes Du Bois's idea, framing it as "racialist" (83); Fanon's she synthesizes as "mental aberration" (58), which many South Africans invariably suffered from; and Rodney's she encapsulates as "the poor of Africa" (31).

Head's Addendum to the Theoretical Response

Head closes the gap in these grand narratives—"mankind's history"— that leave out the specific place of woman in the scheme of things.[10] In spite of her mimicking the narratives, she extends the discourse in a reconfigured world that hones in on a woman's place without being necessarily feminist. As Ebele Eko puts it, "Head's female protagonists come fully into their own only as they accept the male influence as an active part of their consciousness" (217; for a contrary take on Head as a feminist, see Adeola James, 26–33). Head's communal concerns identify her womanist bent in gender matters. When she writes that the "base of it [Elizabeth's relationship with Sello] was masculine" (*Question*, 24), she clearly fuses the feminine and the masculine, thereby redefining the female mind. Further, she identifies religion as a problem area, turning *A Question of Power* into a site for spiritual warfare. This seems prophetic as religious fundamentalism unleashes twenty-first-century terrorism and counterterrorism.

With vested interests as the mother of a black boy and a storyteller, Head, at the acme of her career, differs from her male predecessors. She concentrates on power brokers, those blacks who mimic their masters' tactics and use superhuman means to confine Elizabeth in an unhealthy psychic space, turning the celibate woman into a nerve-wracked voyeur. This space dramatizes colonialism's constant surveillance of the colonized and the paralyzing impact of colonizing the mind. The invasion and occupation of one's home (colonization), as by the phantom figures in Elizabeth's case, is devastatingly humiliating. An exorcism, public and collaborative, is essential in the tedious decolonizing process. To effect this, Elizabeth shifts from the passive to the performative, from the imagined to the actual, from the private to the public, from the punishing home to the therapeutic garden.

Her very life an erasure of the boundaries between nations and states set up by the map drawers, Head, as Elizabeth, concludes *A Question of Power* with a scramble of sorts by claiming the whole of Africa on the last page. Commenting on the work, Head writes:

> My third novel, *A Question of Power*, had such an intensely personal and private dialogue. . . . It was a private philosophical journey to the sources of evil. I argued that people and nations do not realise the point at which they become evil [which] . . . has a powerful propelling motion into a terrible abyss of destruction. I argued that its form, design, and plan could be clearly outlined and that it was little understood as a force in the affairs of mankind. ("Social and Political Pressures," 24)

In addressing these issues, she insightfully unscrambles Africa (and evil) by her very being and her writing. As a mixed product of the scramble, she erases racial lines; further, her exilic, stateless status mocks "tribal," colonial, and national demarcations. Mixing professions as teacher, gardener, and writer, Head dismantles the boxes around which individuals, families, countries, and the globe operate to marginalize. She shifts colonial mapping to the psychological sphere to dramatize its effect on contemporary thought, politics, power distribution, and affiliations.

She recognizes the necessity for the grand theories in accounting for history. The discourses of religion, psychiatry, language, and philosophy, as they relate to Africa, intersect in her writing, giving legitimacy to the cliché that history repeats itself. But in the new historical vision of Head's novel, it is a repetition with a slight difference. Thus, the ambivalent Sello, as monk, monkeying (48) around colonialism when in the brown suit, disrupts Elizabeth's household with his antics and inaction. Imbricated with his strategy to disseminate the seed for the future are the acts of mimicry, simulacrum, doubling, reproduction, re-presentation, as the present imitates the past. Like the numerous birds flying and caroling through the text (116), replication provides flights of fancy and hope. The transplantations, transformations, and reincarnations retain a basic core in a mimetic dance that Taussig would have appreciated in this exposé of unmitigated power.

There are several layers of colonization in the autobiografiction. In the invisible mentalscape made visible through words, Elizabeth occupies her mind with negative thoughts of her own inferiority as a woman, a "Coloured," and a black person. She categorizes herself as other, essentializing Africans by confining them to the powers of darkness in her claustrophobic house. The multiple voices that she alone hears speak to Elizabeth's insecurities as the ultimate other. Unseen, spirit forms have occupied her mind—that is her house—leaving her alienated from her body, land, and home. As black people become a spectacle and spectacular in her mind, her psychic space turns into a site of colonial contestation, where she encounters only uncontrollable, hostile blacks. Her psychic world sharply contrasts with the receptive reality beyond her door, particularly her camaraderie with the feline[11] Kenosi, with whom she works in tandem in the garden.

Kenosi, which in Setswana means "I am alone,"[12] highlights Head's anguish, far back in 1963, at being "left alone to face a horror too terrible to contemplate" ("Letter," 273; see also Gardner, 117). In the novel, the name highlights the creative and spiritual triumphs that Kenosi and Elizabeth, two women, each alone with a child, experience as gardeners and writers. Their relationship is mutually empowering. By novel's end, being alone loses its meaning as disconnection and is transformed by

Elizabeth into a state of spiritual tranquility, which is conducive for writing.

Taking a leap from Setswana into Greek etymology, "*heauton ekenōse* lit. 'emptied himself'" refers to Christ's relinquishing his divinity (OED), a kenosis. Head changes this word to Kenosi in her Setswana English. As Elizabeth's Motswana double, Kenosi encourages her to operate in the public sphere as gardener, enabling the emptying of Elizabeth's mind that induces the calm and peace at the end of the work. As the catlike Kenosi's (*Question*, 89) other, Elizabeth, who Dan thought was "a wilting puppet in his hands" (13), will survive with her nine lives.

In the visible landscape, interestingly, Elizabeth invades Batswana space. Is Elizabeth, as foreign landowner, then, a colonizer colonized? Is Head, as writer, the ultimate power broker, by detailing only selective facts of her story and leaving out details of her own propensity toward evil? Like a self-serving, powerful colonizer, she writes in 1975, "I forcefully created for myself, under extremely hostile conditions, my ideal life. I took an obscure and almost unknown village in the Southern African bush and made it my own hallowed ground" ("Preface to 'Witchcraft'").

As Elizabeth gradually understands that her mind and her body are within her power to control, she becomes less narcissistic and thinks more positively of others by participating in critical food production. The politics of food, a lack of which is a sign of abject poverty, is central to the novel in the rituals of tea drinking, eating, gifts of food, and gardening. The garden, whose abundance is a signifier of wealth, reverses the inadequacy of Motabeng, "the place of sand" (*Question*, 19)—Head's way of advocating Africa's self-sufficiency in food production as a condition of genuine independence.

The Meat of the Matter: Multicolorism and Its Discontents

A Question of Power interrogates the differing nature of power. Like Du Bois, Head believes that the question of race is at the root of the exercise of power. She recognizes this reality in the novel through her representation of dominance: one continent over another; one ethnicity/race over another; the state over the individual; one sex over another; one generation over a younger one; the rich over the poor; the educated over the illiterate; the doctor and nurse over the patient; the teacher over the student; and the husband over the wife. Head reverses some of these situations by dramatizing the power to overcome when one is down. Elizabeth serves as the biracial and bi-cultural victim turned power broker; as the embodiment of the new Africa, she represents the union of Africa and Europe thriving amid traces of other cultures—Asian and Arab/Islamic—that make Africa loosely global and unlike other continents.

In a statement that collapses racism, colonialism, and imprison-ment as sites of power, the "Coloured" Elizabeth remarks to the Dan-ish Birgette about her compatriot Camilla being a "racialist" in the way she insults African men she is supervising in the garden project (*QP*, 82). Camilla, nicknamed Rattle-tongue for the toxic atmosphere she generates with her foolishness, predictably insults the intellect of one of the gardeners, Small-Boy, named for his diminishment. Tack-ling Camilla enables Elizabeth to confront her demons at home, where to hear is to believe—wrongly. Sylvia Walby in "Woman and Nation" deals with "the intersection of gender with citizenship, ethnicity, na-tion and 'race'" (235), issues at the core of *A Question of Power*.

Putatively, Elizabeth is South African, Motswana, white, black, fe-male, masculine, native, and foreigner. She single-handedly defies the idea implicit in the scramble for Africa. Two of the excuses for the scramble were to tackle African barbaric practices, specifically, polyg-amy (or in the Victorian mind, excessive sexuality), and to eliminate internal slavery (though Europe was now enslaving almost the entire continent). Head's biracial status proclaims her married mother's po-lygamous life, since her mother's husband was white. Head's open-ness about "loose" African, male sexuality—Elizabeth's husband is a philanderer on the down low—defines her ambiguity about Africans and Europeans. Polygamy riddled Head's life and preoccupied her fic-tional world. Placed in the untenable position of the tragic mulatto, she makes the best of both heritages.

Witchcraftsmanship: The Psychosocial and Terrorism of the Mind

Head delves into her paternal heritage to produce literary art by in-corporating the African, supernatural take on mental illness. Accord-ing to Fanon,

> This magical structure which permeates native society ful-fills certain well-defined functions in the dynamism of the

libido. . . . The occult sphere is a sphere belonging to the
community which is entirely under magical jurisdiction. By
entangling myself in this inextricable network where actions
are repeated with crystalline inevitability, I find the everlast-
ing world which belongs to me, and the perenniality which
is thereby affirmed of the world belonging to us. . . . The
supernatural, magical powers reveal themselves as essentially personal; the settler's powers are infinitely shrunken,
stamped with their alien origin. (55–56)

Head might have written the above to explain Elizabeth's nervous
breakdown as a type of predatory witchcraft that uncannily promotes
her sense of belonging.

Commenting on Head's depiction of witchcraft, Craig MacKenzie
writes, "Medusa exemplifies the narrowness, the exclusivity of African society. Elizabeth fears that she is an alien in this world. She has a
European fear of "darkest Africa"—the scheming, the witchcraft, the
terrors of the darkness of the African mind and continent to which
she has no access. Her lodestar is her belief in the ordinary person"
(63). However, Head/Elizabeth, a schemer in her own right, is more
complicated than this. Elizabeth frees herself from the sorcerer's entrapment by becoming a sorcerer's apprentice through her reincarnations and initiating herself into the supernatural world to become
part of her father's clan. She graduates to free herself and publicize her
own sorcery—"an awakening of her own powers" (*Question,* 35)—as
she magically transforms real people into spirit forms in her head and
house, thus providing material that can again be transformed into a
text, which her Motabeng audience hostilely receives. Head writes:
"Such a terror was to fill her mind at a later stage that she would look
back on the early part of her life in Botswana and think that the personality who held her life in a death-grip must really be the master
of the psychology behind witchcraft" (21). In Head's subversive version of "Batswana witchcraft [that] only works on a Motswana, not
an outsider" (56), Elizabeth succumbs to the dead owl placed on her
doorstep. Later, she focuses on the constant attack on her head, "black
hands . . . [that] opened her skull" (177), a masculine displacement
of the womb and a hysterectomy. Taussig phrases the idea succinctly:
"Rendering copying synonymous with reproduction, this organ ensures that mimesis fuses as a male secret with origins and . . . with
history as well" (112). As her father's daughter, Elizabeth has become
naturalized as a Motswana, who exposes the experience through her

other heritage—writing. The writer as craftswoman is witchlike, creating an alternate, fantastic world. In the novel, the racial situation comes to a climax with Elizabeth's collision with black life. She spawns surreal characters that act out problems she had confronted since childhood. Her days revert to a simulacrum of the outside world and in the resulting phantasmagoria of terror, she reproduces Sello outfitted as monk with his wife Madonna. Both become reconfigured as the trinity of the spirit, the mind, and the body: Sello, as double dresser, now in brown suit with the killing spirit of bureaucratic non-action;[13] Medusa, his accomplice, with her mind-crippling policy of desexualizing Elizabeth; and the oversexed Dan, whose addiction debases the body. Celibacy and poverty are trivial, with Medusa's racism and Dan's sexism as foci (see Gagiano, 153).

Elizabeth in her manic phase, like some whites, essentializes black life by reducing it to cruelty, barbarism, witchcraft, and kinky sexuality. By refusing to learn Setswana or any other African language, she ineluctably becomes an outsider looking in, "a comrade racialist" (*Question*, 186) of the racist psychiatrist, an untenable position she quickly repudiates by acting like the other African inmates in the asylum. Helen Kapstein sums up the intricate situation thus: "Always liminal and in a state of perpetual motion, madness threatens to be uncontainable. A result of the illicit passage between places or identities, madness unsettles boundaries that the colonial society must then reinstate. The place of madness, instead of another world, is the border itself, and the mad trespasser is continually returned, repressed, and sent back across the border" (72). Against all odds, Elizabeth, the mad trespasser, doubles for the biomythographer, mixing literary genres to replicate her frenzied world. She also imitates Sello the "crop farmer" (*Question*, 28) by gardening, to establish Tswana roots and economic vitalization. To these ends, Elizabeth wills herself to move from the asylum to her home and the garden.

Rooting Out Poverty

The economic perspective is crucial for Head, as it is for Walter Rodney, who emphasizes the place of agriculture in development: "White racist notions are so deep-rooted within capitalist society that the failure of African agriculture to advance was put down to the inherent inferiority of the African. It would be much truer to say that it was due to the white intruders, although the basic explanation is to be found not in the personal ill-will of the colonialists or in their racial origin, but rather in the organized viciousness of the capitalist/colonialist system" (Rodney, 219). Head's response to European superiority complex has similar overtones. In an outburst to the Danish Birgette about African-European continued torturous relationships, Elizabeth makes a stand as an African:

> They [racialists] don't see the shades and shadows of life on black people's faces. . . . There's a magical world ahead of them with the despair and drudgery of semi-desert agriculture alleviated by knowledge. When people stumble upon magic they study it very closely, because all living people are, at heart, amateur scientists and inventors. Why must racialists make an exception of the black man? Why must she [Camilla] come here and help the black man with a special approach: ha, ha, ha, you're never going to come up to our level of civilization? (82–83)

With the use of the pronoun "them" instead of "us," however, Elizabeth seems to distance herself from the "black people" she supports at this stage of her identity struggle. Yet, her driving need for personhood and community leads her to self-help in writing and adapting proven farming methods to improve agriculture in the desert environment.

Eventually, she and Kenosi, as agribusinesswomen, take tentative steps to access power by keeping clear accounts. In her own project that replicates Small-Boy's garden, which is derived from the Englishman Gunner's idea, Elizabeth institutes economic changes through agriculture for her community, thereby documenting a model that the continent can adapt for self-sufficiency. The successful transplantation of the Cape gooseberry from South Africa to Motabeng and the duplication of Thoko's distant farm pumpkin in the nearby garden demonstrate possibilities. The newly located plants mimic human migratory patterns, such as Elizabeth's, that enhance economic prospects and cooperation. Thus, Kenosi, as disciple, successfully holds the fort when Elizabeth is hospitalized.

In her pursuit of agri*culture*, Elizabeth, as agronomist, tries to replicate her recuperative public role in her personal life. The effort to heal both her mind and the soil, the terrains for artistic and food production, is part of a healthy development program. Initially restrained in her unstable house grounded in shifting Motabeng, Elizabeth later contributes magically (82–83) to the transformation of the area into a fertile agricultural space. This mimics the fact that though the interiority of her account lacks a firm base, her subject, in being solidly grounded, generates a great response. As Elizabeth's attachment to the Batswana soil grows, her anxiety and alienation begin to dissipate, and she can participate meaningfully in community economics. Elizabeth's open gardening with its ethical thrust is thus rooted in economics and religion.

Religion—Anticipating the Twenty-First Century

Head eclectically touches five main religions in *A Question of Power*—African Traditional Religions, Judaism, Christianity, Islam, and Buddhism. Their intersections and the interdisciplinarity maintained with her historical and psychological approaches demonstrate Africa's inventive naturalization of religions. She is ambivalent about the consequences, for, in the fantasized world, the different religions cause some form of terror for Elizabeth. I consider Head's stance prophetic, considering the mean-spiritedness of major religions in the new millennium.

Furthermore, Head, according to MacKenzie, "became obsessed with the notion that Seretse Khama, Botswana's president, was both God and the devil at once" (27). She represents him in *A Question of Power* as Sello the monk and Sello in the brown suit, owl and monkey. Virginia Ola comments on this troubling representation: "The fact that the God-like Sello has the vicious and vile Medusa of Greek mythology as his alter ego, and that Dan, after all, is just an extension of Medusa, underscores the complexity of this reality of the battle between good and evil in the world, and in us" (70). Philosophically, for Head, "evil and good travel side by side in the same personality" (*Question*, 98; see 161) and in the same religion.

Thus, in the book's warring section, Head revives the myth of Osiris, the Egyptian god of fertility and the underworld. Head's underworld stands for the wretched of the earth, that substratum of society that peoples Elizabeth's pain-filled, subterranean journey (61). The petrifying Medusa, resurging as the type of woman who mesmerizes and paralyzes other women, attacks Elizabeth, reincarnated as Osiris, as Greek myth (according to Head's rendering) intersects with and imitates Egyptian models. Elizabeth, seemingly impotent without a vagina, as Medusa contemptuously declares (44), stands in for Osiris, victim of a penectomy. Fortunately, as Osiris's double, his jurisdiction over fertility enables Elizabeth to take charge of agriculture and the poor of Africa. Torn apart in a coup involving Egyptian priesthood (40), Osiris is stitched together by Isis, his sister-wife surgeon; this myth comforts the reader of the horrendous biomythology detailing Elizabeth's trauma—she is mentally resilient enough to overpower Medusa finally.

Elizabeth's spiritual struggle, as I have indicated, is also couched in the form of Motswana witchcraft. Her suffering, then, initiates her into African Traditional Religions in which ancestors and predecessors are acknowledged and venerated as pathfinders, as in other religions. Order is restored as Elizabeth takes her rightful place in the sequence of history, simultaneously preparing her son, who participates in the process.

Elizabeth's painful, spiritual journey also links her with the Buddha. After ridding herself of her mental distractions, she finally enjoys nirvana. Through her disclosures, her (pre)occupied mind is emptied, the mark of spiritual and political peace.

Head, in addition, employs a biblical and historical approach in her multilayered realization of Elizabeth, who has been described as suffering from "paranoid schizophrenia" (Evasdaughter, 72). Like the schizoid David (the national fighter taking on the giant Goliath and the murderer who sends Uriah to the battlefront [*Question*, 34; 65]), Elizabeth stands for good and evil, with her "Dr Jekyll and Mr Hyde" personality (57). "She [Elizabeth] accepted Sello's half-concealed revelation of the descent from Buddha to David of the Jews and balanced it against what was recorded of that tumultuous, turbulent life—the innate nobility, the deep God-contact, the peculiar Al Capone–like murder of Uriah and the explosive exposure, an exposure as ruthless and vehement as the murder; the long and tortuous suffering as atonement for the murder" (65). Crossing biblical criminality and punishment with American gangsterism, Head establishes the global repetitions and sameness in history and religion.

Moving from Hebrew scriptures to Christianity and the indigenous religions of Africa, Head represents Elizabeth's nervous breakdown as demonic possession. An iconoclast and a bricoleur, Head intersperses the calculatedly haphazard narrative with ideas of Jesus Christ, as old Mrs. Jones's platitudes replicate Christ's (170) in what Elizabeth finds an irritating imitation. For Elizabeth, Jesus "said the soul was really open territory easily invaded by devils. They just move in, carry on, mess around, and when a man has cleaned up his house, ten thousand more move in. . . . Devils . . . just walk in and smash everything up and then they grin" (192), like cruel Africans, whose "social defects" originate in "carefree sexuality" and "witchcraft" (137).

Masculinizing her spiritual journey and her psychological experience, Elizabeth, the single mother, acknowledges that "Journeys into the soul are not for women with children, not all that dark heaving turmoil. They are for men, and the toughest . . . took off into the solitude of the forests and fought out their battles with hell in deep seclusion. No wonder they hid from view. The inner life is ugly" (30). Defying the odds, Elizabeth, a mother with a son, successfully undertakes a soul journey, as Mohammed's follower. For the novel starts out as a jihad or spiritual striving, as Elizabeth battles the evil forces within her. In a parody of an Islamic paradise, she gazes at her so-called beloved, the African Dan, messing around with "the women of his harem [who] totaled seventy-one" "nice-time girls" (128). With Elizabeth as voyeur, we have seventy-two women engaged in disruptive, illicit sexuality. In this psychosexual turn, polygamy becomes Africanized and Islamized, as Head replicates the misogynistic paradise granted the ardent Muslim man. Dan's imagined paradise, dystopic for Elizabeth, is her Roman Catholic purgatory or Protestant hell. Although it is not "real," as these scenes are hallucinated, the pain is palpable. For inclusiveness, to mark her recovery from all the mental suffering, she openly rephrases "Mohammed's dramatic statement. . . . She said: There is only one God and his name is Man. And Elizabeth is his prophet" (206). Head's deconstruction of the first pillar of Islam addresses female exclusions imposed by religion and patriarchy: as God/Man's prophet, Elizabeth, by word power, humanizes God and becomes a feminized version of Mohammed. This iconoclastic, mirror-image of Mohammed that accounts for the female mind and gives it pride of place astonishingly cloaks the end of the book in a mystically serene and boisterous reflectivity.

A Continental Robe

Protected by clothing herself in the pan-African spirit of Du Bois, Fanon, and Rodney, Head eschews the narrow nationalism fostered partly in an unthinking reaction to the fallout of the European scramble. Indeed, her biracial, peripatetic life is vilified in the initial notion of nation described in Partha Chatterjee's take on the reimagined community: "In fact, here nationalism launches its most powerful, creative, and historically significant project: to fashion a 'modern' national culture that is nevertheless not Western. If the nation is an imagined community, then this is where it is brought into being. In this, its true and essential domain, the nation is already sovereign, even when the state is in the hands of the colonial power" (217).

As Elizabeth visualizes the wrongs perpetrated on her body, mind, and spirit by the exclusionary tactics of the adherents of modern, national culture, she eventually gains power over them through controlling memory by converting the fantastical to the textual, thereby rewriting history. In her "reimagined community," a hallucinated landscape that doubles as "insanity," she creates a domain in turmoil, paralleling the outer turmoil in the state, be it South Africa, her place of origin, or Botswana, the hoped-for paradise. Roller-coasting between her positions of victim and agent, Elizabeth represents the self and her constituency, the poor. Her tortured, fantastical, turbulent life dramatizes the mental impasse, as she, like Margaret in Head's novel *Maru*, despises anything "as narrow as tribe or race or nation" (*Maru*, 16). Through Sello, who says, "I am just anyone" (*Question*, 11), she, as anyone, who ultimately controls Sello by willing him into existence, finds a way out.

Sophia Ogwude neatly sums up Head's grand project to present two choices: "one, the hell of a troubled social set-up manifested in an equally troubled personality, the other a wholesome society in which self-actualization is possible. The relationship between hell and utopian writing is thus shown to be primarily born out of the need to create a reverence for human life by holding up to oneself as well as to others situations and life patterns that are capable of ushering in a better world" (74). To make her point, Head pluralizes the origins of evil, grounding the phenomenon in different national myths, world history, religion, sexism, colonialism, and racism. The tenacity of evil, its global interconnectedness, the continuous desire of individuals and groups for power, which, in its turn, engenders dependency, provide the core of this autobiographical novel, designed to bring relief to the writer as well as to Africa. Elizabeth is colonized and bewitched by egoistic, negative forces. She represents Africa or South Africa, where the guest held the host hostage.

Elizabeth's meltdown is steeped in childhood horrors and "otherhood." A polygamous husband, motherhood, migration, and mental disorder aggravate matters. Excluded from the local power grid, she attracts attention with her difference. Her outcry merges the public and the private, the global and the personal, to enhance continental spiritual health. Literature and history as memory play an important role in her cognitive therapy, enabling her to grab power in Africa.

In a novel fictionalizing autobiography and performing, in effect, a mimesis of a mimesis that alters history, Elizabeth, as a woman alone, resembles her mother, alone and lonely after her illicit sex and mental breakdown. Through learning by imitation, Elizabeth's son participates in familial formation as the fourth generation. As he keeps falling during the mock war of the football that prevented his spectator mother from committing suicide, he unwittingly ensures the survival and victory of his family. To Ketu Katrak, he grounds her in reality (281). Copying his teacher and emulating his mother as writer enable him to produce poetry in a new language that merges the oral with the written—Setswana English. His method and Kenosi's bookkeeping style, "a fantastic combination of English and Setswana" (203), are absorbed by Elizabeth's spongelike, female mind. In her textual unscrambling, Head (as Elizabeth) imitates them, merging Setswana culture with the English language, autobiography with fiction thereby generating interdisciplinary discourses on *A Question of Power.*

In Memoriam
My Sister,
Professor Unokanma Okonjo (1934–2007)
Life is wonderful.

Notes

1. I refer to *A Question of Power* as autobiografiction not just because autobiography is, theoretically, fictionalized, but more because many of the incidents Head includes were fictions of a deranged mind—fictions that happen to be part of her real life, turning autobiography on its head in its union with the novel. See also Helen Kapstein's illuminating comments on Head's shuttling between autobiography and the novel (77–78), and Susan Gardner on Head's made-up life stories, or "biographical legend" (113).

2. I use this term coined by Audre Lorde (see her *Zami: A New Spelling of My Name* [1982]) to refer to *A Question of Power,* as Head did not write the autobiography she had contracted to do in 1984 (see MacKenzie, xv).

3. In our 1981 conversation, Head said that her last name was a convenient translation of her husband's original African name that enabled the family to pass as "Coloured."

4. See Susan Gardner's account of her bizarre relationship with Head.

5. In my 1981 conversation with Head's son, Howard, then a teenager, he predictably found the "sexual hysteria" in the work invidious.

6. Elizabeth's story inverts the idea of the "tragic mulatto" in the movie *Imitation of Life* (Douglas Sirk, 1959), with its self-sacrificing black mother abandoned by her biracial daughter.

7. At the Second Annual International Conference of African Literature, University of Calabar, Nigeria, June 15–19, 1982, when my children and I hosted her.

8. I use this word particularly in light of Lewis Nkosi's attack on the supposedly apolitical nature of Head's writing (see 102). For a brief, impassioned defense of Head against Nkosi's and Nadine Gordimer's criticisms, see Chukukere, 270–71.

9. Many students complain about the denseness and obscurity of *A Question of Power*, which demands many readings for real comprehension. I suggest teaching the text after assigning it as vacation reading, allowing for rereading during the semester when it is taught.

10. Liz Gunner discusses this aspect in her assessment of Fanon (136).

11. Head's use of the monkey and the cat in reference to Sello and Kenosi, respectively, has a colonizer's writerly touch.

12. I am grateful to Sisi Maqagi for this information through e-mail correspondence.

13. Through the outward trappings of skin and clothes, markers for character, Head zeroes in on the occasional superficiality of human perception. See Kapstein's different emphasis on dressing. She deals with the deep implications of South African cross-dressing and its intersection with trespassing and passing (74).

Works Cited

Abrahams, Cecil. 1990. "The Tragic Life of Bessie Head." In *The Tragic Life: Bessie Head and Literature in Southern Africa*, ed. Cecil A. Abrahams, 3–10. Trenton, NJ: Africa World.

———, ed. 1990. *The Tragic Life: Bessie Head and Literature in Southern Africa*. Trenton, NJ: Africa World.

Balakrishnan, Gopal, ed. 1996. *Mapping the Nation*. New York: Verso.

Chatterjee, Partha. 1996. "Whose Imagined Community?" In *Mapping the Nation*, ed. Gopal Balakrishnan, 214–25. New York: Verso.

Chukukere, Gloria Chineze. 1995. *Gender Voices and Choices: Redefining Women in Contemporary African Fiction.* Enugu, Nigeria: Fourth Dimension.

Du Bois, W. E. B. 1976/1903. *The Souls of Black Folk.* Mattituck, NY: Amereon House.

Eko, Ebele. 1986. "Changes in the Image of the African Woman: A Celebration." *Phylon* 47 (3): 210–18.

Eilersen, Gillian Stead. 1995. *Bessie Head—Thunder behind Her Ears: Her Life and Writing.* Portsmouth, NH: Heinemann.

Evasdaughter, Elizabeth N. 1989. "Bessie Head's *A Question of Power* Read as a Mariner's Guide to Paranoia." *Research in African Literatures* 20 (1): 72–83.

Fanon, Frantz. 1963. *The Wretched of the Earth.* Trans. Constance Farrington. New York: Grove.

Gagiano, Annie. 2000. *Achebe, Head, Marechera: On Power and Change in Africa.* Boulder, CO: Lynne Rienner.

Gardner, Susan. 1986. "'Don't Ask for the True Story': A Memoir of Bessie Head." *Hecate* 12 (1–2): 110–29.

Garrett, James M. 1999. "Writing Community: Bessie Head and the Politics of Narrative." *Research in African Literatures* 30 (2): 122–32.

Gunner, Liz. 1994. "Mothers, Daughters and Madness in Works by Four Women Writers: Bessie Head, Jean Rhys, Tsitsi Dangarembga and Ama Ata Aidoo." *Alif: Journal of Comparative Poetics* 14:136–51.

Head, Bessie. 1974. *A Question of Power.* London: Heinemann.

———. 1975. "Preface to 'Witchcraft.'" *Ms. Magazine* (November). Repr. in Bessie Head, *A Woman Alone: Autobiographical Writings,* ed. Craig Mackenzie, 27 (London: Heinemann, 1990).

———. 1979. "Social and Political Pressures That Shape Literature in Southern Africa." *World Literature Written in English* 18 (1): 20–26.

———. 1991. *A Gesture of Belonging: Letters from Bessie Head, 1965–1979.* Ed. Randolph Vigne. London: Heinemann.

———. 1997/1963. "Letter from South Africa." *Transition* 75–76:273.

Heywood, Christopher, ed. 1976. *Aspects of South African Literature.* London: Heinemann.

James, Adeola. 2000. "Bessie Head's Perspectives on Women." In *Black Women Writers across Cultures: An Analysis of Their Contributions,* ed. Valentine Udoh James, James S. Etim, Melanie Marshall James, and Ambe J. Njoh, 13–38. Lanham, MD: International Scholars.

James, Valentine Udoh, James S. Etim, Melanie Marshall James, and Ambe J. Njoh, eds. 2000. *Black Women Writers across Cultures: An Analysis of Their Contributions.* Lanham, MD: International Scholars.

Kapstein, Helen. 2003. "'A Peculiar Shuttling Movement': Madness, Passing, and Trespassing in Bessie Head's *A Question of Power.*" In

Critical Essays on Bessie Head, ed. Maxine Sample, 71–98. Westport, CT: Praeger.

Katrak, Ketu H. 1996. "Post-colonial Women's Colonised States: Mothering and M-othering in Bessie Head's *A Question of Power* and Kamala Das' *My Story.*" *Journal of Gender Studies* 5 (3): 273–91.

MacKenzie, Craig. 1999. *Bessie Head.* New York: Twayne.

Nixon, Rob. 1993. "Border Country: Bessie Head's Frontline States." *Social Text* 36 (Autumn): 106–37.

Nkosi, Lewis. 1981. *Tasks and Masks: Themes and Styles of African Literature.* Harlow, Essex: Longman.

Ogwude, Sophia Obiajulu. 1998. "Protest and Commitment in Bessie Head's Utopia." *Research in African Literatures* 29 (3): 70–79.

Ola, Virginia Uzoma. 1994. *The Life and Works of Bessie Head.* Lewiston, NY: Edwin Mellen.

Parker, Kenneth. 1993. "Home Is Where the Heart . . . Lies." *Transition* 59:65–77.

Ravenscroft, Arthur. 1976. "The Novels of Bessie Head." In *Aspects of South African Literature,* ed. Christopher Heywood, 174–86. London: Heinemann.

Rodney, Walter. 1972/1982. *How Europe Underdeveloped Africa.* Washington, DC: Howard University Press.

Rose, Jacqueline. 1994. "On the 'Universality' of Madness: Bessie Head's *A Question of Power.*" *Critical Inquiry* 20 (3): 401–18.

Sample, Maxine, ed. 2003. *Critical Essays on Bessie Head.* Westport, CT.: Praeger.

Taussig, Michael. 1993. *Mimesis and Alterity: A Particular History of the Senses.* New York: Routledge.

Walby, Sylvia. 1996. "Woman and Nation." In *Mapping the Nation,* ed. Gopal Balakrishnan, 235–54. New York: Verso.

8

A Drama of Power

Aminata Sow Fall's *The Beggars' Strike*

Chioma Opara

The political stance of Senegalese writer Aminata Sow Fall may seem a bit nebulous to a number of critics who have described her as "conservative, political, liberal, social realist, socialist and even 'anti-feminist'" (see Adebayo, 287). But the corpus of Sow Fall's fictional works—*Le Revenant* (1976), *La Grève des bàttu* (*The Beggars' Strike*; 1979), *L'Appel des arènes* (1982), *L'Ex-père de la nation* (1987), and *Le Jujubier du patriarche* (1993)—validates her unalloyed commitment to the cultural, economic, and political freedom of Senegal, a francophone West African country that attained independence in 1960. Like most independent African countries, Senegal has been jostled by Western imperialism and poverty. Senegal has a developing market economy that depends on agriculture. The GNP is abysmally low due to obvious political machinations of selfish and corrupt leaders under the thumb of First World leaders.

The First World/Third World dichotomy is writ large in global political economy. The crass exploitation of African human and mineral resources by the metropolis dates back to the trans-Atlantic slave trade and the industrial revolution. In spite of her rich mineral resources, Africa has remained impoverished in the global capitalist system, condemned, in the words of Ali Mazrui, to "the paradox of retardation" (9). The economic interactions between the First World and Third World countries of Africa, Asia, and Latin America have relegated underdeveloped countries to a dependent subcategory status. Africa has lost control over her economic policies and programs, which are patronizingly superintended and dominated by the International Monetary Fund (IMF) and the International Bank for Reconstruction and Development, otherwise known as the World Bank. In the liberalization of trade in the New International Economic Order (NIEO), the underdeveloped countries have been constrained to abide by the General Agreement on Tariffs and Trade (GATT). This has deepened the economic crisis in the impoverished South, highly polarized from the industrialized North in the global distribution of resources.

The crippling poverty burden that has manacled Africa is of great concern for Sow Fall, who, like her socialist compatriot Sembene Ousmane, is disaffected with postindependence Senegalese capitalist leaders who have bowed to Western imperialism in their capacity as beggars. Sow Fall, as a committed writer, flays Western civilization and its debilitating effects on the rich African cultural heritage. She spurns grossly alienated characters and in some cases yearns for a romanticized pristine African past, devoid of the moral depravity, insensitivity, injustice, graft, and gross venalities perpetrated by the new African leaders.

In *The Beggars' Strike*, Sow Fall revises the parable in Ousmane's political-moral tale *Xala*, which, through its sonorous celebration of beggars, dramatized the annihilating impotence brought about by capitalism. The beggars whom she casts in the binary molds of oppressor/oppressed, tradition/modernity, mystery/temporality, and patriarchal religion/female spirituality appropriate a dramatic posture, underpinned by the varied strategies of power and shifts in power relations.

Beggars in effect constitute the masses in *The Beggars' Strike*, which is set in postcolonial capitalist and patriarchal Senegalese society governed by pragmatic and egocentric leaders, and the relationship between beggars and almsgivers is based on the dynamics of power. In examining the nuances of power in this satirical novel, I will show that power is multicentered, as temporal and infrastructural social power ultimately is submerged by mystifying and supernatural dynamics, shrouded in sacrosanct Islamic tenets. Contrasts and reversals are employed in a parabolic device to flay and deflate a materialistic society that has flagrantly oppressed the physically and economically handicapped.

The social dynamics of begging—often an aftermath of deprivation—are explored in a philistine society that lacks the moral fiber of sublime spirituality,[1] which is antithetical to false religion. Many philosophers have defined religion based on their individual perception of God. Religion, according to John S. Mbiti, is "fully sensitive to the dignity of man as an individual person and creature who has both physical and spiritual dimensions" (274). When religion is false, it is known as religiosity. Religion is as exoteric as spirituality is esoteric. Judy Davis and Juanita Weaver associate spirituality with "a reverence for life, a willingness to deal with more than just rational forces, and a commitment to positive, life-creative generating forces that historically have been associated with a more limited definition of spirituality" (369).

In the main, while spirituality is scintillating, vibrating, and metaphysical, religion appears to be floundering in the tide of hollowness, crystallized in perfunctory rituals. One such ritual in Muslim culture is almsgiving, which in most cases is administered clinically as a means to a selfish end. Alms are given not so much for the sake of the less privileged members of society as for personal aggrandizement. Most people give solely because they hope to receive material and spiritual benefits in the long run. Beggars are in fact viewed as the flotsam and jetsam of humanity, and their well-being is subordinated to government's tourism agenda. These human dregs, who represent the state of the nation in the global scene, are introduced to the reader as a pestilence in the first sentence of the novel:

> *Ce matin* encore le journal en a parlé: ces mendiants, ces talibés, ces lépreux, ces diminués physiques, ces loques, constituent des encombrements humains. Il faut débarrassser la ville de ces hommes—ombres d'hommes plutôt—qui vous assaillent et vous aggressent partout et n'importe quand. (5)

> This morning there has been another article about it in the newspaper: about how the streets are congested with these beggars, these *talibes*, these lepers and cripples, all these derelicts. The Capital must be cleared of these people— parodies of human beings rather—these dregs of society who beset you everywhere and attack you without provocation at all times. (1)

The battle lines are drawn, and the key players in this drama of power are, on the one side, Keba Dabo with his boss Mour Ndiaye, Director of Public Health, emblematized by "the large signet ring" (2); and, on the other, the close-knit phalanx of beggars symbolized by the "running sore," which evokes the sordid station of the handicapped and underprivileged in society.

In her study of a closed Islamic culture, Esther K. Hicks observes the fluid identity pattern for both males and females. "The category of women" includes decrepit men, poor peasants, workers, beggars, and servants (83). Such a society, therefore, classifies beggars as women and consequently derides and represses them. In this class/gender tug of war, the authorities, driven by personal ambitions, chase the beggars off the streets of the capital to a new slum clearance resettlement area, far from tourists' eyes. By this decree, a power distance is created between the ambitious, capitalist officials and the destitute masses, graphically underlining the inequality in power between the two groups.

Subtly interlocked in this running battle are the spiritual directors in the Muslim society known as marabouts. In their capacity as holy men, they mediate between men and Allah (God). The marabout's power is antithetical to social power. Ensconced in an utterly venerated space, the marabout foretells and counsels. Bonnie I. Wright asserts, "A marabout does not increase another's power by attacking that person's opponents, but by protecting the person from the harm that others may intend. Payment for these services is of a far more socially acceptable kind; and the medium of the marabout's power is the word of the Koran" (50). The potency of the marabout's utterances derives from Muslim culture, a facet of patriarchal power. By virtue of the marabout's exalted position in the Muslim society, he is imbued with "the grace of charismatic leadership" and is invariably respected in society, where his word is law.

In *The Beggars' Strike*, we are introduced to Mour Ndiaye's devoted wife, Lolli, on her monthly pilgrimage to the marabout, Serigne Birama. She is traveling on behalf of her husband, carrying provisions as a token of goodwill. This ritual is meant to protect the entire Mour Ndiaye family. Mour Ndiaye's long-standing friendship with the holy man started when Mour was jobless and offered the marabout some refreshing drinking water. The marabout blessed him with these words: "Après dieu, tu m'as porté un secours précieux. La soif allait me tuer. Dieu qui sait ce que tu désires, qu'il exauce tous tes voeux" (Next to God, you have given me most valuable assistance. I would have died of thirst. May God who knows what you most desire grant you all your wishes; 7). Mour's utmost desire then was to find employment. Twenty years later, he still reaps the benefits of the marabout's prayers. Mour's immediate desire is to wield more power; he wants to become the vice president of the republic, and to help reach that goal he has recourse to seeking help from holy men. The authority of the marabout is validated by Muslim tenets and thus supersedes the rational, bureaucratic powers of the top government officials, who vacillate between their official sphere and the hallowed grounds of the consulting seers in the course of their varied supplications, aimed at accreting power.

Sow Fall invests the figure of Mour Ndiaye with mordant irony. Mour uses his hardworking assistant, Keba Dabo, to flush out beggars, including talibés and the marabout's disciples, from the streets of the capital in order to market his potential to the president. Mour Ndiaye himself had once been a talibé of the marabout, Serigne Birama, in Keur Gallo, and like all talibés had probably begged in the street for his and his master's subsistence. By waging a senseless war on these beggars, Mour Ndiaye has unwittingly trodden on the holy men's toes. They invariably condone begging by prescribing almsgiving for their devotees. The *bàttu*, or the begging bowl, a priori constitutes a salient feature in the paraphernalia of the Muslim ritual of begging and almsgiving.

Begging, however, has become controversial within this cultural milieu. While most benefactors depend on beggars to perform their charity rituals, since it is widely believed that "charity opens doors," the status of beggars is very lowly. Not only are they in the disadvantaged position of dependents, but they are trampled upon by the self-styled almsgiving faithful, who may only be making a virtue of necessity in the charitable gesture. As one of the beggars rightly puts it: "Ce n'est pas pour nous qu'ils donnent, c'est pour eux! Ils ont besoin de nous pour vivre en paix" (52–53) ("They don't give for our sake, they give for their own sake: They need us so they can live in peace"; 38). Although begging is practically institutionalized in Muslim society, it is not wholly sanctioned. In the words of Mohamad Umar Chapra, "Islam has prohibited begging and urged Muslims to earn their livelihood" (175). Society is rather enjoined to create an environment for those who wish to work in order that they may rise above begging. Although Mour Ndiaye agrees with the holy man Serigne Birama that "Tout homme a le devoir de travailler" (27) ("It is every man's duty to work"; 18), he ignores the fact that his administration has neither provided enough employment nor established a welfare system to provide for the elderly and the infirm.

The socioeconomic structures of postcolonial African countries, which hardly provide for the jobless and handicapped, force a good number of deprived citizens into complete destitution. Ellie Higgins's study of Mensour Sora Wade's and Diop Mambety's works, which criticize Senegal's neocolonial political economy, examines the "state of apprenticeship" for boys who struggle by begging in Dakar streets and discusses the role of African political elite who collaborate with global institutions for their personal gain (Higgins, 25). Sow Fall's Keba Dabo and Mour Ndiaye surely belong to this crop of depraved political elite who have been absolutely corrupted by power. Tourism, which is an economic alliance with metropolitan countries, appears to be more significant to them than the welfare of the beggars. Mour Ndiaye's vaulting ambition constitutes the driving force behind his putative environmental ethics.

Amply concerned with the welfare of the beggars, the author depicts them as a family of sensible and dignified men and women, thus countering the image, created about them by power-drunk politicians, as unsanitary receptacles for environmental hazard. Clearly, Salla Niang's courtyard provides a meeting place for the beggars. An astute businesswoman, Salla is introduced as "une femme qui a du cran" (14) ("a woman with plenty of guts"; 8). She wields enormous economic power, buying the proceeds of the other beggars at a discount to stock up her shop. Her husband, Narou, who appears to be under her thumb, manages her shop. Salla's dynamism is foregrounded in the depiction of her garments—clean *boubou, pagne,* immaculate little loincloth, and strings of white beads around her hips (12). Salla's clean and tidy inner garments debunk the notion that beggars are synonymous with grime, and the description of them evokes her sexual prowess. There can be no doubt that her sexuality boosts her empowerment. According to rumor:

> Narou est faible.
> C'est Salla Niang qui porte le pantalon.
> Il n'est même pas un homme digne. (19)

> "Narou is a weakling," they say.
> "Salla wears the trousers."
> "He's not really a man." (12)

Sow Fall employs this strategy to masculinize Salla Niang, whose husband, Narou, has purportedly been emasculated. If, according to Hicks's study, beggars belong to "the category of women," Salla Niang has been picked out from that category and empowered like a colossus for political purposes. The masculinization of Salla Niang could be one way of interpreting Aminata Sow Fall's conception of complementarity between the sexes, or Virginia Woolf's theory of androgyny. The feminine and masculine merge in the female hero, Salla Niang, to produce a completely dynamic being who transcends a diminishing gender compartmentalization and bigotry.

In her analysis of Sow Fall's female characters, it is indeed surprising that Aduke Adebayo glosses over the enormous power that Salla Niang wields, failing even to mention her in her study of the book. As she puts it, Sow Fall's female characters "are so unprogressive that they do no credit to any society whether matriarchal or patriarchal. They advocate a return to an idyllic past; which is neither practicable nor desirable" (287). It is salient to point out here that the "idyllic past" is a backward looking utopia that prepares the grounds for positive change. Nevertheless, Salla Niang builds up the community of beggars as well as raising the status of her family. Sow Fall counters the aphorism that women make homes while men build houses. Salla Niang and her husband Narou both reside in the house, which she built single-handedly with the proceeds of her begging.

Appropriation can also be a factor of the imagination. The beggars claim ownership of public buildings and space, which they visit regularly. We learn about Miadabel's hotel, blind Nguirane Sarr's presidential palace roundabout, old papa Gorgui Diop's bank and market, and Salla Niang's hospital. The beggars are, in the main, presented as a vibrant, formidable, eternal, and ubiquitous force rather than as transitory bags of garbage, which can be hurled off at will, as Keba Dabo is inclined to believe. The beggars' essential empowerment, as I pointed out earlier, consists in their enduring existence, which hinges on religious rituals. Consider, for example, the role they will play in Serigne Birama's instruction to the restless Mour Ndiaye:

> Ce que tu veux, Dieu peut te le donner . . . Fais seulement
> le sacrifice d'un beau bêlier tout blanc. Tu l'égorgeras de ta
> propre main, tu feras sept tas de viande que tu donneras à des
> mendiants. (28)

That which you desire is in God's power to grant you and I
think that He will grant it. . . . All you have to do is to sacrifice
a fine white ram. You will slaughter it with your own hand,
you will divide the meat into seven parts and distribute these
to beggars. (19)

It is noteworthy that Serigne Birama wields a great deal of authority in his capacity as a revered marabout. Bruce Lincoln remarks
that "authority is often considered in connection with two other categories, persuasion and force . . . persuasion generally being understood
as the realm of words and the mind, and force that of deeds and the
body" (4). Serigne Birama hands down divine prescriptions in an act
of persuasion encapsulated in epistemic authority. Such prescriptions
from marabouts, considered as Allah's legitimate agents, render the
beggars indispensable in the Muslim community, where a number of
transactions are based on almsgiving. Consequently, beggars are crucial
to the lives of faithful Muslims, who perform this ritual religiously
in the hope that Allah will copiously reward them. Keba Dabo's per-
spicacious secretary, Sagar Diouf, swiftly reminds her boss that he is
only wasting his time in trying to chase beggars from the streets of the
capital, since they have always been there and will remain as part of
the capital until the end of time (14–15). Besides, they are indispensable on moral grounds and cannot be easily jettisoned.

Meanwhile, both Mour Ndiaye and Keba Dabo revel in the eupho-
ria of cleansing the streets of the city of beggars. They believe that
having succeeded in this onerous task, they now have the upper hand.
In the drama of power that unfolds, the author deftly shows the subordination of social and temporal power to the transcendental authority of the marabout, a reflection of Allah's omnipotence. Basking
in his dreams of becoming vice president, Mour Ndiaye takes a trip
to a pastoral town in search of the highly mysterious and charismatic
marabout Kifi Bokoul, who appears to be higher, in the hierarchy of
holy men, than Serigne Birama. One can readily discern the subtle
traces of rivalry between these holy men in the realm of charismatic
leadership. Keba Dabo can hardly hide his jealousy when he learns
that Mour Ndiaye had consulted another marabout. Kifi Bokoul later
goes on a seven-day retreat in the house of Mour's first wife, Lolli.
At the end of his retreat, which underscores the aura of mysticism
about the marabout, the wily Kifi Bokoul assures Mour Ndiaye that he
will have what he desires in one week, on the proviso that he sacrifices

a bull whose coat must be of one color. He is to divide the bull after slaughtering it into seventy-seven portions, and distribute the portions to battu bearers or beggars in the streets. In addition, he should make an offering of three times seven yards of white, nonsilky material, as well as seven hundred cola nuts (58–59). The repletion of the magical number seven, suggestive of Serigne Birama's earlier recommendation of seven portions of meat, further underscores the mystic stature of the embodiment of epistemic power.

The law of retributive justice descends on Mour Ndiaye, who is constrained to run in circles, for he is compelled, as an act of penance, to look for the banished beggars, whom he tries to bring back to the streets for the sole purpose of distributing the seventy-seven portions of meat. The aftermath is an erosion of power out of a pointed reversal. Relegated to the new slum clearance residential area, which is quite far from the morally polluted capital, the oppressed beggars, ironically, enjoy halcyon days in their new home ("la maison des mendiants"; 80). To see them, people travel long distances, analogous to a pilgrimage, to donate generously to charity. In this new abode, the beggars live like princes and princesses. Besides, this new space provides a site for trade unionism. The beggars unionize, in defiance of bourgeois capitalism, shrouded in religiosity or spurious religion. In an ironic twist of fate, the same bureaucratic power that had created a distance to intimidate the beggars now strives desperately to reduce that distance. The beggars, now that there is an obvious reversal of power inflating their lowly stature, are adamant on maintaining the power acquired by the creation of that distance. As Mour Ndiaye tries to plead with the beggars to go back temporarily to the street, Salla Niang, who had been politic enough to convince the beggars to leave the capital instead of contending with continuous harassment by Mour Ndiaye's department, orders the beggars not to step out of their new domain, which has gained the semblance of a spiritual haven. In this abode, the beggars are relaxed and respected and now constitute a visible part of the epistemic authority, which looms large in the Muslim culture. This social mobility and metamorphosis boost the confidence of the beggars, who can now challenge the power-drunk bureaucrats.

Sow Fall in this scene graphically depicts the confrontation between the intimidated oppressor and the assertive oppressed. The male-gendered apparatus of power is dramatically deflated and reversed with the beggars' appropriation of the power of opposition through the medium of a strategic strike. We are told that "pour le moment la force est de leur côté" (118) ("For the moment they've got the power in their hands"; 89). The leader of the strike is Salla Niang, portrayed as a mother of twins and a cook, to underscore the power of female spirituality. Hallie Iglehart notes that "in the Upper Paleolithic and Neolithic eras, women's magical ability to create life and food, plus their menstrual coordination with the cycles of the moon, were regarded as evidence of their intimate relationship with the mysteries of the universe" (295). Imbued with innate female spirituality, which is dynamic, mystical, and integrative, Salla Niang confronts a vehicle of patriarchal religion and religiosity, Mour Ndiaye. Meanwhile, she wears an "ostentatious air of indifference. She goes on stoking up her stove without looking up" (91). One of the characters astutely observes that Salla has the knack of plying the whip without even raising her little finger (86). This underlines Salla Niang's propensity to enormous self-assertion and female empowerment. In a further demonstration of female power, she displays her culinary skill with her cooking pot and ignores Mour standing like á "stuffed dummy" in front of her. Veteran Nigerian female writer Flora Nwapa has stressed the power that woman wields "by the mere fact that she controls the pestle and the cooking pots" (93). This helps to underscore the importance of Sow Fall's delineation of the art of cooking:

> Salla Niang . . . maintenant ouvert la marmite et a jeté dans l'huile très chaude des oignions, puis un bol de pâte de tomate, étendue à l'eau; elle remue, remue sans cesse la sauce bouillante. (121)

> Salla Niang . . . has taken the lid off her cook pot and has put the onions into the hot oil, then adding a bowl of tomato paste diluted in water, she stirs and stirs the boiling sauce continuously. (92)

As she "stirs and stirs," she visibly exerts her brawn in this confrontation. Silence is further employed to heighten Mour Ndiaye's tension. Chikwenye Okonjo Ogunyemi astutely observes that "there is power inherent in some forms of silence, since the other is never acquainted with the subversive thoughts, and she remains a mystery" (186). Salla Niang's silence thus becomes a golden mystery.

Salla Niang particularly stands out as the tower of strength in the community. Sow Fall's graphic portrait of Salla Niang as cook,

mother, and manipulator fits into Chinweizu's militarized phrases—
"the womb's basic power, the kitchen's tactical power, the cradle's
strategic power"—in his polemical treatise *Anatomy of Female Power.*
Invoking a conspiracy theory, he tries to argue that women manipu-
late and control men as husbands, friends, and sons, "from the womb
to the tomb." A woman's power, according to Chinweizu, is "hard to
see, hard to challenge and even harder to overthrow" (23). Although I
do not in the least endorse Chinweizu's hardly concealed cynicism, it
is not difficult to glean the subtle manipulative acts of the wily Salla
Niang in this drama of power. When Mour Ndiaye asks for the master
of the house, she confidently replies that she is in charge (81). There
can be no doubt that Salla is indeed in charge in this new residential
area, such being the enormous power that the dignified, masculinized
"woman being" brandishes. In the end she manipulates and humiliates
Mour Ndiaye, reducing him from the smug and insensitive master to
a groveling beggar, practically on his knees at her feet: the feet of the
"master" of the beggars' house. In the vein of Sembene Ousmane's El
Hadji in his political satire *Xala,* Mour Ndiaye is ultimately reduced
to a powerless cipher.

The two mysterious beings in Mour Ndiaye's conception are Salla
Niang and the rather distinguished blind beggar Nguirane Sarr, who
plays the guitar. Just like cooking and birthing, music and musical
instruments have, from ancient times, been associated with spirits
and deities (Drinker 1982, 45). Elusive, distant, silent, and creative,
Nguirane Sarr, together with Salla Niang, adds to the spiritual ambi-
ence of the beggars' house.

Critics have expressed divergent views on Sow Fall's political
stance. While I would hardly agree with Adebayo, who insists that
"Aminata Sow Fall's writings have no feminist strain in them" (289), I
do subscribe to Julie Agbasiere's postulate that "Sow Fall is a feminist
with a 'subversive' approach" (78). Salla Niang's portrait validates this
claim. Not only does the author introduce Salla before we get to know
her husband, but she is made the master rather than the mistress of
the house. Francis Bacon's dictum that "knowledge is power" is quite
appropriate to Salla Niang's situation. She is armed with knowledge,
which empowers her further. In a flashback, we are apprised of her
experiential power, gained as a maid-of-all-work in the homes of the
oppressive middle class. Having invaded their privacy in this capacity,
she sees through their guiles and hypocrisy. Through her penetrating lenses, we first view the politics of capitalist-patriarchal control,

especially as it affects the woman in the home, who, in most cases, is trapped by the "veil of Islam" and does not dare raise her voice against her husband. In such a society, which sanctions double moral standards, the man is entitled to four wives, as well as mistresses. Because the husband may not obey the Qur'anic injunction that equal attention should be given to all the wives, the elder wife is often shoved aside for the younger one, who virtually supplants her in marriage.

Linking feminist concerns with national matters, like most African writers, Sow Fall simultaneously limns the "torrid heat" in both the public and private sphere. Mour Ndiaye's family is depicted as a patriarchal praxis from the moment Mour announces to Lolli that he is taking a second wife. The patriarchal intimidation of women like Lolli's mother Sanou Cissè, who forbids her daughter to protest against her husband, is starkly contrasted with the assertiveness of the third generation of women, embodied in Lolli's daughter, Raabi. Clearly, Raabi is the analogue of Adja Awa Astou's daughter Rama in *Xala*. These women, including Ramatoulaye's daughters, the "trio" in Mariama Bâ's *So Long a Letter*, come down heavily on the politics of patriarchal power, insidiously spawned by the family hierarchical pattern. Evidently disaffected with her father's capitalist, patriarchal control and shunning patrimonial power, Raabi derides her father, who, in the vein of bourgeois capitalist accumulation, acquires another commodity—a younger wife. However, the new wife, Sinè, diametrically opposed to the quintessential virtuous woman, the first wife, Lolli, smokes and dresses provocatively, thereby challenging her husband's authority. It must be pointed out here that the temperate author depicts some sort of confusion in Sinè's portraiture. Sinè, like Nalla, the heroine of Sow Fall's *L'Appel des arènes*, is a victim of cultural miscegenation. Defiantly articulating feminist rhetoric such as "Je suis une personne et non un bout de bois" (126) ("I'm a person and not a block of wood"; 95), she flies in the face of Muslim tradition, which expects her to be meek and humble. Again, having declared that she is neither "a common-or-garden object nor a sheep," she culminates her revolt by refusing to serve her husband lunch. In failing to exert control over Sinè, Mour Ndiaye finds his stature drastically reduced in the patriarchal power structure. Sinè now assumes power by coercing her patriarchal and narrow-minded traditional husband into submission, in stark negation of social power. This appears to be another case of inversion of power in a Muslim state.

The problem with the practice of Islam today is the warped interpretation of the Qur'an. Several researchers have confirmed that the

Qur'an places women on an equal footing with men both at the spiritual and social levels. This is not surprising, since an ideal, monogamous marriage was contracted between Prophet Mohammad and his first wife, Khadija. Shaped by Jahilia (pre-Islamic ways), the wealthy and independent Khadija not only employed Mohammad to trade on her behalf but proposed marriage to him (Ahmed, 672). In the wake of Khadija's death, Mohammad became polygynous and instituted veiling and seclusion for his wives. While the Qur'an advocates the relegation of women to the private scene, it is specific about husbands giving equal attention to their wives in a polygynous setup. This, unfortunately, is hardly adhered to by most men, who are less concerned with their wives' emotions than with their own machismo. Mour Ndiaye distinctly belongs to this category. Judging from the way he patronizingly relates to his wives, he seems to view women in the Islamic context as the "weaker sex," who should be protected by men, seen as "a degree above them."[2] This Muslim injunction tallies with the Lévi-Straussian view that public and social authority always belongs to men.

A Hadith of Prophet Mohammad, which is not even mentioned in the Qur'an, is purported to state that "a people will not prosper if they let a woman be their leader." Women in this community are not expected to take up leadership positions. As Jamal A. Badawi puts it: "According to Islam, the head of state is no mere figure-head. He leads people in the prayers, especially on Fridays and festivities; he is continuously engaged in the process of decision making pertaining to the security and well-being of his people. This demanding position or any similar one, such as the Commander of the Army, is generally inconsistent with the physiological and psychological make-up of woman in general" (142–43). In an effort to demonstrate that women are unstable during pregnancy and their menstrual periods, the Muslim authorities exempt them from daily prayers and fasting for forty days after childbirth and during their periods. Michael Arnoff and John Clarkin have, however, revealed that although the menstrual cycle is capable of altering behavior patterns in women, it does not impair their performance level (726). In an effort to counter the idea that women are incapable of leading, Sow Fall dexterously pits an anomic state, ruled by incompetent and selfish men, against a wholesome beggars' community, led by a sagacious and virile woman, Salla Niang, who manipulates to conquer. The concept of male leadership is further undermined in Mour Ndiaye's household, where the author ridicules a putative statesman, who is capable of controlling neither a defiant daughter, Raabi, nor a recalcitrant wife, Sinè. In the end, these two women remain at the helm in the revolutionized Mour Ndiaye's household.

Clearly, Sow Fall's political allegory in exploring power as agency and power as episteme, contrasts the spiritual with the religious. Susan Stringer, cited by Rizwana Habib Latha, asserts that if a clear distinction can be made between Senegalese and other female writing, it is the association with religion (23). Sow Fall has gone further than Mariama Bâ in underscoring female spirituality, which is power-related since, according to Charlene Spretnak, "it is a key to the better life" (398). Starkly contrasted with this is religiosity, which is closely linked to polluted social power. The strength of Sow Fall's art lies in the subtle interconnectedness between the various layers of power, at both the horizontal, mundane level and the vertical, esoteric plane that is used by the beggars and women and ultimately empowers them.

Notes

1. In the various definitions of religion, true religion has been at variance with false religion. Spirituality, as I have pointed out elsewhere, is not synonymous with religion, which "concerns itself with the systematic concatenation of rituals, practices and beliefs which may be devoid of moral depth and texture." Spirituality on its own is dynamic and essential to woman's struggle, since it is integrative and metaphysical (see Opara).

2. This degree is Qiwama, which denotes maintenance and protection over woman by man (see Badawi).

Works Cited

Adebayo, Aduke. 2000. "Feminism in Francophone African Literature: From Liberation to Militancy." In *Introduction to Francophone African Literature*, ed. Olusola Oke and Sam Ade Ojo, 275–98. Ibadan, Nigeria: Spectrum.

Agbasiere, Julie. 1999. "Mariama Bâ's *Une Si Longue Lettre:* The Classic and the Critique." In *The New "Eve" in Francophone African Literature*, ed. Julie Agbasiere, 69–81. Enugu, Nigeria: Jee Communications.

Ahmed, Leila. 1986. "Women and the Advent of Islam." *Signs* 11 (4): 665–91.

Arnoff, Michael, and John Clarkin. 1980. "Review Essay on 'Behavior and the Menstrual Cycle' by Richard Friedman." *Signs* 5 (4): 719–38.

Bâ, Mariama. 1981. *So Long a Letter.* Trans. Modupe Bode Thomas. Ibadan: New Horn Press. Translation of *Une Si Longue Lettre.* Dakar, Senegal: NEA, 1979.

Badawi, Jamal A. 1976. "Woman in Islam." In *Islam: Its Meaning and Message*, ed. Khurshid Ahmad, 131–45. Lagos, Nigeria: Islamic Publications Bureau.

Chapra, Muhammad Umar. 1977. "Objectives of the Islamic Economic Order." In *Islam: Its Meaning and Message*, ed. Ahmad Khursid, 173–216. Lagos, Nigeria: Islamic Publications Bureau.

Chinweizu. 1990. *Anatomy of Female Power: A Masculinist Dissection of Matriarchy.* Lagos, Nigeria: Pero Press.

Davis, Judy, and Juanita Weaver. 1982. "Dimensions of Spirituality." In *The Politics of Women's Spirituality*, ed. Charlene Spretnak, 368–72. New York: Anchor Press.

Drinker, Sophie. 1982. "The Origins of Music: Women's Goddess Worship." In *The Politics of Women's Spirituality*, ed. Charlene Spretnak, 39–56. New York: Anchor Press.

Herbert, Eugenia W. 1993. *Iron, Gender, and Power: Rituals of Transformation in African Societies.* Bloomington: Indiana University Press.

Hicks, Esther K. 1996. *Infibulations: Female Mutilation in Islamic Northeastern Africa.* 2nd ed. New Brunswick, NJ: Transaction.

Higgins, Ellie. 2002. "Urban Apprenticeships and Senegalese Narratives of Development: Mensour Sora Wade's *Picc Mi'* and Diop Mamobety's *La Petite Vendeuse de Soleil.*" *Research in African Literatures* 33 (3): 54–68.

Iglehart, Hallie. 1982. "Expanding Personal Power through Meditation." In *The Politics of Women's Spirituality*, ed. Charlene Spretnak, 294–304. New York: Anchor Press.

Latha, Rizwana Habib. 2001. "Feminisms in an African Context: Mariama Bâ's *So Long a Letter.*" *Agenda* 50:23–40.

Light, Andrew, and Christopher Heath Wellman. 2003. "Introduction: Urban Environmental Ethics." *Journal of Social Philosophy* 34 (1): 1–5.

Lincoln, Bruce. 1994. *Authority: Construction and Corrosion.* Chicago: University of Chicago Press.

Mazrui, Ali A. 1980. *The African Condition.* London: Heinemann.

Mbiti, John S. 1982. *African Religions and Philosophy.* London: Heinemann.

Nwapa, Flora. 1998. "Women and Creative Writing in Africa." In *Sisterhood, Feminisms and Power*, ed. Obioma Nnaemeka, 89–99. Trenton, NJ: Africa World Press.

Ogunyemi, Chikwenye Okonjo. 1996. *Africa Wo/Man Palava: The Nigerian Novel by Women.* Chicago: University of Chicago Press.

Opara, Chioma. 2003. "Beyond Patriarchal Religion: The Dynamics of Female Spirituality in Post-Colonial African Culture." Paper presented at ISUD 5th World Congress, Olympia, Greece, 18–23 May.

Sembene, Ousmane. 1965. *God's Bits of Wood.* London: Heinemann.

————. 1996. *Xala.* Paris: Presence Africaine, 1996.

Sow Fall, Aminata. 1981. *The Beggars' Strike, or, The Dregs of Society.* Trans. Dorothy S. Blair. Essex: Longman. Trans. of *La Grève des bàttu.* Dakar, Senegal: NEA, 1979.

————. 1982. *L'Appel des arènes.* Dakar, Senegal: NEA.

————. 1993. *Le Jujubier du patriarche.* Dakar, Senegal: Edo Khondia.

Spretnak, Charlene (ed.) 1982. *The Politics of Women's Spirituality.* New York: Anchor Books/Doubleday.

Wright, Bonnie I. 1989. "The Power of Articulation." In *Creativity of Power: Cosmology and Action in African Societies,* 39–57. Washington, DC: Smithsonian Institution Press.

9

Aesthetics, Ethics, Desire, and Necessity in Mariama Bâ's *So Long a Letter*

Modupe Olaogun

Literature reflects social reality and also mediates it. It is a form through which writers have exposed the social and often naturalized constructions that order people's lives. Since the mid-1960s, African women writers have been transforming a literature that had been dominated by a male point of view. Like the imperial and the colonial ideologies, patriarchal ideology—local or foreign—has been instrumental in creating and maintaining hierarchical social structures. A goal of the feminist writing, particularly of the first wave, was to liberate the woman from a socially relegated position and reinstate her as a historically contingent subject worthy of contemplation in herself. There are African feminist writers whose work preceded Mariama Bâ's *So Long a Letter*: the Algerian Assia Djebar (*La Soif*, 1957), the Ghanaian Ama Ata Aidoo (*The Dilemma of a Ghost*, 1965) and Efua Sutherland (*Foriwa*, 1967); the Nigerian Flora Nwapa (*Efuru*, 1966) and Buchi Emecheta (*In the Ditch*, 1972); the Kenyan Charity Waciuma (*Daughter of Mumbi*, 1969) and Rebeka Njau (*Ripples in the Pool*, 1975); the South African Bessie Head (*A Question of Power*, 1974); and the Egyptian Nawal El Saadawi (*Woman at Point Zero*, 1975, trans. 1983).

The introduction by these writers of female characters into a subject position previously occupied mostly by male characters, along with trends toward politicized readings in feminist, postcolonial, and ideological criticisms from the 1970s and the 1980s, has provoked critical commentaries and theorizations previously unthought of. Eschewing a language that spoke of universal man, feminist and postcolonial criticisms have stressed the particularity of the social world to which the text refers, departing from approaches that treated the literary text as an autonomous object, hermetically sealed from the world. But in emphasizing the political and social discourses in which a literary text is embedded, many of the inquiries have tended to relegate the literariness of the text. Novels, plays, poems, and other literary texts project specific artistic and aesthetic sensibilities that are significant beyond the narrow terms of their political agendas. These sensibilities ought to be acknowledged in the readings of the texts.

Bâ's *So Long a Letter* (1989, translated from French into English in 1981) is a pioneer work in being one of the first novels by a Senegalese writer to give a close portrait of a woman in an Islamic African context. Apart from the multiple languages into which this novel has been translated, it has been made into a movie in Wolof, adapted and directed by Cheik Tidiane Diop and first presented through television to a Dakar (Senegal) audience in 1984 (Azodo 2003b, 426–31). From a brief overview of the critical responses to this novel, this chapter goes on to explore the novel's aesthetic propositions as discernible from the disposition to the notions of morality, necessity and desire, which are connected in the novel. These notions are examined against the contingencies that mediate the characters' responses.

Appreciation of *So Long a Letter* has drawn attention to the clarity of the woman's voice, aided by the novel's poetic language, in a sustained critique of an entrenched patriarchal culture and the traditions that keep women subjugated; Bâ's inscription of the woman's voice in public discourse through her engagement with the novel form; and Bâ's ability to make the voice resonant through her skillful depiction of the postabandonment predicament of Ramatoulaye and connection of this character's emotions and cares to women's experiences beyond the narrative's immediate cultural reference point (Makward, 272; Cham, 89–91; Busia, 89, 91–92).

A particular trajectory of criticism is characterized by what Uzo Esonwanne has described as "anti-feminism." Engendered by a Manichean binary construction of culture in static, essentialist, and eternally opposed forms, this line of criticism has denounced the novel for its feminist interventions and its aesthetic premises (Esonwanne, 82–100). It seems to have found irrelevant the novel's innovative use of existing literary forms, such as the letter, and to have been oblivious to its introduction of new devices—for example, the *tagg,* a Wolof praise form, with a dressing-down complement called *xas,* which Siga Jagne eloquently describes. The assumptions and excesses of this trajectory of criticism have been elaborated by, for instance, Stratton (133–47) and Esonwanne (82–100).

A more balanced criticism of the novel points to the limits of its feminist intervention. Irene d'Almeida, for instance, has suggested that its critique is hampered by the limited reform of the patriarchal tradition advanced by Ramatoulaye, the presumed vehicle of Bâ's ideas, as illustrated in Ramatoulaye's idealization of male children and her expressed preference for them, unwittingly implying that her own female children may be inferior (D'Almeida, 166–67). Similarly, C. L. Innes draws attention to the novel's discourse of nation and proposes that it does not question its supposed model, Léopold Sédar Senghor's cultural philosophy, which had posited that a genuine human civilization would be found in a marriage of the characteristics that he identified in his poetry with Africa and Europe, respectively: emotion versus rationality (Innes, 147–48). Innes's elaboration suggests that Ramatoulaye's exuberant praise of European education, especially its assumption of civilizing powers, is treated unironically by Bâ.

Esonwanne goes further to disentangle the process through which the colonial epistemological machinery, with its channel of colonial education that Ramatoulaye had undergone, shapes the novel's nationalist discourse. Such a deconstructive approach will suggest that the colonial European negative associations of tradition, custom, and superstition, values that it made cognate in the African context, would have encouraged Ramatoulaye's sensitivities about Senegalese traditions and customs. Esonwanne examines the role of polygyny in maintaining the status quo that Bâ finds inimical to women and the family, and the resulting cultural self-criticism. He suggests that polygyny as a sign in the novel points to a class configuration with contradictory inclinations: the bourgeois class, to which Ramatoulaye belongs, is the same class to which the male polygynists who are well regarded in the society and are seen by many as ethical icons—her husband Modou Fall, her friend Mawdo Bâ, and her suitor Daouda Dieng—belong. The contradictions inherent in that class, Esonwanne implies, demand a more thorough self-criticism (88–89, 92–93). In varying degrees, these critical observations have merits, and, where necessary, their details will be taken up in the course of this exploration.

The narrative of *So Long a Letter* dramatizes local-universal and private-public dialogues in which the ideas of what is pleasing and what is moral are juxtaposed with what is desired and desirable and what is imposed by necessity. Through its exploration of the novel's representation of these ideas, this chapter theorizes the literary aesthetic located at the traverse of these dialogues (I define "traverse" below) and attempts to shed some light on some of the tensions represented in the novel, the most prominent one being that articulated by Ramatoulaye in the split between her reason and emotion—"a choice that my reason rejected but that accorded with the immense tenderness that I felt towards Modou Fall" (45). This split is figured in the dualism of Ramatoulaye versus Aissatou, who take different routes to deal with their husbands' betrayal of their respective vows of marriage. At the same time that Ramatoulaye and Aissatou react from opposed impulses on this issue, the two friends gravitate to each other in a bond that redefines a woman's worth outside of male desire and, through this response, reassert themselves.

In like manner, the opposition between the narrator, Ramatoulaye, and her neighbor, Farmata, to whom Ramatoulaye gives the epithet "the griot woman," illustrates the characters' competing conceptualizations of the notions of desire, aesthetic, and morality. As a griotte, Farmata inhabits a social class—formulated as caste—that is subordinate to Ramatoulaye's upper-caste/bourgeois class. The two women's social worlds, nobility versus lower caste, patron versus praise-singer, are contiguous. But as narrators, both characters are interpreters and transmitters of cultural and social mores and are symbolic projections of wider epistemic, aesthetic, and ethical matrices.

The opposition of Ramatoulaye and her co-wife, Binetou, and what each represents in terms of economic necessity versus aesthetic and moral ideals, is a fairly obvious commentary on an often taken-for-granted female solidarity, a commentary that is remarked by Ramatoulaye's daughter, Daba, in her question: "How can a woman sap the happiness of another?" (71). A complicating factor in this opposition is the role of Binetou's mother, who manipulates the younger woman and goads her to seduce Ramatoulaye's husband as a means to gaining economic and social elevation. Similarly, the interaction between Ramatoulaye and young Nabou, and the love-hate tension that marks their relationship, suggests a more nuanced examination of this female solidarity or lack thereof. There are more forces at work than the "female greed and rivalry" and "the vanity, lust and fickle-mindedness of the male" that Mbye Cham adduces as the perpetrators of the malaise attacked by Bâ (95–99). Cham's alignment of these supposed human tendencies along rigidly opposed sexual divisions is Manichaean. Furthermore, Cham's terms imply a universal, readily accessible ethical code that is operational in the world of the narrative, and suggest that morality is the sole determiner of the values to which the characters respond. The novel instead represents a more complex matrix of values that shape the characters' responses. The characters' moral values and choices are mediated by, among other things, necessity, desire, and the notions of what they consider to be ethically valid and pleasing. How the elements intersect and the implications of the tensions they delineate will be elaborated upon. I suggest that the characters' interactions as they respond to the various economic, psychological, and social conditions and desires often involve traverse relations, some of which are productive and others less so.

The word "traverse," as I use it, evokes a combination of the senses of the English word and of the French "traverser." The senses derived from *The American Heritage Dictionary of the English Language* (4th ed., 2000) are as follows: "to travel or pass across, over, or through"; "to move to and fro over; cross and recross"; "to go up, down, or across (a slope) diagonally"; "to cause to move laterally on a pivot; swivel"; "to extend across; cross"; "to look over carefully; examine"; "to go counter to; thwart"; "to deny formally (an allegation of fact by the opposing party) in a suit"; "to join issue upon (an indictment)"; "to survey by traverse." The senses from the French "traverser" are derived from Merriam-Webster's *French-English Dictionary/Dictionnaire Anglais-Français* (2000): "to run through"; "to pass through"; "to penetrate, to soak through"; "to go through, to experience."

Traverse space, as deployed in this exploration, is evocative of the terms employed by Homi Bhabha: "hybridity," "Third Space of enunciation," and "interstices," to describe a new ambivalent space created at the contact zone of cultures. It agrees with Bhabha's theory of ambivalence and the "in-between" space of interpretation and of cultural exchange, which debunks assumptions of a singular authority and of a hierarchical cultural purity (Bhabha 1994, 37–38; 1996, 12–15). But whereas Bhabha's terms focus on bilateral movements, with his Europe-linked postcolonial theorization often positing Europe and Western societies against the excolonized/Others, the traverse space as evoked here suggests polyvalent and multilateral interactions. Traverse space emphasizes equally the contact zone *and* the anterior and the posterior continuums of the subject(s) in contact. Traverse space makes more visible the exchange and surplus values on the different sides of contact.

The concept of traverse space set forth here helps us to see in a dynamic light the pairings and dualisms in the characterization, situations, tropes, and so on in *So Long a Letter*, and the dramatizations of intersections of the local and the universal, the private and the public. Thus, for instance, the contrasting presentation of Aissatou's and Ramatoulaye's immediate responses to their abandonment by their husbands is not necessarily an unequivocal invitation to see these characters as representing model feminism versus non-model. Nor is their imagined coming together at the end of the narrative, with Aissatou, who has long sojourned in the United States of America, arriving in her tailored suit and being nudged by Ramatoulaye to drop fork and knife and dip her fingers into the communal food bowl on a spread-out mat, a projection of a simple hybridity. The women's different responses to their abandonment, and their different circumstances, separate and pull them together. The identity each represents is in formation. Traversing is the notion that best captures a description of their complex relationship and of the many other complex tensions suggested by the novel.

The form of *So Long a Letter* characterizes Bâ's aesthetic project. It is a letter-diary-tagg/praise whose narrative unfolds the experience of Ramatoulaye, who was abandoned by her husband of twenty-five years for young Binetou, their eldest daughter's friend. Ramatoulaye recalls her postabandonment experience on the occasion of the husband's death, five years later, as she undergoes the official mourning prescribed by tradition for him. The whole novel is Ramatoulaye's "letter," which she begins by situating it within the context of an ongoing dialogue between herself and the addressee, Aissatou, her friend from childhood. But what Ramatoulaye puts down, as she herself announces at the onset, is more than a letter. At once her diary and memoir, it becomes an outlet for her grief—an elegy even, considering the intense lyrical and lamenting tone that accompanies the grieving segments—not as much for her recent loss of Modou as for her earlier loss of him when he deserted her and their twelve children for Binetou. Keeping the diary and writing the memoir enable Ramatoulaye to link her abandonment with a number of situations: her widowhood, which subjects her to confinement in her home with her rival, Binetou, for several days for Modou's funeral rites; her loss of some of her material property to the in-laws in the complex mourning custom; a bid by her brother-in-law, Tamsir, to make her his fourth wife; a marriage proposal from a former suitor, long since married, overlooking the intervening years and the emotional gaps between them; and new challenges from her growing children.

From the past, Ramatoulaye recalls her shock at her abandonment, particularly her sudden deprivation of companionship with Modou and the casualness with which Modou's emissaries informed her about his second marriage. This abandonment is contextualized by further recalls to the contrasting happy courtship and conjugal relations that Ramatoulaye initially had with Modou; the near-parallel experience of her bosom friend, Aissatou, in Aissatou's marriage to Mawdo, whose acquisition of a younger wife prompted Aissatou to leave the marriage; and Ramatoulaye's experience as a single parent faced with the responsibilities of bringing up twelve children. In the course of writing her letter-diary/memory/tagg, in which she launches into praises of her friends, acquaintances, and family members, Ramatoulaye receives another letter from Aissatou announcing the latter's impending visit from the United States, where Aissatou is working at the Senegalese Embassy. As Ramatoulaye is signing off her letter, events have moved to the eve of Aissatou's arrival. Ramatoulaye's imagining of the power of the reunion to assert friendship, female solidarity, human communion, and love in sexual and nonsexual terms, along with a reaffirmation of locally generated, individual- and community-sensitive cultural mores,[1] is the termination point of the missive. With this ending, the novel structurally reinforces the element of the imagination as a privileged vehicle of cognition, interpretation, and the will to transform.

The rhetorical and expressive forms in *So Long a Letter* constitute a narration alternating with tagg, apostrophe, and expository reflection. Along with the hybrid vehicle, which is a composite of the diary and the memoir, these rhetorical and expressive forms set the tone of the narrative and dramatize its discursive tensions. They clarify the audience, as well as the contesting desires and ethical and aesthetic ideals dramatized by the narrative. Aissatou, to whom Ramatoulaye addresses her apparently unmailed letter, is a construct for part of this audience, so she does not function only in the capacity of a character connected with the action and the plot; she is a stand-in for other readers. The letter-diary-memoir-tagg addressed to her is a record of a slice of the life of Ramatoulaye, who, at the moment she records a particular experience, has already surpassed the phase that occasioned the record. The hybrid writing, with all of the embedded forms, is like experimental writing, and it represents an analogue of Ramatoulaye's and Aissatou's lives. Ramatoulaye suggests that they are pioneers, as they extend the spans of the indigenous and the foreign forms of education that colonial education has caused to commingle, intersect, and redound—in short, traverse—in their lives. As well, they are pioneers through their expansion of the choices available to women as determined by their chosen forms of independence, though Ramatoulaye's path to her independence is more fraught than Aissatou's. The greatest testimony and monument to Ramatoulaye's claim of this pioneering is the writing itself.

In serving as an interlocutor, especially an imagined interlocutor in the period of Ramatoulaye's mourning, Aissatou's role is most symbolic. In that role, she enables and enriches Ramatoulaye's consciousness, as Ramatoulaye potentially enriches hers—were she to read the outcome. Ramatoulaye celebrates Aissatou, whom she values for who she is, not what she was born as, thus rejecting the arbitrary demarcations of nobility and degeneracy by virtue of birth as prescribed by the caste society. But in her phase of docility and imagined housewifely role, Ramatoulaye does collude with this caste society by indirectly facilitating young Nabou's usurpation of Aissatou's place as Mawdo's wife. Ramatoulaye knows about the plans for Mawdo's second marriage and even lends Mawdo's mother a suitcase on the latter's journey to procure the young wife. While the plans are going on, Ramatoulaye neither informs Aissatou nor raises a voice. She protests only when it is too late. Ramatoulaye's personal weakness at that point—when she has become domesticated—may be adduced for her failure to protest and protect. Her narration of her betrayal of Aissatou in the letter-diary-memoir-tagg then serves also as a form of self-stripping on Ramatoulaye's part, her making of amends to Aissatou. In this episode and its resolution, Ramatoulaye cuts the image of a trickster who unmasks when the performance is over. The source of this tricksterism is a combination of the caste value system and the housewifely docility that underwrite the tricksterism.

Pausing in her narrative to indicate that she is perhaps boring Aissatou by narrating what the latter already knows, Ramatoulaye remarks: "I have never observed so much, because I have never been so concerned" (9). Here she reflects a traverse process involving Ramatoulaye's intersecting of her previous method of cognition with her current form, her using of a known narrative to interrogate another version in order to generate new insight, and her imagining of Aissatou's response to stimulate her analytical process. The sources of this new awareness include Ramatoulaye herself, who constitutes a complex subject, not a sheer victim or a bystander in the ritual of the *mirasse* for Modou. Cham has suggested that the principle of the mirasse provides the framework for Ramatoulaye's *dépouillement*, or stock-taking (91–92). It is important to note as well that Ramatoulaye is an agent here, as it is she who is stripping Modou of the betrayal of which she knows the depth, just as she is stripping herself of the illusions of marriage that had kept her bound to Modou long after the pact between them had been broken, and of the solidarity of the caste class that made her betray Aissatou.[2]

The second source of the new awareness is the psychosocial space that Aissatou and Ramatoulaye share, bridged by the letter-diary-memoir-tagg. Ramatoulaye's decision to keep a diary, which becomes a memoir, and to pay homage to Aissatou through the tagg has made it more exigent for her to be perceptive. The ideal to which Ramatoulaye aspires is expressed in her emotional identification with Aissatou: "Your disappointment was mine, as my rejection was yours" (55). In effect, she intro-, retro-, and circumspects, trades places, and develops her intersubjective faculty. This new circumspection is part of her new creative energy and the source of her moral uplift. However, her inability to control Daba's offensive against Binetou, even though she does not approve of Daba's actions, shows some ambivalence. This ambivalence may go back to her pain over Binetou's hand in the collapse of her marriage.

Ramatoulaye is an important medium through which the audience is sensitized to the concern with aesthetics and ethics and the circumstances that traverse them. At a basic, physical level, Ramatoulaye often refers to Binetou's physical beauty: "Beautiful, lively, kindhearted, intelligent" (48); "Binetou, incontestably beautiful and desirable!" (50). Ramatoulaye equally remarks the physical graces of the men, Mawdo Bâ, Daouda Dieng, Modou Fall, and Ibrahima Sall. She describes Daouda when he comes to woo her in her widowhood: "He was elegantly dressed in a suit of embroidered brocade; he remained the same well-groomed man, meticulous and close shaved. . . . Although a deputy at the National Assembly, he remained accessible, with gestures that lent weight to his opinions. His lightly silvered hair gave him unquestionable charm" (59). It is through Ramatoulaye's eyes that readers also see Ibrahima: "Pleasant features, on the whole. But with remarkably beautiful eyes, velvety, tender in the casement of long eyelashes. One would like to see them in a woman's face . . . the smile as well. . . . He pleased me, and I noticed his cleanliness with relief: short hair combed, nails cut, shoes polished" (84).

In the narrative's emotional desert, overwhelmed by so much hurt, disappointment, and betrayal, passages describing love, contentment, tenderness, and beauty, and the tagg sequences showing appreciation for people and objects, stand out like oases. In the two quoted passages, the privileged characteristics of beauty include a correlation between inner and outer manifestations of being. Ramatoulaye looks for evidence in the individuals' modes of dressing that correlates with their sensory and subconscious projections. The embroidered brocade, short, combed hair, and so on are correlated with the "beautiful eyes, velvety, tender in the casement of long eyelashes," the set of teeth and the smile. Ramatoulaye's picture of physical beauty is characterized by harmony. In the aesthetics Ramatoulaye projects, the opposition of male/masculine versus female/feminine attributes collapses. But she disrupts this photographic notion of beauty through the deliberately ingenuous remarks in respect of Ibrahima: "I let my gaze rest on the set of his teeth. No treacherous gaps. . . . He must be an orderly man and therefore without deceit." The remarks about Ibrahima consist of a sly allusion to Modou, whom Ramatoulaye's mother had found "too handsome, too polished, too perfect for a man" (14). In her long apostrophe to Modou, Ramatoulaye recalls her mother's prognosis: "She often spoke of the wide gap between your two upper incisors: the sign of the primacy of sensuality in the individual" (14). But these readings have little diagnostic power. Ramatoulaye's remark, "He must be an orderly man and therefore without deceit," turns into an ironic joke at the expense of these readers of learned practices, which they turn into physiological and behavioral traits. The remarks about Daouda present him as a performer of roles, thus destabilizing the idea of innate nobility and perfect behavior. Thus the novel dramatizes the ultimate impossibility of totally predicting another human being.

Ramatoulaye created in Modou the embodiment of her sexual, aesthetic, and ethical ideals and her desire for a community of individuals and of a Senegalese nation where her ethical ideal of human equality could prevail. Modou's outward beauty was an element that she projected onto his inner beauty; hence, after age imposes physiological changes on Modou—making him bald and giving him a paunch—Ramatoulaye does not stop loving him. In a tagg to a happier time shared by the couple and their closest friends, Aissatou and Mawdo, Ramatoulaye says of the foursome: "But all of us were made of sterner stuff, with upright minds full of intense questionings that stuck within our inner selves, not without pain. Aissatou, no matter how unhappy the outcome of our unions, our husbands were great men. They led the struggles of their lives, even if success eluded their grasp; one does not easily overcome the burdens of a thousand years" (73).

The struggles attributed to Modou refer to his work initially with the trade union organizations to mediate their demands with the government. After earning a law degree, with its promise of lucrative rewards in private practice, Modou chose the trade unions. His subordination of individual desire to communal needs contributes to Ramatoulaye's respect for him during this period.

However, Ramatoulaye herself is clearly bourgeois. A self-styled spokesperson for the dispossessed, she is unconvincing in this role. In passages most suggestive of a mutually shared and readily accessible moral universe, Ramatoulaye co-opts what she calls the "stoicism" of the physically challenged and the physiologically afflicted: "the blind people the world over, moving in darkness"; "the paralysed the world over, dragging themselves about"; and "the lepers the world over, wasted by their disease" (11). Those whom she evokes are subalterns. If Ramatoulaye is acting as their representative, then she is doing so with unbearable patronage. The power of her gaze objectifies them. What she praises as stoicism and heroism represent a desire not to cause a stir in the status quo. But this desire is one that she projects onto this group of people. In the society, physiological handicap is perceived as individual destiny and those who are affected are sentenced to beggary and penury. Unlike in *So Long a Letter*, the cripples, lepers, and so on who form the cadres of the beggars in the novel by a Senegalese contemporary of Bâ's, Aminata Sow Fall, *The Beggars' Strike* (translated 1981), *do* revolt. They speak on their own behalf. They go on strike one day and refuse alms from the nonbeggar classes in their society, which has instituted almsgiving; their action subsequently threatens a government.

While owning up to the privileges of her middle-class and upper-social-caste background, Ramatoulaye often presents her sufferings as every woman's sufferings. Her reduced family budget following Modou's desertion, the school issues, the minor accidents that befall her children, and the unplanned pregnancy of one of her teenage daughters are some of the travails that she touchingly recounts. But making her single-parent, large family a model is glib and potentially misleading. She says: "The upkeep and education of young children do not pose serious problems; washed, cared for, supervised, my own are growing well" (75). However, Ramatoulaye's upper caste and social class ensure that she is surrounded by powerful people who make it possible for her twelve children to grow well on her teacher's salary: for instance, the doctor, Mawdo Bâ, is on hand at all times to treat her family; Daba and her husband pay the outstanding mortgage on the family's house after Modou's death; and from the United States Aissatou pays for a new car for the family. Ramatoulaye's "stoic heroes"— the beggared classes—have no access to such economic cushioning.

When Modou loses his social vision, Ramatoulaye identifies its derangement with his male ego, rather than seeing operating as well his submission to social stratification by class, which underwrites his middle-class comfort and vanities. As he approaches middle age, Modou experiences a thickening of his midriff. He capitulates to the vanity of appearance, which he once excoriated while fighting for wage-earners. His shortcut to pump his male ego is to strap himself to the image of physical youth by buying the attention of the young Binetou. Why does he not consider exercising or switching to traditional robes to hide his midriff or redirect his energy into grooming the youths who will replace his generation? The effect of Modou's action, as reported by Ramatoulaye, links his sexuality to social performance: "And Modou would dye his hair every month. His waistline painfully restrained by old-fashioned trousers, Binetou would never miss a chance of laughing wickedly at him. . . . Gracefulness and beauty surrounded him. He was afraid of disappointing, and so that there would be no time for close scrutiny of him, he would create daily celebrations during which the bright young thing would move, an elf with slender arms who with a laugh could make life beautiful or with a pout bring sadness" (48). Both Modou and Binetou succumb to the "dream of a rapid social climb" (73), which saps the energies and physical resources needed for a more lasting relationship. A symbolic implication not vigorously pursued in the narrative, due to Ramatoulaye's gender emphasis, is that as a unit of the larger community/ Senegal, the Modou-Binetou pair quite clearly threatens the formation of a productive, ethical postindependent nation.

Prior to her self-reappraisal, Ramatoulaye makes her worth contingent upon Modou's reciprocal desire for her: "You can testify to the fact that, mobilized day and night in his service, I anticipated his slightest desire," she writes to Aissatou (56). Even though she was wrong to place such a limit upon herself, as it dawns on her during her mourning period, some of the narrative's pointed statements signaling traverse discourse can be found in what she says about her longing for Modou; for instance:

> And I ask myself. I ask myself, why? Why did Modou detach himself? Why did he put Binetou between us?
> You very logically, may reply: "Affections spring from nothing; sometimes a grimace, the carriage of a head can seduce a heart and keep it."
> I ask myself questions. The truth is that, despite everything, I remain faithful to the love of my youth. Aissatou, I cry for Modou, and I can do nothing about it. (56)

Modou's philandering with Binetou (his one-time act of waywardness?) happens twenty-five years after his marriage to Ramatoulaye. Although Ramatoulaye is oblivious to this suggestion, she and Modou are partly responsible for encouraging Binetou to come between them. Where is Ramatoulaye when Modou begins to offer Binetou rides home at night? Is she too busy fulfilling her imagined housewife and motherhood roles, or what Azodo rephrases as "wife-craft" and "mother-craft" (2003a, xiv) in order to heighten the supposed values of these roles? Have Ramatoulaye and Modou sustained through the twenty-five years the love and companionship with which they began? Ramatoulaye says she keeps her home in pristine condition. She obviously transfers to her relationship a similar approach. But a relationship is not like furniture that one polishes every other week to maintain its functionality and beauty.

Ramatoulaye seeks to understand the conundrum in which the Binetou-Modou affair/marriage represents a traverse element in her own failed marriage. Her ascription of a logical response to Aissatou versus her own actual emotional response is an occasion of role-playing. Ramatoulaye is doing the reasoning and arguing with herself using her relationship with Aissatou as a prop/catalyst. In this example of mental traversing, there is a strategic use of a fictionalized utterance. The notion that it can be easy to fall in love has a correlate, which is that it can be as easy to fall out of love: Modou leaves Ramatoulaye for Binetou without looking back. The notion becomes a powerful counterpoint to Ramatoulaye's nostalgic melancholia about her lost first love. As the fountain and conduit of both responses at this juncture in her reflection, Ramatoulaye is displaying the range of faculties she can activate in her being—from emotional to rational—to bring about her reorientation and help her emerge from her depression. Ramatoulaye's access to her inner resources does not, however, render Aissatou or the social world with which Ramatoulaye interacts redundant in the processes of self-apprehension and reorientation.

Ramatoulaye will realize her thwarted desire in part through her daughters, Daba and young Aissatou, who choose partners to her moral taste. The daughters' partners are young men who are recommended as much by their comely behavior as by their egalitarian disposition toward women. But the daughters and their fiancés are still young, as Modou and Ramatoulaye had once been, and it is left to a discerning Daba to indicate to her mother that "marriage is no chain. It is mutual agreement over a life's program" (74). Ramatoulaye's desire for marriage is the heterosexual relationship, which she knows is tinged with her idealization of marriage.

Bâ treats as a moral issue Modou's unilateral decision to marry a second wife and desert Ramatoulaye, despite the latter's choice to stay on as his wife, as permitted by their religion. Ramatoulaye makes the inference directly: "In loving someone else, he burned his past, both morally and materially" (12). The story she tells about Jacqueline, another betrayed wife, whose husband philanders openly, places the source of physical pain in the moral realm as well. Referring to Jacqueline's nervous breakdown and physical suffering, Ramatoulaye admonishes doctors: "Often, the pains you are told of have roots in moral torment" (44). To complement Ramatoulaye's hypothesis, the doctor who has impact on Jacqueline approaches her illness differently. This doctor's diagnosis is accompanied by his tenderness and verbal affirmations of the patient's agency. He helps Jacqueline heal first in her soul, then in her mind and body:

> "You must react, go out, give yourself a reason for living. Take courage. Slowly, you will overcome. We will give you a series of shock treatments with curare to relax you. You can leave afterwards."
>
> The doctor punctuated his words by nodding his head and smiling convincingly, giving Jacqueline much hope. Re-

animated, she related the discussion to us and confided that
she had left the interview already half-cured. She knew the
heart of her illness and would fight against it. She was *morally* uplifted. (45; emphasis added)

It is a male doctor who helps cure Jacqueline. On the other hand, Ramatoulaye shifts to a female friend for emotional support after Modou.
The alienation of affection triggered by Modou may have caused
Ramatoulaye to look to a figure of comfort who contrasts completely
with him. Gender counts in this conceptual contrast, for it is Modou's
gender, coupled with his vanity, that has made him a viable candidate
to Binetou, on the prowl for a sugar daddy.

The unnamed doctor with whom Ramatoulaye's evolving consciousness finds affinity is like a conjure man: he succeeds where many
doctors before him had failed in diagnosing Jacqueline. It is not acci-
dental that Bâ uses the word "conjure," which implies the magical, at
the beginning of her narrative, when she addresses the absent Aissatou. The act of conjuration does link Ramatoulaye to the griot(te),
the figure of the alternative narrator who is evoked in this novel. The
relationship between Ramatoulaye and the griot(te) figure constitutes
one of the sites of the novel's aesthetic. The most obvious embodiment of the griot(te) is Farmata, "the *griot* woman of the cowries,"
according to Ramatoulaye, describing her neighbor (67).

Farmata is associated with an approach to life through divination,
intuitive knowledge, propitiatory sacrifice, and tradition, which she
sees as tested and settled practices. She is Ramatoulaye's alter ego.
Ramatoulaye is the woman of the book, until her episteme collides with
Farmata's experience. The latter's seemingly quaint form of knowing
irritates Ramatoulaye, who consigns anything that is associated with
this alternative knowledge to barbarism. Hence, when Farmata suggests that Ramatoulaye's life need not end with Modou's desertion of
her, Ramatoulaye ignores Farmata's reasoning. Instead, she accepts
what she takes to be empirical evidence, the image of herself from the
mirror, which informs her that she is no longer physically attractive,
hence she is undesirable (40–41). The mirror is vulnerable to subjectivity, as what it reports is mediated by what is perceived. Five years
after the mirror episode, an empirically older Ramatoulaye reports a
bath she takes as she awaits Daouda. In a register whose quotidian
directness contrasts with the often lyrical, image-rich register of her

tagg, she effectively relays the impact of this ritual, evoking an image and a feeling opposite to what the mirror had reported years back:

> Today is Friday. I've taken a refreshing bath. I can feel its re-
> vitalizing effect, which, through my open pores, soothes me.
> The smell of soap surrounds me. Clean clothes replace
> my crumpled ones, the cleanliness of my body pleases me. (63)

The passage develops into a philosophical musing about a woman's beauty and the role of personal hygiene in it, and the hard work of the woman thus made beautiful in turning her home into a sparkling edifice in which she naturally performs a managerial role. This rare occasion when Ramatoulaye talks about her own beauty and allows it to be a consideration in the social aesthetics also provokes a rare moment when she openly dramatizes her sexual desires. Shortly after Ramatoulaye's bath, Daouda arrives to profess his love and to propose marriage to her. She describes her feelings as follows: "I opened my eyes wide, not in astonishment—a woman can always predict a dec-laration of this kind—but in stupor. Ah yes, Aissatou, those well-worn words, which have long been used and are still being used, had taken root in me. Their sweetness, of which I had been deprived for years, intoxicated me: I feel no shame in admitting it to you" (65). The degree of Ramatoulaye's transformation between the episode of the mirror and that of the bath points to Bâ's dramatization of the contingencies of subjectivity. One can look hard into the mirror, but there is nothing inherently truthful about its images; the truths of the mirror are mediated by their transmission.

Farmata's divinatory and intuitive knowledge will lead Rama-toulaye to discover her teenage daughter's pregnancy and help her to intervene in time. Against the validity of that knowledge, which Ramatoulaye grudgingly accepts, the rhapsody to the book, as a symbol of Western episteme and a civilization privileged by Ramatoulaye, will seem like hyperbole or a parody by Bâ: "The power of books, this marvelous invention of astute human intelligence. Various signs associated with sound: different sounds that form the word. Juxta-position of words from which springs the idea, Thought, History, Science, Life. Sole instrument of interrelationships and of culture, unparalleled means of giving and receiving. Books knit generations together in the same continuing effort that leads to progress" (32). If this passage entails hyperbole or parody, it is possible to see greater ambivalence at work in Bâ's text than has been suggested by Innes's critique of Bâ's representation of the Senegalese nation and of the European imperial interpositions in its discourse.

Ramatoulaye is closer to Farmata than she thinks. Her evocative style, as in the praise she utters to books, is typical of the griot(te)'s praise form. Jagne uses the examples of Ramatoulaye praising Aissatou and tongue-lashing Tamsir, and the town's praise-singers extolling the Lady Mother-in-Law's new affluence on the radio, to stress the influence of the Wolof's griot(te) tradition and worldview on Bâ's narrative. As elaborated by Jagne, the tagg "operates as a way to show thanks and appreciation; to goad one on to release money; to praise one's ancestry and to ensure that things move smoothly at public functions, despite the fact that sometimes it has the opposite effect" (electronic reference; no pagination). Although Jagne classifies the tagg as a rhetorical experience that takes place between people, the tagg style and principle seem at work in Ramatoulaye's profusions about books and colonial European education. In the passage partially quoted, Ramatoulaye begins with praise to Aissatou, before digressing to the books that Aissatou had studied and books in general: "You had the surprising courage to take your life into your own hands. . . . And instead of looking backwards, you looked resolutely to the future. You set yourself a difficult task; and more than just my presence and my encouragements, books saved you. Having become your refuge, they sustained you" (32). While this digression has a hyperbolic thrust, it is directly relevant to Ramatoulaye's own creation, her "diary." Its writing saves Ramatoulaye. Through it she can exercise power. The apostrophe indirectly becomes self-praise.

Ramatoulaye may be exasperated by the sexual politics of the caste society maintained by the griot(te) tradition, but her romance with the tradition goes deep. She describes Aunty Nabou's journey to the ancestral home, which she criticizes for fueling Nabou's atavistic return to a heroic, sanguinary ethos. This return will make Aunty Nabou trap her grown son, Mawdo, with the young, virginal Nabou, causing Aissatou's marriage to collapse. The ancestral home is presented as follows: "Finally, Diakhao, the royal Diakhao, Diakhao, cradle and tomb of the Bour-Sine, Diakhao of her ancestors, beloved Diakhao, with the vast compound of its old palace" (28). Rather than suggest ironic distance from the griot(te), Ramatoulaye cuts the image of a griotte in this evocation of Aunty Nabou's ancestral home. The repetition of "Diakhao" asserts the defiant presence of this ancestral place;

the plosive sound of the "d's" tempered with the determinate vowels is deep, resonant, and reassuring like the sound of the ancient and enduring *djembe* drum. The unrushed cadence is tender.

Notwithstanding, Ramatoulaye is not the kind of griotte hidden behind Aunty Nabou when the old royal lady is educating young Nabou: "Her expressive voice glorified the retributive violence of the warrior; her expressive voice lamented the anxiety of the Loved One, all submissive. She saluted the courage of the reckless; she stigmatized trickery, laziness, age. Tales with animal characters, nostalgic songs kept young Nabou breathless. And slowly but surely, through the sheer force of repetition, the virtues and greatness of a race took root in this child" (46–47).

A teacher, Ramatoulaye distances herself from Aunty Nabou's kind of education through the mocking tone with which she reports Aunty Nabou's lessons, and through the implied criticism of the heroic narratives which uphold kingdoms, nations, and empires, as typically spun by griots. Bâ is sifting the rhetorical and ethical aesthetics from which she and the oral griots/griottes draw. The sifting implies a clarification of the beneficiaries of the narratives that maintain nations, kingdoms, and races, entities with dubious claims with respect to their presumed harmonious and homogeneous desires. It identifies the violence of the warrior and the anxiety and submissiveness of the "Loved One" waiting for the warrior as gendered categories in a constructed and forced complementariness of the strong male/bread-winner versus the delicate female/housewife-mother. It implies a revision of Aissatou's notion of "polygynous *instinct*" to "polygynous *custom.*"

In a seductive tone, Aunty Nabou goads her young niece to study midwifery, but the sanguinary aesthetic and morality, and the subordination of the female behind this particular use of education, are still the same: "The school is good. . . . Young, sober girls without earrings, dressed in white, which is the colour of purity. The profession you will learn there is a beautiful one; you will earn your living and you will acquire grace for your entry into paradise by helping at the birth of new followers of Mohammed, the prophet. To tell the truth, a woman does not need too much education" (29–30). This passage, like the preceding one, illustrates a nexus of morality and aesthetics. Bâ's traverse aesthetic calls into question the morality undergirding the typically lauded forms of greatness. Aunty Nabou, under the thin veneer of tenderness, shares with the male defenders of the bloodline, the warriors and the noble men of her narratives, an autocratic style.

The notion of the beautiful as it intersects morality is scrutinized in Ramatoulaye's complex relationship with young Nabou. Ramatoulaye does not react to young Nabou with as much bitterness as she responds to Binetou. Both girls have disrupted the older women's marriages, but Ramatoulaye respects young Nabou because the latter works hard to attain a profession, while Binetou takes a shortcut by living off Modou and cutting off his responsibilities. Binetou gets Modou to pay her a regular allowance and to compensate her parents financially in lieu of the income she might have brought them had she not interrupted her education to marry him. Ramatoulaye censures what she perceives as Binetou's amorality in mordant tones; however, her religious charity moderates her anger toward Binetou: "Beautiful, lively, kindhearted, intelligent, Binetou had access to many of her friends' well-off families and was sharply aware of what she was sacrificing by her marriage. A victim, she wanted to be the oppressor. Exiled in the world of adults, which was not her own, she wanted her prison gilded. Demanding, she tormented. Sold, she raised her price daily" (48). "Worn out, Binetou would watch with a disillusioned eye the progress of her friends. The image of her life, which she had murdered, broke her heart" (50).

On the other hand, while young Nabou's midwifery profession may have been appropriated by a male ideology and aesthetic and by class stratification, which the senior Nabou celebrates in the guise of advocating femininity and piety, the efficiency and integrity with which young Nabou subsequently performs her job soften Ramatoulaye towards her. Though young Nabou's snatching of Aissatou's husband is reprehensible against the ethical code drawn by the narrative, she traverses this code—swiveling on it, traveling with it part of the way, crossing it and subjecting it to further scrutiny—through the affinity she strikes with Ramatoulaye and Aissatou in the ethics of work, as underscored by Ramatoulaye's tagg: "Young Nabou, responsible and aware, like you [Aissatou], like me! Even though she is not my friend, we often shared the same problems!" (48)

Young Nabou then, like Aissatou and Ramatoulaye, becomes a figure of the traverse space which connects one individual to another, the individual to the community, the particular to the universal, through a bilateral process of interrogation on the issues of ethics, aesthetics, necessity, and desire. Binetou's mother, "Lady Mother-in-

Law," like Aunty Nabou, abuses her seniority by turning elderliness into gerontocracy with its indiscriminating nature. The antics of the two gerontocrats are like dams on the common stream of mate-making.

The traverse space, which has been delineated so far, is useful for understanding the tensions and affinities depicted in *So Long a Letter.* These tensions arise from divergent claims even when the claims derive from what seems like the same ethical and aesthetic pool. The traverse space reveals, for instance, that Ramatoulaye and Farmata are both griottes after all; yet they have little awareness of how close they are or what separates them, having been made to seem so distant by a time-honored social-caste system and a modern/colonial education system. Ramatoulaye feels enabled by Aissatou, but it is her imagination that has created Aissatou in many respects. She passes across, through, along, and over Aissatou to get back to the self from whom she had become alienated, having been thwarted and traversed by Modou, Binetou, and the polygynous custom. There are contingencies that shape female solidarity and human solidarity, but solidarity is not altogether a capricious category. This exploration contributes to an understanding of the intersections of aesthetics and ethics as these are mediated by necessity and desire in specific social discourse, while also expanding the discussion of Bâ's literary achievement through a closer look at her engagement with aesthetics as theme and form.

Notes

1. Some of Chantal Zabus's observations may be extrapolated to show Senegalese agency even as the novel critiques Senegalese mores. However, Zabus's too-neat categories for contradistinguishing French and Wolof (Senegalese) may seem Manichean: "une méditation entre le parler wolof et le réel ecrit français; entre l'encre et papier; entre le lakh et le thiakry" [a meditation between spoken Wolof and real written French; between ink and paper; between *lakh* and *thiakry*] (96). An emphasis upon Senegalese agency is suggested in her elaboration: "La lettre de Ramatoulaye deviant une véritable pré-texte à la rencontre entre deux femmes. Aissatou sera 'demain' . . . de retour au pays natal. La natte et le bol nourricier, symbols de l'étranger ou hospitalité wolof remplacent 'la table, assiette, chaise, fourchette' qu'une Aissatou occidentalisée exigera immanquablement . . . Inévitablement, leur entretien se déroulera en wolof, la lettre morte mais la langue première 'avant' et après la lettre" [Ramatoulaye's letter becomes a true pretext for a meeting between two women. Aissatou will return to her native country "tomorrow."

The mat and the food bowl, symbols for the stranger and Wolof hospitality, replace "the table, plate, chair, fork," which a westernized Aissatou will certainly demand. . . . Inevitably, their talk will unwind in Wolof, the letter dies but spoken language comes "before" and after the letter⌉ (97).

2. Omofolabo Ajayi-Soyinka reads the hybridity along an interesting axis, seeing in Ramatoulaye's introspection an expansive narrative, which invests the mirasse with wider symbolism. As she suggests, the stripping bare begins with Modou; extends to Ramatoulaye and not just what her life means in the context of her nuclear or extended family but as a woman in her society; and extends further "to all of Senegalese culture⌈, which⌉ is subjected to a thorough and critical soul-searching examination" (160). This interpretation is in line with the argument of this chapter.

Works Cited

Aidoo, Ama Ata. 1965. *The Dilemma of a Ghost.* London: Longmans.

Ajayi-Soyinka, Omofolabo. 2003. "Negritude, Feminism, and the Quest for Identity: Re-Reading Mariama Bâ's *So Long a Letter.*" In *Emerging Perspectives on Mariama Bâ: Postcolonialism, Feminism, and Postmodernism,* ed. Ada Azodo, 153–74. Trenton, NJ: Africa World Press.

Almeida, Irene Assiba d'. 1986. "The Concept of Choice in Mariama Bâ's Fiction." In *Ngambika: Studies of Women in African Literature,* ed. Carole Boyce Davies and Anne Adams Graves, 161–71. Trenton, NJ: Africa World Press.

Androne, Mary Jane. 2003. "The Collective Spirit of Mariama Bâ's *So Long a Letter.*" In *Emerging Perspectives on Mariama Bâ: Postcolonialism, Feminism, and Postmodernism,* ed. Ada Azodo, 37–50. Trenton, NJ: Africa World Press.

Azodo, Ada. 2003a. "Introduction: The Phoenix Rises from Its Ashes." In *Emerging Perspectives on Mariama Bâ: Postcolonialism, Feminism, and Postmodernism,* ed. Ada Azodo, ix–xxxiii. Trenton, NJ: Africa World Press.

———. 2003b. "Postscript: From the Author to the Nation." In *Emerging Perspectives on Mariama Bâ: Postcolonialism, Feminism, and Postmodernism,* ed. Ada Azodo, 419–38. Trenton, NJ: Africa World Press.

Bâ, Mariama. 1989. *So Long a Letter.* Trans. Modupe Bode-Thomas. Oxford: Heinemann. Translation of *Une si longue lettre.* Dakar, Senegal: Les Nouvelles Éditions Africaines, 1980.

———. 2003. "The Political Function of Written African Literatures." In *Emerging Perspectives on Mariama Bâ: Postcolonialism, Feminism, and Postmodernism,* ed. Ada Azodo, 411–16. Trenton, NJ: Africa World Press.

Bhabha, Homi. 1994. *The Location of Culture.* London: Routledge.

————. 1996. "Aura and Agora: On Negotiating Rapture and Speaking Between." In *Negotiating Rapture: The Power of Art to Transform Lives*, 9–17. Chicago: Museum of Contemporary Art.

Busia, Abena. 1991. "Rebellious Women: Fictional Biographies—Nawal el Sa'adawi's *Woman at Point Zero* and Mariama Bâ's *So Long a Letter.*" In *Motherlands: Black Women's Writing from Africa, the Caribbean and South Asia*, ed. Susheila Nasta, 88–98. New Brunswick: Rutgers University Press.

Cham, Mbye. 1987. "Contemporary Society and the Female Imagination: A Study of the Novels of Mariama Bâ." *African Literature Today* 15:89–101.

Djebar, Assia. 1957. *La Soif.* Paris: Julliard. Trans. by Frances Franaye as *The Mischief.* New York: Simon and Schuster, 1958.

El Saadawi, Nawal. 1983. *Woman at Point Zero.* Trans. Sherif Hetata. London: Zed Books.

Emecheta Buchi. 1972. *In the Ditch.* London: Barrie and Jenkins.

Esonwanne, Uzo. 1997. "Enlightenment Epistemology and 'Aesthetic Cognition': Mariama Bâ's *So Long a Letter.*" In *The Politics of (M)Othering: Womanhood, Identity and Resistance in African Literature*, ed. Obioma Nnaemeka, 82–100. London: Routledge.

Head, Bessie. 1974. *A Question of Power.* London: Heinemann.

Innes, C. L. 1991. "Mothers or Sisters? Identity, Discourse and Audience in the Writing of Ama Ata Aidoo and Mariama Bâ." In *Motherlands: Black Women's Writing from Africa, the Caribbean, and South Asia*, ed. Susheila Nasta, 129–51. New Brunswick, NJ: Rutgers University Press.

Jagne, Siga Fatima. 2004. "Djotaayi Dieguenye: The Gathering of Women in Mariama Bâ's Fictional World." *Wagadu* 1 (1); http://www.web .cortland.edu/wagadu/issue1/mariama.html.

Makward, Edris. 1986. "Marriage, Tradition, and Woman's Pursuit of Happiness." In *Ngambika: Studies of Women in African Literature*, ed. Carole Boyce Davies and Anne Adams Graves, 271–81. Trenton, NJ: Africa World Press.

Njau, Rebeka. 1975. *Ripples in the Pool.* London: Heinemann.

Nwapa Flora. 1966. *Efuru.* London: Heinemann.

Sow Fall, Aminata. 1981. *The Beggars' Strike, or, The Dregs of Society.* Trans. Dorothy Blair. Essex: Longman. Trans. of *La Grève des bàttu.* Dakar, Senegal: NEA, 1979.

Stratton, Florence. 1994. *Contemporary African Literature and the Politics of Gender.* London: Routledge, 1994.

Sutherland Efua. 1967. *Foriwa.* Tema: Ghana Publishing.

Waciuma, Charity. 1969. *Daughter of Mumbi.* Nairobi: Kenya Literature Bureau.

Zabus, Chantal. 1994. "La Langue avant la lettre: *Une si Longue Lettre* de Mariama Bâ." *Notre Librairie* 117 (April–June): 95–97.

10

Reading Masculinities in a Feminist Text

Tsitsi **Dangarembga's** *Nervous Conditions*

Helen Nabasuta Mugambi

Tell us what it is to be a woman so that we may know what it is
to be a man.

—Toni Morrison

Masculinity . . . does not exist in isolation from femininity—it
will always be an expression of the current image that men
have of themselves in relation to women.

—Arthur Brittan

Tsitsi Dangarembga's *Nervous Conditions* is one of the most complex
and insightful coming-of-age narratives in the postcolonial African
literary tradition. It intricately weaves the lives of diverse characters
in a Shona community to highlight the challenges of growing up
female in a patriarchal and colonized world. Trapped in the poverty
of the homestead, a result of the historical displacement of indigenous
peoples from their fertile land by colonial forces,[1] Tambudzai, the
daughter of Jeremiah and Mainini, struggles to obtain a Western education in a patriarchal environment that does not value girls' education.
It is only after her brother Nhamo unexpectedly dies that Tambudzai
is allowed to go to school, taking her brother's place in the mission
school run by her father's brother, the revered but controlling,

ultramasculine Babamukuru, who is also father of Nyasha and her brother Chido. During Tambudzai's stay with Babamukuru and his wife, Maiguru, her awareness of colonial evil and gender oppression is intensified through her sharp observation, augmented by insights from the rebellious Nyasha, her alter ego.

With this plot line in mind, it is easy to see why critics have analyzed *Nervous Conditions* primarily as a postcolonial feminist text. Most readings have focused on the novel's denunciation of the perversions of colonialism (also implied in the title[2]) and the feminist struggle against patriarchy. The feminist strand is elaborated in sequences ranging from comments by younger women such as Tambudzai, who condemns patriarchy for making the woman "a victim of her femaleness" (115), to homilies by matriarchs on the state/fate of femaleness in a patriarchal society (e.g., 16, 101–2). Early in the novel, for instance, the words uttered by Tambudzai's mother not only typify the matriarchs' keen awareness of women's oppression; they reveal a consciousness of the process that propagates subjugation: "This business of womanhood is a heavy burden. . . . How could it not be? . . . When there are sacrifices to be made, you are the one who has to make them. And these things are not easy; you have to start learning them early, from a very early age. The earlier the better so that it is easy later on. Easy! As if it is ever easy" (16). Such feminist sensitivity and resistance appear throughout the novel, from the homestead setting to the mission residence and the transnational world beyond Shonaland. Before going to the mission, Tambu observes her mother's poverty-ridden life, fights Nhamo over his chauvinism, and argues with her father about her education. Furthermore, reminiscent of Janie and her grandmother's lament, in Zora Neale Hurston's *Their Eyes Were Watching God*, that black women are the mules of the world, Tambu not only contemplates her own mother's words, she watches them materialize as Nhamo arrogantly and repeatedly demands that his sisters carry his luggage home from the bus stop. After exposure to the mission, Tambudzai's own cumulative conclusion is insightful in its expansion of the novel's transnational feminist significance: "The victimization I saw was universal. It didn't depend on poverty, on lack of education or on tradition . . . what I didn't like was the way all conflicts came back to this question of femaleness. Femaleness as opposed and inferior to maleness" (115–16). This declaration is particularly illuminating. It points to the intensification of the heroine's painful awareness of the dichotomous construction of gender, and, in particular, of masculinity as a major force in women's oppression.

Declarations in this vein point to the significance of the novel's male characters and hint at the necessity to explore this feminist novel as a masculinist text. Indeed, the novel contains multiple indications towards such a reading. The opening paragraph cautions us not to be too categorical about whose, or which, story the narration is. The narrator, Tambudzai, initially claims that this is her story and the story of her fellow women: Mainini (her mother), Maiguru (her uncle's wife), Lucia (her aunt), and Nyasha (her cousin). However, her claim culminates in the declaration that "the story of my brother's passing and the events of my story cannot be separated" (1). This pronouncement is rephrased more explicitly in the final sentence of the novel: "but the story I have told here is my own story, *the story of four women whom I loved, and our men*" (204; emphasis added). Taking the cue, therefore, that these gendered lives are inextricably intertwined and that conflicts in the novel stem from the dichotomies forged between maleness and femaleness, we can surmise that Tambudzai could also characterize her narrative as *"the story of our men and the four women whom I loved."* This rephrasing shifts our focus toward the construction of masculinity and the male characters, who have so far received little critical attention beyond their presentation as agents and representatives of patriarchy. Moreover, this revision of Tambudzai's words underscores the many ways in which the novel is an exploration of the construction of masculinity in a dichotomous relationship to femininity.

Approaching a feminist text as a masculinist text does not, however, mean concentrating exclusively on the attitudes and acts of the males in the novel. On the contrary, such a reading also involves looking at the ways women resist or facilitate masculinities, all of which are integral to the construction of maleness. Furthermore, probing real or imagined oppositions between genders as polarizing constructions facilitates more accurate perceptions of masculinity re-productions. Arthur Brittan, in the epigraph to this chapter, reiterates the gender boundaries in the well-known hypothesis that masculinity is always constructed in opposition to femininity, mirroring men's current vision of themselves in opposition to women (113–14). In *Nervous Conditions,* Dangarembga skillfully explores and interrogates different manifestations of gender positions that support this hypothesis. Furthermore, she goes beyond the binary hypothesis when she systematically orchestrates a range of masculinities against femininities but simultaneously undermines the essence of each by dramatizing their capacity for volatility. Through this interrogation of simple gender dichotomies, the novel also epitomizes gender polarization, elaborated by Sandra Lipsitz Bem, who defines gender polarization as "the ubiquitous organization of social life around the distinction between male and female" (80). In her elaboration of the problematic aspects of this social process, she notes: "Gender Polarization operates in two related ways. First, it defines mutual exclusive scripts for being male and female. Second, it defines any person or behavior that deviates from these scripts as problematic—as unnatural or immoral from a religious perspective or as biologically anomalous or psychologically pathological from a scientific perspective" (80–81). Through female characters who transgress into conventionally defined male territory and male characters who exhibit some conventionally feminine traits, *Nervous Conditions* simultaneously replicates and interrogates such mutually exclusive gender scripts. Dangarembga employs the historical context of the novel's Shona community to undermine or deconstruct the clearly demarcated gender boundaries along which masculinities and femininities can be plotted.

In this chapter, I explore Dangarembga's multifaceted presentation and critique of masculinity. I argue that the author's presentation of masculinity constitutes an interrogation or deconstruction of maleness and an attempt to blur the boundaries of the attendant male/female dichotomy that contributes to gender polarization. I contend that in the process of challenging manifest notions of masculinity, the author propagates a sense of balance and underscores the need to alleviate the oppressive masculine forces undergirding the nervous condition thematized in the text. My analysis operates on the premise expounded by Judith Butler, that gender identities exist only as performance. In her renowned book *Gender Trouble*, Butler states: "There is no gender identity behind the expressions of gender; that gender identity is performatively constituted by the very 'expressions' that are said to be its results" (25). Noticeably, "gender as performance" is visible throughout *Nervous Conditions*, where Dangarembga has unambiguously created characters who explicitly or consciously perform or are described as performing femininities or masculinities.

In order to lay bare Dangarembga's skillful and multilayered exposition of masculinity, my discussion commences with a normative presentation of masculinities before proceeding to analyzing how masculinity is explored and critiqued. Having identified Babamukuru,

Tambudzai's uncle, as the chief icon of masculinity in the text, I analyze his performance of masculinity before comparing and contrasting the other characters' performances vis-à-vis Babamukuru. In the final part of the chapter I highlight the shortcomings of the polarized gender positions and the search (or reach) for a relatively gender-neutral balance necessary for mitigating the postcolonial "nervous condition." The discussion relies heavily on textual evidence to highlight Dangarembga's unique contribution to our understanding of both the theory and practice of masculinity.

Normative Masculinity—
From Masculinity to Masculinities

In an excellent review of the literature that grapples with defining masculinity, Kenneth Clatterbaugh points to scholars' confusing use of the term "masculinity," which he concludes is a "subterfuge" because it subsumes too many variables.[3] "Masculinity," for purposes of this discussion, refers to the characteristic performances and attitudes that gendered society attributes to the male. Indisputably, *Nervous Conditions* embodies enacted definitions of masculinity, which transcend confusing theoretical terminologies. Dangarembga orchestrates the lives of the male characters, individually and collectively, so as to counter a simplistic view of masculinity and reveal ways of reading the many variables responsible for pluralizing masculinity. She reveals, for instance, the interplay between colonial and patriarchal indigenous forces in the creation and destabilization of men's perceptions and experiences of manhood. Such interplay of forces sets the stage for appreciating the novel's presentation of pluralized masculinity as performance. A close look at the array of the highlighted males in the narrative—Babamukuru, Jeremiah, Nhamo, Chido, and Matimba, Tambudzai's teacher—points to the inadequacy of lumping together all males, in this text or in any context, as the "patriarchy." It is true that society's normative ascriptions to the "man," ascriptions that constitute masculinity, are also used as justifications for the power structure of patriarchy. However, it is equally true that even in the homogeneously heterosexual Shona community of the novel, not every male is endowed with those characteristics of masculinity in the same manner or to the same degree as every other male. More significantly, the novel makes it clear that few males consistently act masculine at all times. Thus, masculinity becomes more a matter of performance than of being, and as such, substantiates Butler's view of performed gender identities.

It may be useful to briefly outline the characteristics of masculinity as ascribed by gendered social convention and as they emerge from the text. A particularly instructive moment eloquently characterizes these ascriptions of masculinity. In order to appease Babamukuru (who can no longer tolerate what he considers his daughter's masculine behavior), the narrator, Tambudzai, contemplates her conscious effort to counteract Nyasha's perceived masculine tendencies:

> I could see that my uncle was growing more and more disappointed with his daughter. In fact, it became very embarrassing for me, because I had grown quieter and more self-effacing than was usual, even for me. Beside Nyasha, I was a paragon of feminine decorum, principally because I hardly ever talked unless spoken to and then only to answer with the utmost respect whatever question had been asked. Above all, I did not question things. . . . I did not think that my reading was more important than washing the dishes. . . . I was not concerned that freedom fighters were referred to as terrorists, did not demand proof of God's existence nor did I think that the missionaries, along with all other whites in Rhodesia, ought to have stayed at home. As a result of these things that I did not think or do, Babamukuru thought I was the sort of young woman a daughter ought to be. (155)

This introspection takes place toward the end of the novel as a culmination of Tambu's experience in gender survival strategies. It might also explain why in most of the novel, women are expected to appear or act controlled, commanded, provided for, and protected. To put it a little more positively, though no less perniciously, faced with masculinity, femininity is supposed to consist of emotion, compliance, obedience, acceptance, submission, dependency, tenderness, and silence. Above all, Tambudzai's enactment of the feminine to counteract the masculine testifies to the "gender as performance" theory while demonstrating Dangarembga's skills in reproducing and blurring the boundaries within the masculine/feminine dichotomy. In this instance, the author subtly employs two female cousins to embody or perform both the masculine and the feminine.

The masculine or "real" man stands in contrast to the feminine "virtues" performed by Tambu. He is expected to reason and achieve and, in the process, command, control, assert, protect, possess, and provide for women. Indeed, in several instances, most of the big battles between the genders occur when women refuse—or are perceived as refusing—to conform to these ascriptions. Refusal to conform is seen as a threat to the propagation of masculinity.

However, four qualifications need to be made before I proceed with this assessment. The first, as suggested above, is that the traits mentioned are manifested in performance, which varies not only from individual to individual but also from situation to situation. This, in fact, presents the rationale for characterizing the traits in action rather than in descriptive terms. The second qualification is that masculinity and its ascriptions should be seen within cultural and political contexts. Thus, in *Nervous Conditions* masculinity should be seen not only within the Shona-African perspective but also within the colonial and Christian missionary perspectives that provide the historical setting of the novel. Third, as in all gendered/gendering perceptions, masculinity is propagated as a point from which to "other" what defines a woman. Thus, in view of the gendering of roles, all the traits of masculinity could be seen as performed toward women, who are supposed to be passive recipients of the men's agency. Dangarembga's genius lies in her ability to both reproduce and undermine these constructions of interdependent genders. Fourth, and most important, nearly all the traits of masculinity mentioned above have negative and destructive aspects. Reason is matched with inflexibility, command with imperiousness, control with dominance, assertion with aggression, protection with confinement, possession with greed and avariciousness, provision with meanness, and the ambition to achieve with ruthlessness. Hence Babamukuru seems to represent extreme versions of unbridled masculinity.

Masculinity: The Case of Babamukuru

Babamukuru (the Great or Big Father) could be regarded as the epitome through whom the traits of masculinity may be seen in their highest concentration. A top achiever, he has overcome the odds of race and economic deprivation to become a highly Western-educated, thoroughly professional man of considerable circumstance and authority. Tambudzai's insights point to Babamukuru's masculine image: "You never thought about Babamukuru as being beautiful or ugly. . . . He didn't need to be bold anymore because he had made himself plenty of power. Plenty of Power. Plenty of money. A lot of education. Plenty of everything" (50). In his early appearances in the novel, Babamukuru perceives himself as a provider and minder of his nuclear family—Maiguru (his wife), Nyasha (his daughter), and Chido (his son)—and of his feckless brother Jeremiah's family, to which Tambudzai (the narrator) and her siblings belong. Babamukuru consciously asserts his position as sole provider, oblivious to Maiguru's contributions to the family finances. When Maiguru takes exception to what she regards as a case of excess in his expenditures, he counteracts by asking rhetorically: "If I, as head of the family, don't provide food, who will provide?" (122).

Nor will he brook any questioning of or opposition to his status, authority, and power, as may be seen in his heated outburst to Nyasha in the fight scene: "I am respected at this mission. . . . We cannot have two men in this house. . . . Not even your brother there dares to challenge my authority" (114–15). Similarly, he fumes at Tambudzai when she is reluctant to attend her parents' wedding: "'I am the head of this house. Anyone who defies my authority is an evil thing in this house, bent on destroying what I have made'" (167). This absolutist insistence on his masculinity and godlike authority is Babamukuru's damning trait. It brings out the negative aspects of masculinity suggested earlier. What would have been his reasonableness freezes into intransigence and inflexibility. His idea of controlling and protecting his children degenerates into a neurotic tyranny over, and even violence toward, them (103–15). Indeed, his entire presence in his family appears to be suppressive. The reader is hard put to remember a single occasion when Babamukuru says a tender word to either of his children. Instead, "We hardly ever laughed when Babamukuru was in earshot, because, Maiguru said, his nerves were bad. His nerves were bad because he was so busy. For the same reason we did not talk much when he was around either" (102). In Babamukuru, workaholism becomes a characteristically masculine trait of the exaggerated desire to achieve. In other words, despite his positive qualities, his failure to establish a balance between his performance as a "man" and as a human being not foreclosed by prescriptions ends up bringing misery to his children, his wife, and himself.

There are, however, a few moments when Babamukuru manages to detach himself from unmitigated masculinity. Sometimes he seems to be capable of moderating his inflexibility in the face of new experiences. Thus, the death of Nhamo forces him, belatedly, to acknowledge and act on Tambudzai's need for quality education (46–47), just as his wife Maiguru's protest walk-out (173–75) prompts him to treat her with more regard and respect in their future interactions (e.g., 180). Similarly, Nyasha's nervous breakdown seems to elicit genuine concern from Babamukuru, despite the bitter fights (verbal and physical) that they engage in before this tragic development (191–201). As stated earlier, however, flexibility, concern, and tenderness are traits that convention ascribes to femininity. That they should manifest themselves, to however small a degree, in the prototypical/stereotypical masculine character of Babamukuru undermines the binary oppositions of feminine/masculine.

Masculinity: The Case of Other Male Characters

Babamukuru is not alone among the male characters in displaying this mixture of traits. A touching example of the mixture of feminine and masculine traits in a male character is found in the vignette of Tambudzai's green mealies (corn). Mr. Matimba, the schoolteacher, is a typical figure of control and authority when he stops the fight between Nhamo and Tambudzai (23). Soon after that, we see him in tender and close solidarity with Tambudzai as he plans for her to sell her mealies in Umtali. He also turns into a soft and persuasive, not to say submissive, negotiator/mendicant for Tambudzai when confronted by the critical white customer in the city who is willing to buy the mealies (27–29).

This last incident points to the threat of symbolic emasculation that the experience of colonialism poses to the colonized male. Mr. Matimba may be authoritative and assertive (i.e., masculine) on his own turf in Rutivi; however, he is in an emasculating situation (i.e., feminine) when confronted by an agent of the dominant, colonial power. Babamukuru endures a comparable experience of challenge and helplessness when he is confronted with racism at Tambudzai's predominantly white Sacred Heart School (194–95). Such incidents point to the author's suggestion that even the performances of masculinity or femininity are subject to broader frameworks of power relations, and it is not always accurate to assume that because patriarchy is in power, all men are powerful all the time (Kimmel and Messner, viii).

In terms of masculinity, the opportunistic, ne'er-do-well Jeremiah can be seen as a direct foil to Babamukuru's shining, masculine qualities. Jeremiah is portrayed not only as a lazy, self-pitying semiliterate but also a shameless alcoholic cadger. From the outset, his masculinity pales in comparison to that of Babamukuru, who is described as a "man not afraid of hard work." Jeremiah, for instance, shuns the conventionally masculine chore of repairing the family roof, leaving it to his daughter and Lucia. It is also significant that upon being taken under Babamukuru's wing, Nhamo, embarrassed by his father's chronic dependency, explicitly disowns him, proudly declaring, "I shall no longer be Jeremiah's son" (48). As Jeremiah himself confesses, Babamukuru has done and continues to do everything for him and his family (31, 45). The nadir of Jeremiah's dependency (a supposedly "feminine" trait) is dramatized when he is ordered by his sister to kneel before Babamukuru to thank him for deciding to take Nhamo under his wing (46). Fascinatingly, while Babamukuru is portrayed as assertively performing masculinity throughout the novel, his brother, Jeremiah, parallels this performance only through staging an imagined masculinity. For instance, symbolic of his failure to keep a roof over his household, Jeremiah fails to carry out repairs to the kitchen roof but effectively enacts for Babamukuru an imagined participation. "You should have seen us! Up there with strips of bark and the fertilizer bags, and tying the plastic over the holes. Ha! There was a big job there, a big job" (154). He thus shamelessly takes credit for the "masculine" job accomplished by the two women. Tellingly, earlier in the story, while Babamukuru returns as a successful "warrior" with academic accomplishments from England, his brother, spear in hand, can only *perform* the warrior dance, around the car of the newly arrived brother. Jeremiah represents failed masculinity and appears more pathetic because Babamukuru, the model by which the other males' masculinities may be measured, towers over him.

Nevertheless, there are several levels of the performance of masculinity in which Babamukuru's actions run parallel rather than in contrast to those of Jeremiah. They are unanimous, for example, in their privileging of the male child, Nhamo, over his sister Tambudzai.[4] We also see similarity in their tyrannical suppression of their daughters. Even more surprising, in the light of Babamukuru's education and residence abroad, is the almost identical manner in which the two men treat their wives as invisible or insignificant. These negative traits point to the conspiratorial transformation of masculinity into monolithic patriarchy, most likely the result of early socialization into polarized gender attitudes. The resultant internalization of sexist attitudes never seems to go away, even in males as educated and sophisticated as Babamukuru. It can erupt at the slightest female challenge, as in the case of Babamukuru and Nyasha. Furthermore, it is an indication that the colonial system, of which Babamukuru is a byproduct, is no more ultramasculine than the indigenous patriarchal structure. By using two differently situated brothers, Dangarembga expands the range of definitions of masculinity.

Nhamo, a budding product of both the indigenous and colonial systems, is a pathetic case of the internalization of distorted masculinity and inflated egotism, which translates into insidious male chauvinism. Not only does he look up to and admire the authority figure of Babamukuru, but he appears to have fully absorbed the "masculine" notions of his father about the inferiority of women. When Tambudzai drops out of school, the explanation of her plight is obvious to the chauvinist Nhamo: "Because you are a girl. . . . That's what Baba said, remember?" (21). His chauvinism does not stop at acceptance of masculine superiority but extends to active violence towards his sisters. He bosses them around about carrying his luggage, as indicated above, and beats them when they demur (9–10). His destructive tendencies appear at their worst when he starts stealing the mealies that Tambudzai has grown and is trying to sell to raise the money for her school fees (21–22). One cannot help sharing Tambudzai's indignation and rage, which drive her to fight her craven brother on the playfield (22–23). After he is taken to the mission, Nhamo's bloated ego and his perversity worsen with colonial pretensions. These more than justify the narrator's seemingly outrageous opening statement: "I was not sorry when my brother died" (1). Nhamo's early exit from the text may be an indictment of the sneaky, opportunistic chauvinism that he represents, for the narrator begs us not to judge her too harshly for her unkind sentiments towards her brother's death.

On the other hand, Chido is a curious mixture of nonperformance (reminding the reader of Jeremiah) and passive and uncritical acceptance of the patriarchal status quo. Indeed, he seems to be his mother's son. Chido's appearances in the novel are infrequent, perhaps reflecting his ineffectuality within the family and the way he is dominated by the supermasculine figure of Babamukuru. Babamukuru definitely accords to Chido privileges denied his sister Nyasha, such as the luxury to associate with peers of the opposite sex. Nevertheless, in the narrator's consciousness, Chido is also certainly overshadowed, not to say eclipsed, by Nyasha. According to patriarchal convention, Chido is supposed to "protect" and discipline Nyasha and Tambudzai, but, in the face of his insipidity, the narrator sees the proposition as ridiculous: "Poor Chido! I do believe he felt obliged to carry on the tradition in the normal, unanalytic male fashion, because when we refused to be subdued and laughed at him instead, he reverted to his usual lovable self" (109).

This does not, however, deter Chido from forcibly taking away Nyasha's cigarette, grinding it out, and admonishing his sister, in true patriarchal fashion: "You are the daughter. There are some things you must never do" (117). His most decisive performance in the novel, however, is when he assists his mother to hold Babamukuru off Nyasha during their tragic tussle (115). Since both Chido and Maiguru, representing male and female agents, engage in restraining Babamukuru, their act can be read as neutral. In the conventional categories mentioned earlier, it can be classified neither as feminine nor as masculine, but simply as human, an expression of gender balance.

Women and Masculinity

Most of the female characters actively engage in masculinity (de)construction at the same time that they participate in executing "the mutually exclusive scripts" (Bem, 80) of gender polarization. Their engagement with masculinity ranges from passive acceptance, through admiration, aspiration, and emulation, to active and confrontational challenge. Significantly, most of these responses are toward Babamukuru, the identified icon of masculinity.

Passive acceptance of masculinity is associated mainly with the older women in the novel, especially the two matriarchs, Maiguru and Tambudzai's mother, Mainini (Younger Mother). In these two representatives of traditional African femininity, we see the essence of ultimate deference to masculinity and, ultimately, to the patriarchy. The most disturbing element in these women's approach to life is that although they articulate the injustices and prejudices in their society, they appear to consciously accept them. Tambudzai's mother succinctly states the philosophy of acquiescent submission in her homily to Tambudzai on what the mother calls "the weight of womanhood": "This business of womanhood is a heavy burden. . . . How could it not be? Aren't we the ones who bear children? When it's like that you just can't decide today I want to do this, tomorrow I want to do that, the next day I want to be educated! When there are sacrifices to be made, you are the one to make them. And these things are not easy; you have to start learning them early. . . . What will help you, my child, is to learn to carry your burdens with strength" (16). These words sound like a classic catalogue of subjugated "femininity," but even more strikingly, they anticipate Maiguru's explanation of her own subservience to Babamukuru: "'I glimpsed for a little while the things I could have been, the things I could have done, if—if—if things were—different. But there was Babawa Chido and the children and the family. And does anyone realize, does anyone appreciate, what sacrifices were made? As for me, no one even thinks about the things I gave up'" (101–2).

Although it is easy to understand and accept Mainini's passive res-ignation to the tyranny of the system, given her poverty and lack of choices, it is much harder, at the outset, to sympathize with Maiguru's apparently masochistic self-sacrifice. The reader expects Maiguru to have known better than to abase and efface herself before the imperious Babamukuru. This does not seem to be a necessary part of the need to take care of her husband and her children. However, as it transpires in the course of the story, Maiguru's self-effacement is calculated (as is the case with Tambu) to boost Babamukuru's ego, which, in its ab-solutist masculinity, cannot stand anything like self-assertion. Maigu-ru's ritualistic fussing over Babamukuru at the dinner table is a graphic illustration of her exaggerated and demeaning playing up to her hus-band's bloated masculine image (80–82). As on several other occasions when the action is not simply human but masculine, the narrator hints to the reader how Babamukuru responds to his wife's ministrations: "Babamukuru tucked in *manfully*" (82; emphasis added).

Two important observations shed light on women's apparent but-tressing of masculinity through submission. The first is that the so-cialization into polarized gender positions, observed above in the men, is even more pervasive in the women, who are sometimes obliged to perform submission as a means of abating the "nervous condition." The novel hints in numerous places that the "script" of "femininity"— what women should and should not be or do—is even more explicit than in the case of masculinity, thus accounting for the sometimes physical fights between the sexes when women express resistance against rampant masculinity. Such fights also find expression in direct insightful, metatextual observations: "It stung too saltily, too sharply and agonizingly the sensitive images that women had of themselves, images that were really no more than reflections. But the women had been taught to recognize these reflections as self and it was frightening now even to begin to think that, the very facts that set them apart as a group, as women, as a certain kind of person, were only myths; that generations of threat and assault and neglect had battered these myths into the extreme, dividing reality they faced" (138). Obviously, mission school and college education or overseas training (where masculinity also reigns supreme to various degrees) seem to only reinforce indigenous indoctrination regarding gender scripts. Nevertheless, recognition of the falsities in these scripts forms a powerful basis for my second point, the possibilities of transformation glimpsed at through various characters.

The basic optimism of the narrative hinges on the fact that the passive women's submission to masculinity is not entirely without variation and nuance, or even change. The sometimes bold and explicit changes attest to the dynamic nature of masculinities, if they are indeed constructed against an ever-changing femininity. We get a glimpse, for example, at how the supposedly passive matriarch Mainini, like the young Nyasha, resists masculinity control, in her case by becoming anorexic and refusing to do housework. Additionally, Mainini tactfully defies her husband, Jeremiah, and manages to establish a functional solidarity with her daughter, Tambudzai, whom Jeremiah wants to bar from traveling to town to sell her corn. To Jeremiah's order to tell Tambudzai that she is not to go to town, Mainini retorts: "'And why should I tell her such things? . . . The girl must have a chance to do something for herself, to fail for herself. . . . You know your daughter. She is willful and headstrong. . . . She must see these things for herself. If you forbid her to go, she will always think you prevented her from helping herself,' she continued, recovering her sense of direction. 'She will never forget it, never forgive you'" (24–25). This decisive articulation is so powerful that it leads to the only instance in the novel when Jeremiah gives in to his wife or his daughter, with his simple "Then let her go" (25).

Strikingly, this incident is almost a mirror image of a later sequence where Maiguru firmly rejects Babamukuru's implicit request that she endorse his objection to Tambudzai's joining the convent school. Maiguru's lucid argument against Babamukuru's assumptions on this occasion is not only a reflection of her incipient "emancipation" and an act of female solidarity with Tambudzai, but also a search for balance in the face of Babamukuru's absolutist polarization of gender. She argues:

> I don't think that Tambudzai will be corrupted by going to that school. Don't you remember, when we went to South Africa everybody was saying that we, the women, were loose. . . . It wasn't a question of associating with this race or that at the time. People were prejudiced against educated women. Prejudiced. . . . I am disappointed that people still believe the same things. . . . I don't know what people mean by a loose woman. . . . All I know is that if our daughter Tambudzai is not a decent person now, she never will be, no matter where she goes to school. And if she is decent, then this convent should not change her. (181)

Maiguru's extended speech could be regarded as completely out of character, unlike anything that we have seen of her up to this point. But it is convincing stylistically and thematically, as she is a changing woman, gradually beginning to face up to the patriarchy and its masculine absolutism.

Maiguru's active engagement with her husband's masculinity is extended and subtle, ranging from verbally criticizing and protesting some of his excesses (e.g., 122, 171–72, 182) to physically restraining his violence and aggression (114–15), and even walking out on him when his insensitivity becomes intolerable (173–75). Later in the narrative, we are told of "Maiguru's progress with respect to her emancipation and the way Babamukuru was coping with his more adamant wife" (196). Clearly, the women's engagement with masculinity destabilizes their men's identity performances.

A few details, however, should be considered in the case of Maiguru's intervention in the violent scene between Nyasha and Babamukuru. First, it is an act of direct and decisive opposition to masculine violence. Second, it indicates the delicate balance between Maiguru's actions and her words. Although her restraining actions are definite and firm, her words are intended as a plea to soothe Babamukuru: a manifestation of curious ambivalence in the face of masculine chauvinism. Third, and more important, Maiguru's intervention on Nyasha's behalf on this occasion is one of the few times that we see Maiguru in solidarity with her daughter. Most of the time, it appears that Maiguru conspires with her husband's controlling masculinity against Nyasha. For example, together they forbid Nyasha from reading *Lady Chatterley's Lover* (75, 81). Though their decision could be a consequence of the official opposition to that novel during their residence in England, they nonetheless present their decision in unison. This uncharacteristic betrayal by a mother exacerbates Nyasha's problematic relationship to masculinity, especially Babamukuru's extremist brand of it.

For Nyasha herself is an extremist. She is undoubtedly the most explicit and most intelligent opponent of masculine chauvinism in the novel. Her militancy is seen in all her attitudes, reflections, words, and actions, culminating in her shocking and pathetic punching of her father (115). The reader would expect a feminist text to approve of, if not to applaud, Nyasha's struggle against the patriarchy. But, although not condemning Nyasha, the discourse of *Nervous Conditions* does not appear to approve of her actions either. Indeed, that she ends up as a nervous wreck is one indication that her rebellion, as the narrator remarks, "may in the end not have been successful" (1). The comments of Tambudzai, Nyasha's greatest admirer, repeatedly underline the same point: "You had to admit that Nyasha had no tact. You had to admit she was altogether too volatile and strong-willed. You couldn't ignore the fact that she had no respect for Babamukuru" (116).

Nyasha's character raises a lot of questions. Why do her traits militate against her struggle, and in the end threaten to destroy her? What, in effect, are the implications of her challenging battles against her father's programmed masculinity script? Of course, we cannot overlook other complicating factors, such as Nyasha's alienating childhood in England and her feverishly sharp and analytical intelligence. Furthermore, her analytical power, reasoning abilities, and inquisitiveness are all perceived by Babamukuru as masculine and therefore as a threat to his manhood. In masculine terms, however, Nyasha's tactical undoing is that she tries to fight masculinity by claiming or appropriating that very masculinity, especially in its negative aspects, such as absolutism, arrogance, and aggressiveness. The basic problem in Nyasha's approach is that although she is convinced that chauvinistic masculinity, as she sees it in her father, is wrong, she still assumes that the best way to confront it is by using the same stances or tactics that she deplores in it.

It is also fascinating that Nyasha is a great admirer of the gender-transgressive Lucia, about whom Babamukuru says, "that one, she is a man" because she dares to invade the patriarchal meeting. The narrator tells us that Nyasha is "pleased with Lucia" after her confrontation with Takesure at the patriarchs' meeting (159). Lucia is also one of the characters whom the narrator considers to have been "liberated" from the excesses of masculine oppression. However, although Lucia is a fighter like Nyasha, Lucia adopts a wide and flexible range of strategies that enable her to handle each situation as it arises. Although she can physically twirl Takesure's ears to stop his telling lies about her, she can also petition Babamukuru for a job to reduce her economic dependency (156–57). This does not prevent her from reprimanding the patriarch for dictatorially forcing her sister into a wedding and persecuting Tambudzai for refusing to attend the farcical ceremony (170–71). Realizing that her lack of education limits her ability to express and assert herself, Lucia goes to adult night school, where she performs brilliantly. In other words, whereas Nyasha, the inflexible, theoretical, "men-must-be-fought" inexperienced feminist, hurls and hurts herself against the granite of masculinity, Lucia, the practical tactician, scores empowerment points (even from Babamukuru, who appears to compliment her gender border crossings) by flexibly fighting each masculine challenge as it arises (160). It is not only her inflexibility, as compared to Lucia, that intensifies Nyasha's nervous condition, but her symbolic attempts to appropriate Babamukuru's place. At the mission, Babamukuru is expected to serve himself first and to start eating before the rest of the family. On one occasion, Nyasha transgressively starts to eat before her father. Again, while visiting at the homestead, both Maiguru and Babamukuru decline to sit on a chair presented to them in Tambudzai's mother's room. The narrator tells us:

> We all gazed at the chair upon which Maiguru steadfastly refused to sit and wondered what to do with it. My mother suggested that Babamukuru would be more comfortable on the chair, but he claimed that the bed was more ideal for sitting on. My mother was very distressed that neither my uncle nor my aunt, in fact nobody, would sit on that chair. . . . In the end Nyasha, whether she intended to be rude or not, got up off the floor, where she had been sitting beside her mother.
> "Well, I'll be more comfortable here even if no one else will," she announced, planting herself in the chair. (130)

It is no wonder Babamukuru consistently feels threatened by his daughter, as is evident in the fighting scene, where he justifies his excessive violence toward the frail Nyasha (115). An even more vivid contrast to Nyasha's tactless inflexibility is dramatized through her alter ego, Tambudzai. Nyasha, who occasionally refers to her father as "the man," appears to subversively lay claim to Babamukuru's place, whereas Tambudzai simply admires him and aspires, not to replace him, but to become like him. Nyasha despises and contradicts Babamukuru (and, indeed, the submissive Maiguru), whereas Tambudzai explicitly confesses to respecting and emulating him: "I entered our bedroom, vowing earnestly that I would be like Babamukuru: straight as an arrow, as steely and true" (88). This attitude in the leading character and narrator, whom the reader expects to be the main reflector of the significance of the narrative, is admittedly problematic, especially as it appears to persist throughout the novel. In the final chapter, for example, the now supposedly sophisticated young lady muses: "I was and would remain Tambudzai, the daughter. Babamukuru was still and would always be the closest thing a human being could get to God" (199). To a purely feminist reading, this is perplexing unless of course it is taken as sarcasm, a reading that the context does not quite warrant. In masculine performance terms, however, Tambudzai's attitude to Babamukuru could be taken as a desire to perform and achieve his positive attributes, stereotyped in polarized gender frameworks as "masculine," when in reality they are simply human attributes. Tambudzai aspires to education, independence, wealth, and power (183) as possessed by Babamukuru, and tellingly describes Babamukuru's identity, as "illusive." Furthermore, even though she takes pride in successfully performing the role of an ideal (subservient) daughter, she effectively turns a relentless gaze (a conventionally male privilege) toward Babamukuru and, through authoring her own story, participates in the male authorship privilege. In essence, she becomes the quintessential contemporary African woman writer, Ifi Amadiume's "male daughter," grappling with productive ways of textualizing masculinities.

In the final analysis, Dangarembga consistently enacts masculinity in order to highlight its pitfalls and its complexities as well as to dismantle the gender polarization transmitted through cultural norms. At the same time, the narrative and interpretive style (from the female point of view) employed in the novel throws open the door to many other possibilities of interpreting and theorizing what it means to be masculine in a postcolonial context. It can be concluded though, that what the novel dramatizes is not simple masculinities but *distorted notions of* maleness. The author is also proposing that there are neither masculine nor feminine qualities but only positive/empowering performances and negative/debilitating performances. In the novel, we see time and again that positive developments take place when the agents, whether female or male, adopt positive approaches, such as generosity, solidarity, tact, flexibility, determination, and clear thinking. On the other hand, mayhem and entrapment ensue when the characters indulge in inflexibility, aggressiveness, passivity, and narcissistic egotism. The point is best made with Tambudzai, the heroine/narrator, who apparently survives and triumphs amidst the chaos, symbolically replacing the self-destructing Nhamo and Nyasha and offering a viable alternative to the entrapped matriarchs, Maiguru and Mainini. Tambudzai is able to blend and balance the positive qualities necessary for her empowerment and survival. Through Tambudzai's story, Dangarembga succeeds in laying bare the challenges of knowing what it means to be female and, in the process, illuminates the complex meaning(s) of masculinity. Thus, *Nervous Conditions* unmistakably responds to the call (quoted in the first epigraph) from the traditional story narrated by Toni Morrison as part of her Nobel lecture: "Tell us what it is to be a woman so that we may know what it is to be a man" (28).

Notes

1. Through the voice of Tambu's grandmother, Dangarembga effectively provides a family history (and indeed a history of the nation not available in history books). This oral history sheds light on the root cause of the poverty of the homestead: "Your family did not always live here. . . . We lived up in Chipinge, where the soil is ripe and your great grandfather was a rich man in the currency of those days. . . . Wizards well versed in treachery and black magic came from the south and forced the people from the land. . . . At last the people came upon the grey, sandy soil of the homestead, so stony and barren that the wizards would not use it. There they built a home" (18).

2. See essays particularly in "Critiques of Postcolonial Rhetoric" and "Postcolonial Subjectivities," sections 1 and 3 of Willey and Treiber. See also Charles Sugnet.

3. See Kenneth Clatterbaugh's comprehensive discussion.

4. Even though Nhamo is older and would naturally be more privileged, we know that Babamukuru's son Chido, though younger than Nyasha, is accorded privileges denied to his older sister.

Works Cited

Bem, Sandra L. 1993. *The Lenses of Gender: Transforming the Debate on Sexual Inequality.* New Haven, CT: Yale University Press.

Brittan, Arthur. 1997. "Masculinity and Power." In *Key Concepts in Critical Theory: Gender,* ed. Carol C. Gould, 113–19. Atlantic Highlands, NJ: Humanities Press.

Butler, Judith. 1999. *Gender Trouble: Feminism and the Subversion of Identity.* New York: Routledge.

Clatterbaugh, Kenneth. 1988. "What Is Problematic about Masculinities?" *Men and Masculinities* 1 (1): 24–45.

Dangarembga, Tsitsi. 1989. *Nervous Conditions.* Seattle: Seal Press.

Kimmel, M. S., and M. A. Messner, eds. 2004. *Men's Lives.* 6th ed. Boston: Pearson, Allyn and Bacon.

Morrison, Toni. 1994. *The Nobel Lecture in Literature, 1993.* New York: Alfred A. Knopf.

Sugnet, Charles J. 1997. "*Nervous Conditions:* Dangarembga's Feminist Reinvention of Fanon." In *The Politics of (M)othering,* ed. Obioma Nnaemeka, 33–49. London: Routledge, 1997.

Willey, Ann Elizabeth, and Jeanette Treiber, eds. 2002. *Emerging Perspectives on Tsitsi Dangarembga: Negotiating the Postcolonial.* Lawrenceville, NJ: Africa World Press.

11

Sindiwe Magona

Writing, Remembering, Selfhood, and Community
in *Living, Loving, and Lying Awake at Night*

M. J. Daymond

In the early 1990s, just at the time when South Africans were turning toward democracy, Sindiwe Magona published three books in rapid succession: two volumes of autobiography, *To My Children's Children* (1990) and *Forced to Grow* (1992), and, between them, a collection of short stories, *Living, Loving, and Lying Awake at Night* (1991).[1] In all three works Magona is concerned with representing selfhood and its formation within a particular community, and there are signs in the short stories that her thoughts were beginning to turn to the larger concept of a heterogeneous social collectivity. Her autobiography indicates the extent to which her exploration of community and self-formation in her fiction is guided by her own experiences, and it indicates too how and why Magona chose to deal with such matters in writing—fictional as well as autobiographical.

Magona wrote her autobiography while in exile in New York.[2] Besides the ache of absence, the depredations of apartheid during her life were such that a sense of loss permeates her sense of self: "I am the result of a series of losses, lacks and lapses" (*To My Children's*, 16). But at the same time, she rejoices that her loss was never total, claiming that her childhood meant that "there has always been a place to which I belonged with a certainty that nothing has been able to take from me" (1). This place is Gungululu, a village in the Eastern Cape. There, life was carefree for children: it was a "people-world, filled with a real, immediate, and tangible sense of belongingess. . . . I was not only wanted, I was loved. I was cherished" (3). Magona describes the guidance she received from her mother and grandparents (her father was a migrant worker in Cape Town). She gives particular attention to the place of storytelling in her upbringing. Her delight in it, and her grasp of the underlying structures of folk tales as well as their social functioning, would shape all of her own writing: As Magona puts it: "I can see clearly how *iintsomi* [folk tales] are an essential and integral part of the socialization of the child among amaXhosa. . . . Central to the stories . . . was the bond of love with the concomitants: duty, obedience, responsibility, honour, and orderliness; always orderliness. Like the seasons of the year, life was depicted full of cause and effect, predictability and order; connectedness and oneness" (6).

When she was five, Magona's parents decided that the family should move to Cape Town, where her father worked. They settled first in Blaauvlei, an informal settlement near Retreat on the wind-swept sand dunes that spread north and east of the mountain and the Cape Town city bowl. There, people were developing new ways of living in modernity and of drawing together as a community. As Magona depicts it, a feverish excitement about life in Blaauvlei replaced the orderly tranquility that the child had known in the village, but it was still a happy time; as she puts it from her adult perspective, she and her age-mates reveled in the "vibrancy, throbbing aliveness, and . . . [the] many-faceted complexity. . . . [t]he filth, squalor, poverty, shabbiness, [which] sharpened [their] . . . senses" of their world (37–38). Then, just as she completed her formal education and embarked on adult life, "[t]hat well-knit, lawful community" was scattered "willy-nilly like grains of sand during a whirlwind" (92). Her family was compelled to move to a newly built township, the cruelly named Guguletu (our pride). Without any choice in the matter, she and her family found themselves living in proximity to but not in community with others. She writes that it was "a massive dislocation. . . . I found myself in the midst of a conglomeration, rather large in number, of ill-assorted people, strangers brought together by the zeal of the government to control our lives" (92). To bring home the contrast with Blaauvlei, "where she had grown up knowing almost everybody in the community" (92), Magona writes of her first encounter with urban "thugs . . . fearless, and feared, a law unto themselves" and ascribes her loss to the apartheid government's "unwavering pursuit . . . [of] the destruction of African family life, communal life, and all those factors that go toward the knitting of the very fabric of a people" (92).

Later in adult life, Magona found a kind of community that can be seen as something of an antidote to the uniformity and anonymity of township life, but it was not materially based. Its formation began when she studied through Unisa and, at the SACHED tutorials,[3] met a heterogeneous group of like-minded students with whom she attended support classes. Although her class was not representative of broader developments in the country and was often subjected to racist accusations of transgression when they met in premises officially designated for white use, she began to recognize that a common purpose could overarch diversity and that "whatever group you were locked into by law had no bearing on one's studies and the attainment of one's goals" (106). This can be seen as the first of Magona's consciously "transcultural" steps (Jacobs, 50).[4] She took another when she was drawn into Church Women Concerned, a "multi-racial, multi-denominational, inclusive [grouping] of all faiths" that espoused "reconciliation." Although at that time their objective was, Magona says, "a fond dream put forward as a testimony of faith" (*To My Children's*, 125), it too enabled her to envisage a new kind of community in South Africa. What Magona begins to grapple with is a matter to which Mamphela Ramphele has pointed: people in a modern democracy usually belong to many "subnational units" that control their loyalties and direct their enterprise, and they may even find themselves belonging to "multiple and sometimes competing communities" (2). This, Ramphele says, is particularly true of South Africa today, where "individual human rights and traditional communal obligations coexist in a state of tension" (3).

While loss is her autobiographical refrain, Magona does not render her life in tones of self-pitying regret; her narration is lively, colloquially sophisticated, humorous, often angry or self-critical but always informed by rational good sense. Her narrating voice is a talkative one, for she uses what Innes and Rooney have called "spoken writing," which "pays attention to forms of vocalisation" and in which "speechmaking . . . [may] become its mode of address" (210). Magona grew up in a largely oral culture, and her autobiography indicates that, besides a love of her people's orature, she had, by the time she entered adult life, developed a sharp ear for the idiosyncrasies of individual speech. This delight in what can be rendered through what were then the alternative discourses of daily life carries into her short stories and her later novel, and her predilection seems always to be to capture the complexities of how people, and women in particular, speak to each other (or themselves) about their circumstances, their thoughts, and their dreams. The story cycle "Women at Work" in *Living, Loving, and Lying Awake at Night*, for example, depicts a group of African women thrown together because they are employed as live-in domestic workers in adjacent white suburban households. In a sequence of separate monologues (except in the first story, which is told in authorial and figural narration), they each tell a seventh woman, Atini, who has recently joined their circle, about their lives, their work, each other, and their relationship with their white employers.

There is a sequence in her autobiography that indicates where Magona's chosen focus on women's speech, as well as her subject matter, had its origin. Magona's parents were able to pay for her formal education until she had qualified to teach in primary school, and her family rejoiced as she entered the ranks of the small, poorly paid African professional class (Daymond 1995, 566). Her career was brought to an abrupt end, however, by an unexpected pregnancy and marriage to a man whom she represents as irresponsible; he left her with three children to care for, nowhere to live, and no job. Her only option was to put her children in her mother's care and to take on work as a housemaid in the homes of white families in order to feed her own. She first worked as a live-in maid for three families before "opt[ing] for sleep-out jobs" (*To My Children's*, 138), which meant that she lived with her mother and children in her mother's house in Guguletu and traveled to and from the white suburbs by bus each day. It was during these bus rides that Magona listened avidly to the talk of other domestic workers—whom she calls "brilliant story-tellers" who were not too "dumb to understand their exploitation" (139)—and it is their power to represent their circumstances in the form of stories that she remembers in "Women at Work." The result is filled with the spirit that Magona had heard on the buses: astute observations lit by the women's racy and sometimes angrily resistant humor about working in white suburban households.

But the "Women at Work" cycle does not begin with personalized speech; the protagonist of the first story, "Leaving," is not even named, and it is not until the end of the cycle that a reader knows for sure that she is the same person as the woman called Atini who addresses the reader directly in the second story. The third-person narration of "Leaving" focuses on the circumstances (poverty, drought, and a neglectful husband) that compel a young rural woman to leave her starving children to the care of their grandmother and to go to the nearest town to find work; more particularly, the focus is on the perceptions and conflicting thoughts and emotions of this woman as, without being able to explain herself to anyone except herself, she abandons her immediate function as a mother in order to ensure the survival of her children in the only way available to her. She is doing what is unthinkable in her community, and as she climbs out of the valley where her homestead is, she imagines to herself what will be said about her: "witch . . . wanton . . . slut" (*Living*, 8). As David Callahan says in his close reading of these stories, in being unnamed, she seems to "exist as a personification of many women, a representative of the rural Xhosa woman" (90). The second section of *Living, Loving, and Lying Awake at Night* begins with a strikingly similar story, "Flight." Without explaining the reasons for her flight, it depicts another young married woman's hurried ascent of a mountain in order to escape from the valley where her husband's family lives. In this way, although it does not begin a set of stories that are as integrated as those in the first section, "Flight" picks up the powerful theme of entrapment and escape: "Women's escape is built into the emotional geography of the short tale as of the book as a whole" (Callahan, 96). Such a theme is a powerful diagnostic tool for a writer concerned with race and gender in self- and community formation, but to understand the full significance of Magona's choice of narrative mode as well as her subject matter, it is again helpful to turn to a particular sequence of her autobiography, her account, in *Forced to Grow,* of how and why she began to write.

Magona recounts that, as a member of Church Women Concerned, she found herself much in demand as a speaker at public protest meetings, which were proliferating after the student uprisings of 1976.[5] At these meetings she spoke with a passion—"spill one's bleeding guts out, baring one's soul, one's pain to complete strangers"—that made it intolerable to have to deal with ignorant and complacent responses such as "'What can we do for you people?' [and] 'What do your people want?'" (*Forced,* 167). These formulations contained an arrogant obliteration of her identity and were the reason that she found herself so "[t]ired of trying to convince others I was a human being" (182) while her efforts were thwarted by the pre-given categories of thought drawn on by those whom she was addressing. She decided to abandon the public platform. Public speaking had led to her being subjected to the silencing with which Gayatri Spivak engaged when she asked her now famous question about the subaltern: whether "the oppressed can know and speak for themselves" (74). Magona was permitted to speak, but only from one of the hegemonic, discursive sites available to black women in their self-representation, and even this meager license entailed a dilemma that Spivak points out when she characterizes the intricately related but different meanings of *Darstellung* and *Vertretung* (both translated as "representation") as "the contrast, say, between a proxy and a portrait" (71). It is because she has been rendered a powerless proxy who cannot be heard that Magona decides to abandon the public platform; the problem is not her lack of words but the racial and gendered discursive habits of her white listeners, which make them unable to hear her. Magona says that at that time she still, however, felt compelled to respond to events around her, and so she turned to writing as the mode of expression (if not of communication) that suited her better; she says that she felt that as she wrote, her only consideration need be "my feelings, my truth" (*To My Children's*, 183).

In making this shift, Magona is describing her own encounter with historically nuanced questions about speech and writing as modes of communication between self and others. As Innes and Rooney point out, Western culture has made rather different assumptions about its own practices in this regard from what it presumes about Africa: "[I]n the history of Western metaphysics, speech has been accorded privilege over writing in that it is equated with origins and presence while writing is regarded as derivative, as 'copy.' . . . [But within] a colonial/post-colonial history . . . it is writing that is accorded privilege over orality . . . [as] the sign of authority, learning, power, legitimacy . . . progress and technology" (209). Magona's own experience bears out this reversal as she finds that speech cannot, in her circumstances within apartheid, grant her a "presence," an authority, an individualized legitimacy or agency, and so she turns to the privacy of writing and its greater communicative integrity.

In her sense that what she needed was the privacy of writing, Magona can, besides negotiating racism, also be seen to have been reaching for the particular scope that writing offers women coming from a gendered, oral culture. In this context, writing becomes simultaneously a refuge and a site of subjectivity and agency in a way that the Zimbabwean writer Yvonne Vera has so thoughtfully articulated:

If speaking is still difficult to negotiate, then writing has created a free space for most women—much freer than speech.
There is less interruption, less immediate and shocked reaction. The written text is granted its intimacy, its privacy, its
creation of a world, its proposals, its individual characters, its
suspension of disbelief. It surprises in the best carnival way,
reducing distances, accepting the least official stance. The
book is bound, circulated, read. It retains its autonomy much
more than a woman is allowed in the oral situation. (3)

The gendered implications of choosing to write, which Vera brings
out, may not have been immediately present to Magona, but once she
came to explain why her turn to writing in 1978 did not inaugurate
her career as a writer (which began in 1990), gender certainly was
part of her reckoning. She says that in the 1980s one or two small
pieces were published, but "despite such encouragement, I did not
embark on a writing career. . . . I did not know anyone like me who
did. Even the Xhosa writers I knew of were much older, all men,
none of whom lived in or near Cape Town" (*Forced*, 184). The measure of her potential that Magona uses here tells her that writing
is the province of Xhosa men (she is not succumbing to the racist,
colonial view that only white people were sufficiently civilized to
write), and this suggests that while writing had become privately
necessary to her, its public form was, within her own culture, still an
alien and transgressive aspiration for a woman. Her self-positioning
within her cultural options may help in understanding why, when
she turned from public speech to writing, she chose to make the
illusion of speech, of the oral mode, paramount. She opens her autobiography by speaking as a grandmother, claiming that she wants
to give her great-grandchildren a sense of who they are by telling
them "the story of your past" (*To My Children's*, preface). She then
acknowledges the turn to writing at which she has arrived. Their
heritage "is an oral tradition," but contemporary circumstances
mean that she has to "keep, for you, my words in this [written]
manner" (1). As a storytelling Xhosa grandmother, Magona speaks
from a position overtly imbued with authority in her culture, but
hers is also a hybrid position in which she is, as Pumla Gqola points
out, "playfully engaging with Xhosa creative traditions" and allowing her readers to register the "centrality of innovation" in her undertaking (55).

The conjunction of having been received as a "proxy" rather than a person, of moving away from orality and yet sustaining the presence of voice, of grappling with the gendered associations of writing for publication, and Magona's particular circumstances at the demise of apartheid, make her turning to writing a complex move to explore. In first embarking on autobiography, she was in one sense still engaged in "trying to convince others I was a human being" (182) and in counterasserting her individuality against those who reduced her to a symptom of black peoples' needs. If writing autobiography enabled her to adumbrate her individual humanity to her "children's children" (a listening-reading position that can be widened to include those prepared to "learn or re-learn" [Gqola, 61] the discourses and reading strategies through which to hear her), then fiction may be said to have allowed her to create "portraits" of women as characters who are simultaneously representative and individual beings. This is what makes the opening of "Women at Work" so fascinating, for by beginning her first volume of fiction with a story about a woman whose anonymity renders her a representative figure and then shifting in the next story to this woman's own speaking voice, Magona signals clearly the scope that fiction gives her. It is the scope first of all to create a gathering of "unexpected speakers" (Gqola, 62) and through this move to create individual speakers who may resist the stereotyping to which black women had been subjected. This is a resistance that Magona herself had tried to achieve by speaking on public platforms but that had been denied her by her audiences' inability to hear. She spoke, but who listened? Now she uses spoken writing to invite her readers to listen in a new way. This might, of course, not follow automatically from her narrative mode, and so Magona supports her project by deploying Atini, the active listener to each of the monologues, as the reader's surrogate in the text. She enacts a listening, which the reader may be enabled to emulate.

The process by which this is done can be traced in some detail. In the second story, "Atini," when this character begins to speak for herself about her employment by Mrs. Reed, she uses a direct address to the reader that positions the narratee as a "you" who is not an alien entity but "my friend" (12), as Atini puts it. This is an important change from the autobiography, which, while it begins and ends as a potentially inclusive vocalized address to "my children's children," contains embedded scenes in which "Magona's narrating position shifts . . . so that it is not [always] the voice of the grandmother that we hear" (Gqola, 62), and in these scenes, the reader may be positioned as "other." Then, in the third story of the "Women at Work" cycle, in which Stella is the speaker and addresses her monologue to Atini rather than the reader, the narrative situation changes yet again. Now the location of utterance is explicit as the two women sit face-to-face in Atini's khaya (a small room in an outbuilding at the back of the house), and from now on Atini remains the narratee as each of the women visits her and talks. She becomes the reader's surrogate in the text, and her implied responses (she never speaks directly) have the potential to guide the reader as well as to prompt the other characters to further speech.[6] This device is what positions the reader alongside Atini—we hear the women's monologues with her, through her circumstances and discourses—and it does much to disrupt and even destroy the silencing power of the hegemonic discourses within which Magona had had to speak on the public platform.

Once the monologues addressed to Atini are under way, Magona's narrative probes the factors that both hold this circle of women together and divide them, and in doing so she explores the connection between what Spivak has called "the subject as individual agent" and "the subjectivity of a collective agency" (72). From the outset, and although these women "begin to imagine a countervailing, self-regulating community life for themselves" (Daymond 1995, 333), it looks unlikely that they will form a cohesive group that can adequately promote their common interests, for their monologues are a series of surreptitious confidences that enact their entrapment as live-in domestic workers. On the other hand, while they have to speak their thoughts in secret, they are shrewd, like their township-dwelling sisters to whom Magona had listened on the buses. The first priority of the women who speak is to keep their words away from their white employers, so Stella makes her clandestine visit to Atini only when she has seen Mrs. Reed's car drive off. These women cannot have the pleasures of free and openly shared speech that Magona had so enjoyed when she traveled to and from work on the buses. But there is another side to the secrecy of these monologues, for, as Sheila reveals when she speaks, these women have to keep their utterances concealed from each other too, or at least learn to be skeptical about what is said in confidence. The signal comes when, having spent much of her visit talking to Atini about Mrs. Reed, Sheila says in insouciant self-contradiction: "Let me give you a tip. Friend, don't listen to anything the other maids tell you about the woman you work for. Or her husband. Sometimes people tell you things and it's because they're jealous, that's all. These maids here are full of rubbish. You just go on doing your work—keep your mouth shut. And when they tell you things—listen with one ear only" (29).

In Magona's inquiry into the kinds of bonds that may be formed between oppressed peoples, this is her clearest indication of why this group of domestic workers, women who have so many interests in common and so many reasons to unite, is unlikely to form a community that will find "the subjectivity of a collective agency" (Spivak, 72). Their lives and interests are too thoroughly governed by their employers, and, like enslaved people everywhere, even while they know and speak to each other about their own exploitation, they are compelled to see their interests as best served by outward subservience to their masters. By the 1980s, which seem to be the period of these stories, trade unions had begun to win the legal right to represent registered black workers in South Africa, and projects to educate domestic workers, always the bottom of the proletarian heap, had also begun.[7] It is again Sheila who mentions this: "Have you heard about how maids should not let the white women call them girls or servants anymore? And we should join a group to fight for our rights? Do you think that can happen? White women can learn not to call us girl? . . . Me, myself, I don't think so. I really don't think so" (25). It is understandable that a change in her employer's language should be of more immediate concern to Sheila than is group solidarity leading to protopolitical action, for the latter is beyond her experience. When she says that she is sure that their employers have "groups" because they are able to keep wages uniformly low, Sheila identifies unerringly the political cohesion behind her oppression and its management: "they treat us the same because they know [from their groups] what that same is" (26). But Magona makes it clear that this relatively uneducated woman cannot really envisage the converse—that maids' "groups" could claim matching powers, and eventually even compel their oppressors to accept the principle of equal rights. Although these women, like their counterparts whom Magona encountered on the buses, express what Innes and Rooney call a "knowing otherwise" (210), this knowledge had not yet entered the public counter-discourses of the day in South Africa. So Magona chooses to use an educated, articulate, angry, and much younger woman, Joyce, to give an analytical formulation of what Sheila and the other women experience. Joyce says that although some employers might be charitable, low wages are "an insult to the maid's dignity, and an assault to her self-esteem. . . . Pay her and pay her justly. Then and only then does she become—even in the eyes of the medem—the adult that she is" (42).

Atini's first monologue has already indicated that a lack of trust is another important reason why the community that these women form is limited in what it can achieve in the short term. She explains that two months after she had arrived from the country, she was employed by Mrs. Reed as a stand-in for Imelda, who had to go to her distant rural home to care for a sick parent. When Imelda failed to return within the stipulated time, Atini found herself replacing Imelda permanently. As she tells us, the other women did not like what they saw as Atini's duplicity, and her own conscience was troubled until she thought about her starving children and the reasons why she had come to town for work in the first place. But competition over jobs is not the only source of distrust in this group of women. By the time Atini has found a job in town and the occasion for the monologues has been established, Imelda has gone, and thus is not given a monologue. When she later returns, she is excluded from the women's circle because, in her anger at having been supplanted at work, she does what she is already disliked for—she takes revenge by spreading malicious rumors about Atini and the other women. Her story does, however, emerge between the lines of the other monologues, and it is one that indicates, yet again, how these women's conditions militate against the mutual trust that would enable them to organize in their common interests and create a collective agency.

Besides Sheila's warning Atini about Mr. Reed, several other speakers hint that her employer's husband takes a sexual interest in the black women who work in his neighborhood: Virginia says it is rumored that he "tries tricks on the maids" (39) and that Imelda had called the Reeds "dirty inside" (36); the older woman, Lillian, indicates that she felt pity for Imelda, who was clearly pregnant and then suddenly was not; but it is Sophie who tells Atini the brutal truth—that when Mrs. Reed took Imelda to her doctor to terminate the pregnancy, she also saw to it that Imelda was sterilized. Mr. Reed has abused Imelda and perhaps other women sexually, but it is Mrs. Reed who presumes to exercise absolute control over her servant's body, and it is only months later that Imelda realizes why she cannot conceive and why her fiancé no longer wants to marry her. The monologues indicate that the other maids, and at least one white employer, have watched and understood these developments but have not intervened. This is probably because the black women knew their powerlessness—they lacked the civic and political rights to bring the Reeds to justice—but also because these women are part of a group that is divided against itself. At least one of them, Virginia, does not want to disturb present arrangements; she indicates her reasons when she asks Atini, "Has your medem asked you to stay in? I used to stay in a lot for them; before Imelda worked there. They pay well for stay-in" (38). The chance to earn extra money (this "stay-in" work is usually babysitting at night) takes priority over matters like justice and group solidarity. What this confirms of course is that these working women are silenced in public as a community; they do not lack words, but they lack the means in the sociopolitical system of getting themselves heard.

Atini concludes the cycle with her own "Reflections," in which she says that she feels she has exchanged "the hell of starvation" for another hell, that of being "a slave" (60), and that she and the other women are probably permanently trapped. She sees no way out and can cite laughter as their only way of making life tolerable; their shared misery is not itself a bond that can lead to subjective and collective agency. This unproductive bond is haunted throughout the cycle by another bond, that between a mother and her children, which is usually powerful but in these contexts can be ambiguous and even debilitating. It is experienced by the women in two forms in the sociopolitical system within which they work: the domestic worker's relationship with her own children, and her relationship with her employer's children. Caring for these white children would have been part of her duties, and these duties would have been emotionally complex in that her infant charges would still be innocent of the racism that frames their connection. Atini says in her "Reflections"—again spoken directly to the reader, who is now addressed as "my child" (51)—that her own children are surviving, that she has seen the three older children in the village only once in the two-and-a-half years she has worked for Mrs. Reed, and that she tries to see her two younger children on her weekly day off as they are now living in a local township with a woman whom she pays for her services: "I am not saying I pay her enough; but where would I get the money to pay anyone enough?" (54). In the light of the importance to Atini of her responsibilities to her own children (it was her reason for action and it now forms the basis of her relating to us as she speaks), it is interesting that Magona does not depict directly what would be an ironic mirror relationship between these women at work and the white children of the households they serve. The role of black women as nannies to white children, as surrogate and often beloved mother figures who are spurned when the time comes, haunts South African life; it still awaits fictional exploration from a black woman's point of view. Atini touches indirectly on this relationship when she reflects with quiet irony that she can "see the problem of the white woman opening her home to the black woman and trusting her completely—with children, with everything in the home, and with one's very life" (58; also *Mother,* 82–83), and it is the focus of Joyce's angry general observation: "Mornings see all the women in their uniforms taking white children to school. What a sight; until you ask yourself who takes the black child to school. And the white woman knows the black woman working for her has children. . . . [W]hy is she not bothered by this mother in her house[?] . . . [Because] in the eyes of the white women they work for they are children, worse than children: children grow up but domestic workers remain children to their death" (*Living,* 44). What we do not encounter is Atini face to face with Mrs. Reed's children (for whom Virginia is keen to babysit) or any of the other women reporting directly on their interactions with the children of the families for whom they work. And so the issue has a subdued rather than full presence in the cycle. This observation is made not as a reproach to Magona, whose autobiography indicates that she has experienced and thought hard about the issue, but in order to indicate how carefully she has sustained her chosen focus in "Women at Work." In relation to their white madams, who have the authority of the patriarchal apartheid system behind them and who, as Jacklyn Cock has argued, benefit directly from a gendered oppression of black women, these women are powerless, and yet in relation to their own families, each of them may have had to take on a degree of agency that enables them at least to sustain their children's lives. Given the burden of depicting a sustained practical choice that is enslaving and carried out within circumstances of powerlessness, any dramatization of the complicating question of affection between a black woman and her white charges might, in a delicately fragmentary form such as a short-story cycle, have served to deflect Magona's central narrative point. Perhaps if we wish to learn to read Magona historically and adequately, in the way that Gqola has called for, we must concede that, as with the laughter which masks their misery, these women know, besides their own exploitation and the boundaries of utterance imposed on them by apartheid, the limits of what they can bear to reveal even to themselves and each other about their circumstances.

The opening story of the second section of *Living, Loving, and Lying Awake at Night*, "Flight," indicates that, as in "Women at Work," bonds, bondage, entrapment, and escape are to be the interwoven themes of this section. "Flight" is narrated by a child, probably a little girl, as she and her friends are playing with rag dolls, and the use of her perspective enables Magona to leave unanswered our questions about why the young woman in her "new-wife-length dress" (64) that the child is watching seems to be running away. Instead, the focalizing child gives herself wholly to her churning desire to see the woman, who she senses is a prisoner, succeed in her bid to escape. The child simply delights in the natural world's collaboration with the escapee as she sees her finally "waft into the wall of mist" (64) that has come far enough down the mountain to hide the woman from her pursuers. Even in adult life, as the concluding reflections indicate, the narrator is unable to forget "the thrill I felt watching her escape" (65). This brief reflection from the present moment of narrating inaugurates the attention of the stories in this section to the function and functioning of memory, an activity that Magona introduces through her narrator in many of the stories. Remembering—the act of recovering and questioning the past from the perspectives of the present—is what links these stories with both Magona's own autobiographical explorations of her past selfhood in formation and her peoples' present moving away from subjection to apartheid and toward the creation of new personal and collective identities.

The functioning of this opening story makes for a many-layered comparison with that of "Leaving," which opens the first section of *Living, Loving, and Lying Awake at Night*. Like other stories in the collection, it acknowledges a crucial, century-long shift in the lives of African women from a rural to an urban context. Because the narration of "Flight" is limited to the child's perceptions and responses, there is no indication where the young woman will seek refuge, but readers can speculate (guided by long-standing cultural practices) that if she is indeed escaping marriage and if her family is a rurally based one, she would be unlikely to return to them, as they would be constrained by custom and the value set on family alliances to return her to her marriage family. Instead, she would be likely to seek the anonymity and the opportunities of a town. But when the stories that follow "Leaving" take up this move to town, the women protagonists are no longer depicted as alone, as was Atini, nor are they located in the half-life of domestic servants in a white suburb. Now the stories attend to the mixed blessings of family life in the townships, and, while the question of women's suffering and need to escape continues, the core issue shifts to the establishing and sustaining of rules by which these new communities may live. Understanding new cultural practices and assessing their viability is where memory is so important. Again, this matter is enriched by Magona's own experiences, for it is what she focuses on in her autobiography when she records her family's forced move from Blaauvlei to Guguletu—the breaking up of a coherent community that had been self-ordered and orderly, and the need for displaced people to replace what has been destroyed.

Secondly, both "Flight" and "Leaving" function as an "articulated joint" (Calvino 1997, 116). This phrase is Italo Calvino's way of explaining the necessary presence of a signal to the reader that the narrative has now launched into the realm of fiction and will use the liberties of invention that fiction allows to a writer. The freedom of this realm is evident when Magona, echoing her use of a generic figure of escape in "Leaving," uses her child-narrator in "Flight" as a device through which she can naturalize a severance from concerns of the daily social context and focus on an idea and an emotion. And this gap between fiction and the quotidian leads to the final point in this comparison: "Flight" also stands opposed to "Leaving," for in it the thrill of claiming individual liberty is allowed to override considerations such as a responsibility to others, whereas in the earlier story the protagonist's maternal responsibilities were at the core of her actions. These differences suggest that as a volume, *Living, Loving, and Lying Awake at Night* will examine from multiple angles its central concern with selfhood in a regulated community, and particularly with women's entrapment and escape, and that the stories can be read as speaking variously to each other in this concern. This variety means that we can read Magona's stories not just for her protagonists' understanding of and grappling with questions around "self" and "community," but for the range of Magona's own analysis and creation as it can be seen through the narrative modes that she uses.

The next story, "The Most Exciting Day of the Week," takes up, in its portrait of the ordered week of a newly urbanized community, the question of how the sense of responsibility that directs Atini in "Leaving" but is apparently ignored in "Flight" might be inculcated in a child. Furthermore, it asks the crucial question of how this might be done within a community that is simultaneously resisting the apartheid laws of the land, laws that should uphold the principles of individual morality but, in their racist decision of whose interests should frame the law, do not do so. Again Magona uses a child's experience for her story, but this time the child's thoughts are more continuously filtered through the narrating adult, who is remembering the pleasures of her early life. This means that the reader is guided to compare the knowledge that emerges from innocent encounters with the ways of the world to the knowledge that might be needed in adult life. The remembered routines of the week teach the child to trust her "inner place, the place of knowing and understanding. The place where joy and all thoughts of gladness dwell" (69). The child consciously draws on this knowledge when she resists the dullness of her formal education by consoling herself that her "real" life begins after school hours, but the story also takes us beyond her immediate defenses to show that what she learns through the routines of home life are what Magona adumbrates as her most important mainstay. For example, when the child gives her waking self entirely to the delight of listening to the gurgling, bubbling beer that her mother brews and sells each Friday night, she imagines that the beer whispers to her as it ferments and yearns to "complete its journey. . . . 'Please let me be. Please let me be'" (67). "Let me be" is *the* desire at the heart of selfhood, and as this wording indicates, fulfillment of being will be at issue for the child. Through the beer's song, Magona is able to connect sensuous delight to the formation of a regulatable social identity. The child's delight in the beer's secret whispering is vital to her in a further sense, for her mother's township brewing is illegal. This means that the family's life is ordered around a purpose that the apartheid state, in measures that both abrogate traditional cultural values and practices and deny economic survival to many, does not permit. There is a profound conflict between the social unit's choice of how to constitute an orderly world and the punitive regulations that the state has imposed on them, but the child will always be guided through this conflict (if not protected from its consequences) by the trust that she has learned to place in her "inner knowing and understanding."

When the narration embarks on events in the mother's Friday night shebeen, which (however dubious its delights) is presented as an enterprise that is undertaken with care by the child's parents, Magona can use her narrator's memories to further explore the complexities of ordering a life. Once she has drawn her readers into validating the family's focus on beer-brewing, she then conveys both the security of this rationally ordered life and the thrill of bending or straining its self-chosen controls. When the local factory sirens have sounded the end of the working week, Friday night in the township is given over to the carnivalesque. For the adult drinkers who come to the family's shebeen, the night offers an excess that wipes out the grind of the working week, and for the child who hopes to be sent to the shop on small errands for her mother's customers, it also offers a delight in excess. On these errands, she can escape to the bright lights of the main street beyond the township, territory that is usually out of bounds for children at night, and can do so knowing that the customer who has sent her to the shops is likely to reward her too generously, for, as the adult narrator puts it, "a drunk hand is a more open hand" (74). Always present in such excursions and observations, however, is a grasp of the family's own norms of order and responsibility against which the exciting night and its transgressions are to be measured.

While some of Magona's stories present transgression as a necessary part of a lively child's education in selfhood and community life, others look at the other side of the coin: the destructive consequences of witting and unwitting transgressions. The rules that manage sexuality and family life in rural communities are ineffective when men come to cities as migrant workers and are compelled to live in the single quarters known as "the zones" in the townships of Cape Town (109). This is the context of the shocking destruction of innocence, and the weight of the knowledge that may replace it, that is presented in "It was Easter Sunday the Day I Went to Netreg." The perspective of the unnamed first-person narrator is such that, for most of the story, it seems that the destructive act Magona is concerned with is abortion, but at the last moment she springs her trap and we discover that the pain and horror of incest is also at issue. Mother and daughter discover that, fifteen years apart and unknown to either of them (or to the man), they have each been seduced and impregnated by the same man. Commenting on the melodrama of this final revelation, David Callahan suggests that it is a forceful metaphor of apartheid's "closing down of healthy human development . . . [and] the living death that the system produces" (99). In this connection, it is notable that the abortion is organized by the mother's white employer, who drives them to the house in Netreg where it is performed and who is the one who later pays for the young woman to study midwifery. When read in conjunction with the stories in "Women at Work," this employer's involvement (which is a more benign version of Mrs. Reed's having Imelda sterilized) sets up ambiguous echoes of the power relations and the burdens of knowledge that were explored through Atini, her colleagues, and their employers. How much did this employer, Sue, know about what she was doing? Was it because she was ignorant of the reason for the abortion that she could signal so cheerfully to the young woman that she "was not angry" (104)? Or does her smiling, compared with the mother's tight-lipped anger and the grandmother's accusations, suggest that although she treated her maid as a "person" (106), and although she knew what had happened, she had not exerted herself enough to imagine the trauma that mother and daughter were going through?

Told in the first person by the woman who had at fourteen endured an abortion and the realization that the man responsible was her father, the narrative concludes with the adult reflecting on her multiple losses. She measures her realizations that she would never be able to enjoy sex or to have children, and that as a midwife she would be relegated to caring for the infants of other women, against her feelings on the day of the abortion, and she asserts that the innocence she lost that day outweighs all the other wrongs done to her. This might at first seem like self-pity, but in the context of stories such as "The Most Exciting Day of the Week" and "Two Little Girls and a City," the protection of a child's innocence stands as one of a society's foremost obligations. As the former story suggests, "innocence" in Magona's writing does not require an overly protected life, nor does it uphold the idea of children being angelic creatures whose purity can only be sullied by their encounters with the adult world; nor does the concept place a value on childish ignorance. Rather, "innocence" requires a relationship of trust between the child and her community, the people in her unfolding world, so that that world may make sense to the child who is exploring it. This is where things can go so badly wrong, as the latter story indicates.

The gradual or sudden destruction of innocence is also the point of a series of portraits that Magona creates in stories named after their protagonists. In "Lulu," pregnancy is again the trigger; in fact, this story reads as an alternative to what might have been done to remedy the circumstances of the narrator of "Netreg" had incest not been involved (that is, the adoption of her child and a hasty marriage to a much older man), and it also indicates briefly the unhappy alternative to the newly married woman's escape in "Flight." But "Lulu" is not about a physical escape to new circumstances so much as about an inexorable imprisonment that finally becomes the imprisonment of being permanently "retarded" (100). When the child narrator first meets her, Lulu has been sent to relatives in town by her impoverished family in the country, and the demands made on her as she adapts to life in a township are hard: first she must accept that her formal education will not be continued; then, when she is made to earn her keep, she has to learn to comply with the demands of the white women for whom she works as a nanny; and lastly, when she becomes pregnant, she has to accept the loss of her baby and being married off to a much older husband. As the young narrator observes at the time, these customary and sanctioned demands may dim but do not obliterate Lulu's robust beauty. It is the unconscionable consequences of apartheid that destroy her. In their last encounter, some years after they have been compelled to move to different townships, the narrator finds that Lulu is now a mere shadow of herself, permanently damaged by something, no one knows precisely what, that happened when she was taken into police custody during the authorities' heavy-handed attempts to quell a township riot.

Echoes of these polarized options, of being "new-born or . . . crazed" (116), are again present in "MaDlomo," but this time the protagonist is an urban, educated woman who is finally defeated when the customs supporting marriage, to which she has tried loyally to adhere, are turned against her. Narrated by MaDlomo's neighbor, the story is a portrait of a once-beautiful woman whose spirit shines out through poverty, tuberculosis, and her own drinking. Her sense of being partly responsible for her own plight has led MaDlomo to accept the woman that her country-born husband brings home as a second wife, and she tries to reconcile herself to the system of polygamy in which he was raised: "Long into the evening MaDlomo would regale us with accounts of the virtues of being a senior wife" (122). Only when the younger woman refuses to abide by the rules governing cohabitation and seniority does MaDlomo literally turn her face to the wall and die.

In the third of these portraits, "Nosiza," Magona takes up the contrast between the material circumstances and opportunities of black women and those of their white employers that informs "Women at Work," but now the focus is on the children of such women. In the eyes of the girls at her school in the township, Nosiza is "luckier than most of them" (85), for her mother's employer allows her to share the servants' quarters at the back of the house in the white suburb (which was against the law). From there, Nosiza has absorbed much of the education that has been given to her age-mate, Karen, the youngest child in the white family. But for Nosiza this is not a bountiful life, for it means a daily encounter with her "mother's enslavement" (85) and constant reminders that, whatever her abilities and deserts, she will always be positioned as second-best compared to a white child. Rather than prompting her to try harder, the verdict that she feels has been passed on her leads to her suicide, and the question a reader is left with is why Nosiza was compelled to accept such a verdict. In the monologue given to Joyce in "Women at Work," Magona gives a powerful portrait of a young woman who refuses the devalued subject position imposed on her by apartheid (and Atini later reveals that Joyce's exceptional faith in herself has been rewarded with a scholarship to study abroad), but in "Nosiza" her focus is on a young woman who cannot resist. It is not for a reader to pass judgment on either protagonist; rather, we must recognize the care with which Magona uses her fiction to recognize both possibilities and to show how powerfully and insidiously racist thinking can damage selfhood.[8]

Much as we might want to read stories of women who successfully resist oppression, an honest recognition of what goes against the grain is something for which Magona's writing is always to be valued. In "Women at Work," for example, she invites her reader to see that in their way white women are as trapped in a dehumanizing system as are their black employees, and conversely to acknowledge that while a "medem" may be doing the right thing in helping her servant to buy a house in the township, her charity is also putting what feels like a noose around her maid's neck. The balancing of sympathies in the portraits of black and white women is evenhanded, but the relationship can never be symmetrical in the face of the huge material and political disparities of power that shape their circumstances, and Magona is careful to keep her exploration of both sides of a case within the realities of the world she represents.

Magona's critical insights into relatedness within inequality become the structuring principle of "Two Little Girls and a City," in which the narration cuts between matching scenes of black and white children at play, particularly Nina and Phumla. It charts in comparable detail the rapists' killing of the little black girl at the back of some shops and of the little white girl on a beach, and the desperation, followed by grief, of their respective families is carefully balanced. Against the writer's equitably sympathetic handling of horror, the historically significant difference toward which the story is ultimately directed emerges near the end when public memory is in question. The English newspapers, radio, and television, filled with "holy ire" (153), publish the full story of Nina's murder, so that ten years later, when the story is retold, "not a few remember the name . . . [even in] Guguletu" (154). But in that very township where Phumla had lived and was killed, "no one knows the name of the little girl found in a rubbish drum at the back of the butcher's shop. They don't know it today for they never knew it then" (153). The discriminatory distinction made in the realm of public discourse between a murder that is considered newsworthy and therefore a tragedy that will be remembered, and a murder that can be dismissed as a familiar part of everyday brutality, brings us right back to Magona's decision to use writing in order to represent her engagement with identity and community. As she had once tried to convey to her audiences when she made public speeches, all South Africans are human beings together, and their lives should be valued equally. This is momentarily registered in the story when the police realize that Phumla's father has come to the spot where his mutilated child has been found, and they all become "just ordinary men, human beings: no more and no less" (150), but fellow feeling does not spread beyond the murder site. The story of the two little girls' killing was generated by events almost half a century ago, but Magona gives to the narrator, who is remembering both sets of events, an anger that still rises because of the different public recording of and responses to what happened. One murder generated public outrage: "CLEAN UP SEA POINT . . . screamed the headlines for weeks after" (153), whereas after the other the tide of humanity simply closed over Phumla's dead body. In the 1980s, public organs of record such as newspapers followed the ideology of apartheid and habitually denied the commonplace but foundational need to treat people and the places where they live with equal respect. Against this brutality, Magona pits an individual act of remembering. In today's moves towards heterogeneous nationhood, this society's need for a basic recognition of equality remains a matter that will be difficult to recognize, attain, and sustain without a new public ethos, and such an ethos must arise from single individuals such as Magona's narrator, and then from a collectivity of such individuals.

Magona's volume begins each of its sections with stories that use powerful means of moving the reader into their fictionality. This inaugurating "articulated joint" also creates expectations of what will be a fulfilling conclusion to the collection. In other words, it may be preparing readers for the mode that Magona uses in the concluding story, which seems at first to be a documentary presentation rather than a fictionalized recollection of actual events. "Now That the Pass Has Gone" raises a very similar question to the one at the heart of "Two Little Girls": is public memory adequately concerned with the value of each individual life in South Africa? This time, however, Magona comes at her question through public rejoicing rather than a community's or a single person's anger. The story is set in 1987, the year in which the hated Pass Laws were finally repealed, and, like the previous story, it is generated in order to reject the selective memorializing evident in newspaper headlines. In this case they "S-C-R-E-A-M-E-D: THE PASS HAS GONE" (156). Because the reader is not urged to remember that the "I" who narrates both is and is not Magona herself, the narrator seems at first to be the author, who is merely documenting the event. It is not until she allows her mother to explain her refusal to join in the celebrations (because she considers it more important to remember what the Pass Laws had once done to individual people she had known) that it becomes evident that the story will consist of events that are creatively linked by the writer's imagination (rather than the narrator's observations) in order to interrogate the meaning of what is happening. When her mother recounts a passing encounter ten years earlier with a young man, China, who was in Umtata desperately trying to secure another contract to work on the mines so that his young wife and children in the drought-stricken country would not starve, the narrator begins to understand the extent of the control over people that was wielded through the hated *dompas*. Even the young man's right to search for work, and through it his family's chances of survival, were controlled by the pass, and so the mother is right to insist that while the document might be abolished, its effects will continue into the new dispensation and must be understood rather than forgotten. Here, too, echoes from earlier stories come into play, for China's efforts to feed his starving children, for example, are reminiscent of Atini's desperate decision to find work in town in order to feed her starving children.

Two kinds of repetition from one story to the next are at work in stories like "Two Little Girls and a City" and "Now That the Pass Has Gone." One kind works toward a recognition of various human endeavors to survive and to form communities that support and regulate individual selfhood, while the other works toward the importance of remembering, recording, and comparing those efforts and is done largely through Magona's narrators who are engaged in acts of memory. The multifaceted consistency of Magona's approach to social history makes itself felt through this dual connection. Her concern is always with the ways in which a personal story may both support and pull against the (his)story that a community has to create for itself in its local life and as part of a growth toward a larger collectivity such as a nation. In the words of Elaine Young's comment on *Push-Push and Other Stories*, Magona "complicates [the] . . . status [of events] as social signifiers" (105); in the final story, her narrator's mother demonstrates that at every step of the way, the public (meaning primarily readers) has to learn to hear what individual people have to say about their own oppression and about the bonds that unite and those that divide them. In any nation, but especially in one composed of the heterogeneous, "multiple and sometimes competing communities" (Ramphele, 2) to which a democratic South Africa is striving to give space, identifying and hearing the voices of those customarily excluded from public discourse have to be constantly relearned. Sindiwe Magona writes in order that all readers might understand this task and that South Africans might succeed in it.

Notes

1. Magona records that she first wrote her autobiography as one volume and that it was divided into two volumes for separate publication at the suggestion of her publisher, Marie Philip, who also asked Magona if she would write short stories for an interim publication. These materialized as *Living, Loving, and Lying Awake at Night*. The publication of *Forced to Grow* was delayed until after the short stories so that *To My Children's Children* might "have a full life" (Meyer, 221). Magona also lists, as her current projects and hitherto unpublished writing, a play, *Vukani!* (Wake Up), which was performed on World AIDS Day in New York in 2003; a novel provisionally entitled *Anatomy of Infidelity;* and a verse "biography" about her parents (Meyer, 222). She has also published stories for children and has translated into isiXhosa the first volume of her autobiography (1995).

2. After Magona had won a scholarship to Columbia University and had completed an MA, she returned to South Africa. She could not find

suitable employment, and when offered a post at the United Nations, she decided to leave South Africa with her children.

3. Unisa (the University of South Africa) offered degrees by correspondence to people of all races. It supplied material by post, but there was no organized personal contact between students and lecturers or among students. Magona explains that SACHED (the South African Council of Higher Education) helped to fill this vacuum by arranging, on a voluntary basis, support tutorials for those who needed assistance with their part-time studies. It provided books, advances for tuition fees, access to libraries at some universities (municipal libraries were closed to black people), tutors, rooms with tables and electric lights, a kitchen and bathroom, and, above all, "the opportunity to meet, interact with and get to know people who were classified differently from me" (*Forced*, 102).

4. Jacobs quotes Lionnet (8) to argue that Magona inhabits "'a complex syncretic cultural system [that] comes to replace two or more ostensibly simpler cultures'" (Jacobs, 50). My suggestion is that while working with women from other racial groups, Magona was actively exploring the implications of this complex overlaying of cultures and that her questioning was a kind of agency indicating that she no longer simply occupied an allocated subject position.

5. The student protests, which began in Soweto in June 1976 (initially against the use of Afrikaans as the medium of instruction at black schools), spread rapidly to other cities such as Cape Town.

6. Magona says that her first wish was to write plays, but "each time I wanted to write I would see my life before me" and so she decided to write her autobiography and "get this stupid thing out of the way" (Meyer, 226).

7. COSATU (the Congress of South African Trade Unions) was formed at the end of 1985; the implications of the absence of legal recognition for domestic workers until the early 1980s are given by Suzanne Gordon, who was one of the organizers of the Domestic Workers' and Employers' Project.

8. Magona's major fictional undertaking to show how a character might challenge the mental confines of racism comes in her novel *Mother to Mother* (1998). She imagines the self-questioning grief and guilt of a Xhosa mother whose son has been found guilty of the murder of a young white American woman in a Cape Town township, and, working again in the first person, has this mother invite the dead girl's mother to cross from her utterly different context and history and to recognize the long-term factors that might have led to her daughter's death. The stories in *Living, Loving, and Lying Awake at Night* show the beginnings of Magona's interest in creating points of contact between polarized lives, but on the whole they reflect a racially stagnant world.

· Works Cited

Callahan, David. 2004. "Closure, Survival and Realism in *Living, Loving, and Lying Awake at Night:* South Africa, Magona and Realism." In *Sindiwe Magona: The First Decade*, ed. Siphokazi Koyana, 83–104. Pietermaritzburg: University of KwaZulu-Natal Press.

Calvino, Italo. 1997. "Levels of Reality in Literature." In *The Literature Machine*, trans. Patrick Creagh. London: Vintage.

Cock, Jacklyn. 1984. *Maids and Madams: A Study in the Politics of Exploitation*. Johannesburg: Ravan Press.

Daymond, M. J. 1995. "Class in the Discourses of Sindiwe Magona's Autobiography and Fiction." *Journal of Southern African Studies* 21 (4): 561–72.

———. 2002. "Complementary Oral and Written Narrative Conventions: Sindiwe Magona's Autobiography and Short Story Sequence 'Women at Work.'" *Journal of Southern African Studies* 28 (2): 331–45.

Gordon, Suzanne. 1985. *A Talent for Tomorrow: Life Stories of South African Servants*. Johannesburg: Ravan Press.

Gqola, Pumla Dineo. 2004. "Forced to Think: Innovation and Womanist Traditions in Sindiwe Magona's Wor(l)ds." In *Sindiwe Magona: The First Decade*, ed. Siphokazi Koyana, 51–66. Pietermaritzburg: University of KwaZulu-Natal Press.

Innes, Lyn, and Caroline Rooney. 1997. "African Writing and Gender." In *Writing and Africa*, ed. M. H. Msiska and P. Hyland, 193–215. London: Longman, 1997.

Jacobs, J. U. 2000. "Cross-Cultural Translation in South African Autobiographical Writing: The Case of Sindiwe Magona." *Alternation* 7 (1): 41–61.

Lionnet, Françoise. 1995. *Postcolonial Representations: Women, Literature, Identity*. Ithaca: Cornell University Press, 1995.

Magona, Sindiwe. 1990. *To My Children's Children*. Cape Town: David Philip.

———. 1991. *Living, Loving, and Lying Awake at Night*. Cape Town: David Philip.

———. 1992. *Forced to Grow*. Cape Town: David Philip.

———. 1995. *Kubantwana Babantwana Bam*. Cape Town: David Philip.

———. 1996. *Push-Push and Other Stories*. Cape Town: David Philip.

———. 1998. *Mother to Mother*. Cape Town: David Philip.

Meyer, Stephan. 1999. "Interview with Sindiwe Magona." *Current Writing* 11 (1): 79–90.

———. 2006. "We Would Write Very Dull Books if We Just Wrote about Ourselves: Interview with Sindiwe Magona." In *Selves in Question:*

Interviews on South African Auto/biography, ed. Judith Lutge Coullie, Stephan Meyer, Thengani H. Ngwenya, and Thomas Olver, 219–30. Honolulu: University of Hawai'i Press.

Ramphele, Mamphela. 2001. "Citizenship Challenges for South Africa's Young Democracy." *Daedalus* 130 (1): 1–17.

Spivak, Gayatri Chakravorty. 1994. "Can the Subaltern Speak?" In *Colonial Discourse and Post-colonial Theory: A Reader*, ed. Patrick Williams and Laura Chrisman, 66–111. New York: Columbia University Press.

Vera, Yvonne. 1999. Preface to *Opening Spaces: An Anthology of Contemporary African Women's Writing*. Oxford: Heinemann; Harare: Baobab Books.

Young, Elaine. 2004. "Identity and Community: Sindiwe Magona's *Push-Push and Other Stories*." In *Sindiwe Magona: The First Decade*, ed. Siphokazi Koyana, 105–26. Pietermaritzburg: University of KwaZulu-Natal Press.

12

Every Choice Is a Renunciation

Cultural Landmarks in
Ken Bugul's *Riwan ou le chemin de sable*

Aissata Sidikou

> Do not listen anymore to other people's idle gossip. We must
> tell our own stories to ourselves, know them, and evaluate
> them. . . . Let's not let others analyze us and decide for us
> anymore. . . . Let's discover ourselves on our own.
>
> —Ken Bugul

The Senegalese Ken Bugul is now established as one of the most
prominent francophone female writers. She has written several novels:
Le Baobab fou (1983), translated as *The Abandoned Baobab* (1984);
Cendres et braises (1994); and *Riwan ou le chemin de sable* (1999), which
won the Grand Prix littéraire de l'ADFL and was chosen as one of
the one hundred best books from Africa in the twentieth century.
These three books constitute an autobiographical trilogy of Bugul
navigating between Africa and Europe in search of an image and a
space of her own. The search continues in *La Folie et la mort* (2000),
De l'autre côté du regard (2003), and *Rue Felix-Faure* (2004).

Born Mariètou M'Baye, the novelist adopted the pseudonym
Ken Bugul, which in Wolof means "no one wants" or "no one

loves," concealing her name and her female identity to avoid possible negative criticism, especially when she writes about issues and behaviors that are still taboo in some African societies. Though the author does not say that she adopted the pseudonym in keeping with African tradition, she indeed explains in an interview with Bernard Magnier (1985) that the Wolof give this name in order to protect children of women who keep having stillborn babies. The practice of name concealing occurs in many West African societies. Parents can conceal a child's name for protection against the evil eye or any harm that may possibly befall a child during its development. Oftentimes, individuals choose to hide their true names to protect themselves from enemies or from the potent medicine of rivals. Bugul's decision to use a pseudonym thus speaks volumes about the way the author chooses to position her self in literary space.

In her first novel, the autobiographical *Abandoned Baobab*, Bugul exposes the trials and tribulations of a young girl faced with Western values embedded in the colonial system of education. As Nicole E. Meyer suggests, the girl "suffers a traumatic separation from her mother" (191); her childhood dreams go unfulfilled because of the absence of the mother, emphasizing the lack of those African standards that are supposed to give her direction throughout her life. Traumatized by the mother's abandonment, she leaves Senegal as an adolescent to attend a professional school in Brussels, a place that later becomes the site of her descent into hell as she is confronted with racism, drugs, sexual exploitation, and an identity crisis. Her alienation and yearning to belong unfold with intensity and despair. She then returns to her village to find the baobab, symbol of her cultural roots, dead.

This yearning continues in the next novel, *Cendres et braises*, also autobiographical, where the central character returns to Africa to connect to "the" mother, not yet "her" mother, because she has just discovered her: "Elle était la Mère, et maintenant, presque trente après, je la découvrais" (She was the Mother, and now almost thirty years later, I was discovering her; 13). The novel illustrates a return to the mother, to the roots, to the natal environment, and to the potential of facing psychological trauma and cultural issues. But *Cendres et braises* also highlights the central character's difficulty in adjusting to African life; as one cannot be what one cannot see, she cannot find herself or affirm herself. She meets a French businessman named Y, falls for him, and returns to France with him as his mistress, reliving her dream of the fashionable, luxurious life of the exotic African woman. Unfortunately, she is an object and a possession in the eyes of the Frenchman, who subjects her to humiliations, sexual exploitation, and all sorts of physical abuse.

Bugul finally situates her central character in Senegal in *Riwan ou le chemin de sable*. The work is the compelling story of her physical and spiritual return from Europe to Senegal. In her constant search for self and identity, she becomes the twenty-eighth wife of a Serigne, an old, revered religious leader. She finds acceptance and sexual and spiritual gratification in her new life. Being the Serigne's wife ensures her privilege, integrating her in her society, where she finds her identity and is finally able to reconcile with her past and her mother. During her experience at the Serigne's and in the company of his other wives, she finally learns to appreciate what it is to be a woman and to enjoy that status. The text also gracefully interweaves stories of women from different backgrounds, as the author stylishly presents female conditions. *Riwan* is not only a text on finding oneself; it is first the story of a final return to the source that leads to rehabilitation and self-assertion. It is a renunciation of everything that the woman used to be. Most of all, it is a cultural, political, and sociological text that provides information on critical issues that pertain to the status of women in monogamous and polygamous relationships in West African societies.

This chapter will examine how *Riwan*, by tapping cultural signs in history and sexuality, brings these signs to the center and positions Africa in the debate on identity and sexuality. How do the female protagonists, by embracing or rejecting their cultural landmarks, renegotiate their status in their environments? What do women represent in the narrator's assessment of the issues raised, and what roles do they play in her reconnection to self? What voice does the narrator speak with, and to whom is she speaking?

The privileged expression of African women's art is verbal. This is true particularly of precolonial societies, where talented women excelled in composing and singing songs ranging from praise-songs, defaming songs, and poems to lullabies and proverbs. In many West African societies, *griottes*, for example, are oral historians who inherit verbal mastery, *la parole*, from their parents, using it to entertain their communities as educators and critics. Like *griots*, they also recite complicated genealogies and epics, learned over many years from the *jesere dunka* or the master *griots*.

This verbal art serves many purposes. It creates and endorses ways of life that firmly unite a community in its aspirations, hopes, and endeavors. Functioning as a literary, political, cultural, and philosophical reference, it informs people of their strengths and weaknesses, their myths, legends, and beliefs, as guides for the future. The verbal art reinforces whatever ties they share and positions them in their society as well as the world. Values, concepts, and restrictions are exposed in this form of literature, which serves as the ultimate source and foundation for a continuing education for children, adults, and the community. Whether practiced by women or men, verbal art has greatly influenced the written literatures of Africa as a source of inspiration in the constant search for individual or communal identity. This dynamic was destabilized when French colonialism imposed itself on many societies.

On the African continent, European colonialism was a planned economic, political, and cultural enterprise that aimed at conquering territories and reducing their people to physical and mental subordination. This foreign system turned communities into abstractions with a new set of foreign values that were incompatible with basic African values. The system upturned the establishment, and this is most evident in education. By imposing insidious and less obvious aspects of the French educational system on African children, the colonial administration consciously designed a structure that would later prove painful to many African intellectuals who blame their cultural alienation on an education that had no room for inserting their African heritage.

With the imposition of European education came the burden of discrimination and the broadening of the patriarchal system. Women who formerly played a privileged role in education in their societies were now barred from French instruction simply because of their gender. Men were encouraged to attend the new schools because the urgent need for the new power to conquer and colonize called for French-educated Africans who would help in the domination and exploitation of their communities. Men thus became the *porte-parole* of the foreign social, political, and economic system, enjoying additional power with their new status. Besides becoming clerks, nurses, translators, teachers, and soldiers, they strengthened the French system, which excluded women. In the resulting confining space, the alienated women struggled to understand their position and status. It was only in the early eighties that a new literature by women emerged from francophone Africa to give the younger generation of women an opportunity to raise their voices and question the establishment without fear of ostracism. Thus, precolonial, colonial, and present experiences shaped the writings of most of the women writers who were products of French colonialism. It is against this background that Ken Bugul exposes her social, historical, and political positions in her connections to Senegalese society, Africa, Europe, and the world.

In an interview with Claire Bourget and Irene Assiba d'Almeida, Ken Bugul claims that her main objective is "d'écrire quelque chose que j'avais vécu" (to write something I had experienced); not surprisingly, in most of her novels she speaks about women's issues from the perspectives of children, adolescents, and women. She addresses not only Africans but also those who have distorted ideas about Africa and its people. In *Riwan*, one gets a unique perspective on the type of relationship the central character intends to have with herself, men, and especially women. Her marriage to the Serigne grants her a cultural, traditional, and spiritual identity through which she justifies her existence and enjoys her sexuality.

She chooses to marry the Serigne for what he represents and provides. Marrying him means embracing her origins: "Years had gone by and I had left the village for the big foreign educational centers. But I knew that even though I was absent, people were taking care of things for me. Those who stayed in the village carried on the role of those who had left for different reasons, hoping the latter would one day come back to take their place and pay their debts. *And* I had left because I thought that I did not want to live like the others, I thought I could not" (115; all translations are mine). Naively believing in the myth of Western education contributes to separating one from the group, the community, but most of all one's language. As a young woman, the narrator is convinced that she is different from the "others," those who stayed home and who probably did not experience the circumstances that prompted her to leave home for a "better" world, a "civilized" life and education. Though she was gone, she still claims a place in her community, as evident in the use of the conjunction "et" in the French version of the text, suggesting integration rather than intentional separation.

The narrator's French education fixed her as an object in time and space, restraining her because it failed to give her the right tools for self-definition. In trying to define herself, she finds out that she is unwittingly part of a system that maintains predetermined and contradictory representations that she must fight. Back home and with the assistance of the Serigne and the community of women, she can finally make the choice to be an African woman with cultural landmarks. Her choice exposes her to sounds, personal images, smells, and visions that offer comforts unattainable for her in foreign lands.

The outcome is not one unique tradition and worldview, but an intersection of experiences. For her identity choice to be effective, the narrator has to reject her European identity, which objectifies and demeans her. After this step, there can be a renewal with the rehabilitation of the self in the integrated space. This completes the transformation that unites the self, ensuring self-acceptance. Finding cultural landmarks means applying unprecedented measures to an unprecedented situation. It also means justifying her marriage with the polygynous Serigne, even though such a decision (Western-educated women marrying non-Western-educated, polygynous men) does not seem widespread in Africa.

Riwan is indeed a rebuilding of a fragmented soul. Instead of the search taking place in Europe, as in the earlier novels (*The Abandoned Baobab* and *Cendres et braises*), this time the narrator is on a quest to belong to an African and a female space, a language, and a higher state of mind. Faced with many choices, she knows what she wants for herself and from her society, realizing that choice is not surrender but a formation. Her choices are made easier because she is among those she can identify with, those who are close to her thoughts and spiritual specificities. These are the women, her co-wives, in whom she sees the mother who abandoned her years before. Her choices help her bond with the mother, finally acknowledging her as mother, and, indirectly and symbolically as the core of the cultural landmarks and language she lacked. Her recognition of her cultural landmarks is a condition for reconnection. One may say that marrying the Serigne and becoming his twenty-eighth wife is a drastic way of embracing her culture. However, reconnection takes place uncompromisingly to ensure that she rejects her fragmented selves.

The narrator is finally in touch with herself, her community, and, more importantly, her mother, whom she finally refers to as "my mother." This *prise de conscience* comes after she is able to immerse herself in her culture through her marriage, which grants her the possibility of being able to see and to sense. Through recognition and reconnection, she gains power, and she is in harmony with her environment, burying the apprehension, pain, and loss she suffered. Her power of perception is apparent on almost every page. It appears in words such as "aperçut" (saw), "apercevoir" (to see), "regarder" (to look), "fixer son regard" (to gaze at), "observait" (observed), "voyait" (saw), "regardant" (seeing), "sembla avoir remarqué" (seemed to notice). Coupled with images of seeing are others associated with various sensations of touch: "la main," "les mains" (the hand, hands) and colors, "bleu" (blue), "jaune" (yellow), "rose" (pink), "vert" (green), "blanc" (white), and "rouge" (red). These infuse life into the experience of the narrator, clothing her with a new, explosive self. The narrative voice thus exposes a Senegalese set of values as cultural landmarks.

The sexual act is cultural. Her sexual encounter with the Serigne is an act of "spiritual resourcing" that galvanizes her; importantly, at this crucial moment, she refers to her mother for the second time as "ma mère" (my mother) (167) instead of "la mère" (the mother). By caring for people and humanity, the Serigne seems to have the nurturing qualities of a mother. Following the sexual experience, the narrator is able to recognize signs, links, and relations. His presence and his love reveal her to herself, enabling her to reattach herself to humanity. The Serigne and the mother are therefore metaphors of healing, revival, and integration. "Thus, the Serigne had offered and given me the possibility to reconcile with myself, my environment, with my origins, my roots, my world without which I could never survive. I had escaped the death of my own self, this self that did not belong to me alone. This self that also belonged to my kind, to my race, my people, my village and to my continent" (167–68). It is because of the importance of this cultural connection and because "the self does not belong to her alone" that the narrator introduces the story of the marriage of her friend Nabou, another choice presented in *Riwan*.

Nabou Samb's marriage exposes not only another choice, but also a cultural dynamic within a sociological framework. Its sensational ceremony exposes a material and social security and an economic dynamic that certain women need and expect in a marriage. Nabou seems to prefer the marital status, as she made a choice to pursue marriage rather than continue her studies (118). Her marriage is a discursive way of exposing knowledge of the primordial culture in which one evolves and to which one belongs or would like to belong. The story establishes cultural specificity and recognition that one is moving toward the right pole. The narrator's identity is formed not only by what she sees, but also by what she knows. By witnessing Nabou's wedding, she now knows details of how marriage is celebrated in her society, what it means, and how it affects people. She has the capacity to see, and she realizes that her people see her. Perception here is no longer "the masculinist gaze that disavowed her presence" (190), or even the imperialistic gaze that reduces her into a body to be tamed and scripted on or an exotic body to be displayed. In *The Abandoned Baobab* and *Cendres et braises*, her body was exposed to the gaze of men who held material power and could control and desecrate it. In *Riwan*, she finally discovers her self by seeing around her and through others.

Another interesting character is Sokhna Rama, who is given to the Serigne by her parents at a tender age, as a testimony of their faith in and commitment to him. Rama is the victim of the law of "accepter, subir, obéir" (to accept, to be subjected to, to obey; 152), which is also the philosophy behind the *Ndigueul*, or "un abandon total de son soi" (total abandonment of oneself; 31). As a young girl under parental control, she is expected to accept her parents' choice of a husband without protesting. Her lack of commitment to her parents' religion pushes her to commit the sacrilege of betraying the Serigne when she has a sexual encounter with her village beau. All she really has in mind throughout her stay in the Serigne's village is Mbos, a place of sensual pleasure (86), where she first felt some sort of sexual curiosity.

Unlike the narrator, who can now choose to act, Rama has no choice but to accept the Serigne with her father's coercion (51). Unable to control her desires like the other women, she cheats on the Serigne (134–35). Since she is not with the Serigne through the orders of the Ndigueul, she gives the Serigne some pleasure because she also likes taking hers. Predictably, she never sees the Serigne as a spiritual being or an ideology as most people do; instead, she sees him as a man from whom she can get her sexual enjoyment. "Rama assumed her role and enjoyed it not because she wanted to enter Paradise, but for pleasure. She liked giving pleasure to the Serigne because she felt good by doing it" (134). Because she is young, vivacious, and sexually inexperienced, Rama cannot control her sexuality like the other women. This leads her to stray away from the community and lose her soul because she does not know how to channel her eros. The author seems to imply that Rama does not understand that in this religious-oriented environment, the realm of the mind is directly connected to that of the body. Part and parcel of the concept of the Ndigueul is total surrender to the Serigne who is supposed to represent the principle of oneness and integration; he is the one who keeps people together, and he is the respected source of energy who offers all to everyone, women and men. Rama's decision to move away from the space constructed by

the Serigne and her rebellion against authority break the myth about
the Serigne and protest a life that is not sexually fulfilling for her. Her
action casts doubt over the Ndigueul and the Serigne who represents
it. Her transgression stands as a twist of reality, as her community
sees it. By affirming her individuality and subjectivity in the face of
culture and history, Rama's character offers a new vision for women
and a new discourse that must be considered by men of all ages. Unfortunately, her tragic death can be read as a transfigured harmony.

Rama's being chained to her youth and sexual desires is reminiscent
of the experience of the central character in *The Abandoned Baobab*,
who suffers from jealousy and sexual carelessness. As an inexperienced
young girl, Rama is unfortunate not to enjoy the "first night" and
the material acquisitions granted by marriage; that is why she envies
Nabou: "Ah! Rama! Combien de fois elle avait rêvé de faire un mariage
comme celui de Nabou Samb!" (Ah! Rama! How many times had she
dreamt of a marriage like that of Nabou Samb! 85).

Because the Serigne takes another young wife and no longer sexually fulfills Rama's desires, she becomes anxious to find a man who can
gratify her. Unlike the other wives, she is motivated by sexual pleasure
instead of spiritual inspiration (135), necessitating her tragic end. Unlike the narrator and Nabou, who "succeed" in marriage, Rama fails
because she does not embrace the Ndigueul. Her story continues to
be told orally, to memorialize the foremothers who must be inscribed
in history, but also to warn young girls. Weaving her story into the
written text recreates her voice and memory and contextualizes her
in a myth worthy of female knowledge.

Like Rama, Riwan, the title character, is in chains (though his,
unlike Rama's, are real), and it is worth mentioning that he looks
strikingly like the narrator when he is brought to the Serigne (25).
Although not compelling as a character, he plays a tremendous role in
rendering the spiritual power of the Serigne. Just as he has healed the
narrator, the Serigne is the only one who is able to heal Riwan after
he is brought in chains like a violent madman. As a spiritual guide, the
Serigne shows his power and connection to Riwan, who has attained
the spiritual apex. In the interview with Bourget and d'Almeida,
Ken Bugul suggests that "[l]e personnage de Riwan est inspiré du
Ndigueul. . . . Riwan est tellement imprégné du Ndigueul qu'il ne
se sent plus homme, ni femme, ni rien du tout. Il s'oublie" (Riwan's
character is inspired from the Ndigueul. . . . Riwan is so embodied by
the Ndigueul that he no longer feels himself as a man, or a woman.

He forgets himself; 357). This model of Riwan fits the narrator's ideal of genderless and selfless individuals. She thus elaborates a criticism of existing regulations and proposes utopian elements in order to further this historic metamorphosis of Riwan. The fact that Riwan is a man reveals that both woman and man can suffer disorder but in different ways. In the Mourid faith, man gets his salvation through the Serigne, while woman gets hers through her husband;[1] hence, Riwan's cure comes from the Serigne.

Interestingly, this Serigne is an educated and refined intellectual who treats people with humanity and gives them hope. "The Serigne was particularly considerate of children and the misfits . . . all those abandoned were his friends. Like a mother, he is a nurturer" (140). He is not seen as flesh, but rather as one who helps the narrator assert her freedom and transcend her insecurities. Transcendental, he brings out the difference between the pure and impure, order and disorder. As a spiritual force, he is the only one capable of healing and exorcising Riwan, who is fired up by a madness that comes from the gods.

The narrator seeks the Serigne's closeness to a higher being (190): "At the Serigne's, there were no jokes about the husband as it was supposed to be in general. The Serigne was not a simple husband. There was another connection, another relationship essentially based on the Ndigueul, and that relationship was more important" (129). The Serigne symbolizes the Ndigueul way of life. Indeed, he himself is a way to life, and a way to the self. He functions as the superhuman force that must bring the lost woman back to her senses, hence the sensual and radical language of the novel. By bringing the narrator back to her senses, he grants her an identity, functioning as the link between her and the other women.

As the narrator states, the Serigne is "un repère spirituel et intellectuel mais pas comme un être de chair et de sang" (a spiritual and intellectual landmark but not like a being of flesh and blood; 151). He provides the narrator with the ability to define herself, thereby preventing her from sinking into the complications of a destructive history. If she can escape that history, her past, she will have a future. Finally, as his wife, she attains a higher state of mind, being venerated, through him, by her people and rehabilitated by the other women in the compound:

> Everybody was trying to please me: to get the favors of the Serigne, because through me the Serigne is being honored. The spouse who is intellectually so close to the Serigne was

herself almost like a Serigne. All of a sudden, I found myself being a grande dame in this village where I had been rejected, despised. The Serigne had allowed me to regain my place, this place that no one could hold, this empty place amidst my own, in the center of my existence. It was also important for my mother. This rehabilitation, my rehabilitation, was also hers. She had secretly suffered from what I represented, from what the sand path had buried, like the gossipings, the "sous-entendus" and the misunderstandings. In a way I was more than rehabilitated; I was accepted. I was gaining weight; I was becoming more attractive. (168)

From the individual presentation of women, the author moves to a community of women. Apart from the narrator, Nabou Samb, Rama, and the mother, other women carry weight in *Riwan*. The women are faces at first (26), but as the novel progresses, the faces and hands become whole. The narrator seems surprised to see so many faces at first, but later we get to know them by name, profession, age, class, history, pains and sorrows, ambitions, jealousies, and rivalries. Although the women are mostly the Serigne's wives, they appear to be self-determined and economically independent, and more importantly, they do not take up their husband's personality. Instead, they negotiate power in a female environment. Though this environment seems closed, they have a moral and mental responsibility toward themselves and others. The narrator seeks to navigate this space as well, even though the Serigne provides her with spiritual bliss.

> More and more I needed to be with them. I felt good around them. I was realizing that I could speak differently, laugh differently, be different, all natural. Without prejudice. They saw me as I was, and did not expect anything from me. With them, I had felt an internal rehabilitation, a possibility of exorcising alienation. For a while I no longer knew how to speak, be and laugh. . . . I had always loved the company of women, not always as persons of the same sex, but distancing myself, with a different gaze. I saw them as different beings while in their company, and they, most of the times, gave me weird sensations and feelings. (33)

The narrator likes the women because she finds her mother in them; she is one of them. In fact, through the women, she is searching for a history that goes to the memory of women. They nurture her and she reciprocates. By doing so, they maintain history and its transmission. Now that she is back from Europe for good, she has absorbed the feeling of belonging to a community and speaking the language of that community. She has finally come to terms with her alienation, and she is now distanced from the delusional fragmentation and anguish she experienced in Europe. Her new sense of accomplishment will lead to the simple joy of human relationship. She adheres to this important poetic and spiritual moment, realized through a female presence and space, relishing the voices, gossip, secrets, memories, and connections. It is this aspect of bonding that Rama had not envisioned.

Even though the Serigne lives few steps away in his own dwelling, in their space (the women live in their own closed quarters) the women freely embrace and assume their sexuality and the narrator enjoys being part of it. Artisans of their fate, the women lead their own lives and make their own choices in a space that allows them to speak the common language of sexuality. Being with the women gives her a sense of self and complicity that she did not have previously with her mother, with Africa. This reconnection through the hands of women, the language of women, the body of women, the space of women, and the vision of women is healthy: "I enjoyed this women's space so much and I, more and more, want to stay with them. They taught me secrets on serenity through their reactions when confronted to the day-to-day events that happen around them. Sharing one part of my life with these women was worth one thousand yoga lessons or transcendental meditation" (178). However, this idealized space is not always positive and rewarding. To avoid generalizations and the romanticizing of this space, the author introduces the example of a character, Sokhna War, whose polygamous experience is unsuccessful (178). If the narrator could identify herself with the women, War is forced by her co-wives to live marginally as a stranger because of the violence and the petty naggings that sometimes stem from jealousy and irresponsibility in polygamous situations. The polygamous space in which Sokhna War evolves is mired in debasement and scorn. It is nothing like the one in which a woman can enjoy the company and performance of other women.

The narrator, who considers herself "evoluée" and "civilisée" (emancipated and civilized) because she had attended French schools, is stunned to realize that co-wives can live together harmoniously, in an environment that promotes "une apparente sérénité" (a seeming serenity), thus contradicting earlier discourses that shaped her thinking:

How could eight, twelve women share the same room and the same man?

I, who belong to the generation of those who went to the Others' school, could not understand nor admit this. With all the men I had been with, jealousy, acknowledged or concealed, had gnawed at me to the bone, and it was more familiar to me than any other feeling.

How could these women, most of them beautiful and young, live in the same compound? Yet, I was also born in a compound shared by two women. I was taught there to dream of a different compound, a compound where I would be alone. (36)

This passage clearly gives the narration a dynamic configuration. The author exposes two antithetical spaces that determine women's behavior. The space with several women promotes consciousness, return, memories, and the future, whereas the other space underscores abstraction and delusion. The latter space misleads her into becoming a "not-I," an egocentric separated from her community by a system that neglects or misrepresents her truth: "How I regretted to have wanted to be something else, a quasi unreal person, absent from her origins, to have been led astray, influenced, and deceived, to have played the emancipated woman, so-called modern, to have wanted to believe in it, to have missed things, to have screwed a life, maybe. Because I was told to reject what I was, when I could have remained myself and still be open to modernity" (111). The legend, the story, and the many cultural landmarks, especially the narrator's choices and Nabou's marriage, are subversive texts of resistance against what the narrator sees as European and "modern African" women's myopic view of what African discourses must be. These texts underscore the recounting of history, the narrator's story, the history of her foremothers, which are important for reconnection and for future generations. The historical trajectory unfolds in the following sentence: "C'était cela la tradition de ma mère, de la mère de ma mère" (That was the tradition of my mother, of the mother of my mother; 108). The narrator sees the polygynous environment that keeps the women from the outside world as a sociopolitical space where they insist on rising to the occasion by bonding. She finally discovers that polygyny is not just about sex, or being dependent on the husband; polygyny is a system where man is not invoked, as woman becomes the center: "I very much enjoyed the moments I spent with them. We exchanged ideas and recipes, we discussed politics, oh yes, politics, we discussed life cost, youth education, the good to be done and the bad to be avoided" (176). These women are not disturbed in their psyches like the so-called modern women of the city whom both the narrator and the author criticize. Here the narrator enjoys the openness, friendship, and effectiveness of the group. Consequently, they feel good in their bodies and minds, promoting rather than demeaning their interactions with one another. They live the truth that they, women, are lovable and valuable. The narrator discovers the power of friendship between women who share the same culture and roots. She describes her emotions as she connects with them, and she describes how the women identify at many levels with their interests, values, and aspirations. She learns what it is to be a woman and a Senegalese. The collaboration between women and the power they get from one another is historically important, and by discussing several women from different backgrounds, the author encourages a feminine culture.

Deep camaraderie reinforces the yearning for that space of consciousness, emphasizing the dynamic of collaboration that unites the women, with every individual accomplishing her duty. The group of women reflects an affective and intense unity where the "we" is felt like a reality, symbolizing one's discovery through interaction with the other. By being with the other women, the narrator discovers an internal reality transcendentally imposed by the everyday action of the group; this constitutes the core philosophy of *Riwan*. Women, as individuals or groups, participate in strengthening their camaraderie by each bringing the knowledge that will help create new roles or reflect what they want themselves to be.

To promote harmony in the group of women and in the mind of each woman, Bousso Niang,[2] another female character in *Riwan*, mimics sexual acts through dance. She shows sensuality and ease in her sexuality:

> Being neither the Serigne's daughter, nor his wife, Bousso Niang was liberated from belonging to a family structure that is codified by attitudes and rigid and determined behaviors. Bousso Niang could allow herself to laugh hard, swing her hips, and push up her firm and already high breasts with a willful and accentuated arching of her back. Bousso Niang loved to sing and dance ... she would dance erotic dances that would make them [the women] utter fake offensive exclama-

tions and wiggle with excitement. Bousso Niang would press her hands on her full thighs, and her wrap-around pushed up all the way to her groin, she would throw her butt back and imitate the rotating movements of a fan. Thus leaning back, she would turn her head to watch herself, and enjoy the spectacle of her own body in fury. She would finish her dance with a spasm that imitated the sexual act and would walk away as if nothing ever happened. Bousso Niang was a liberated woman. This was not the case for the Serigne's wives. (88)

In a therapeutic move, the group relishes Bousso's irresistible force and language, which makes them vibrate against their will. Because Bousso Niang is not bound by the Ndigueul, or dependent on anybody, she is her own free agent with the creative uses of her body as language. Bousso Niang is "liberated" as she has sexual superiority over the Serigne's women who must observe a moral status because of their dedication to their holy husband and the Ndigueul. She is vital to their being, as sex is vital and healing to the human. Her sexual freedom speaks to the women who seldom engage in sexual activity with the Serigne; they can take their sexual pleasure in the actions of Bousso Niang. Her performance is neither pornographic nor vulgar, but a poetic discourse on the body that taunts and subverts the traditional order. Bousso Niang functions as a "sexual counselor," a role that can be found in many societies in West Africa. Society automatically grants permission to individuals such as Bousso to play a liberating role. She performs and entertains, subversively taunting the establishment in order to remind it of its hypocrisy as far as sexuality is concerned; however, there is the possibility that the Serigne is not aware of what is going on on the other side of his fence.

Throughout *Riwan* there is an invention of spaces of identity through cultural landmarks. These are essential, for the identity of the "modern" woman must spring from the source—the mother. Identity is deeply rooted in the mother tongue, through which one is fully realized. The language of the colonizer is only an accident of history, and as such, it serves the individual in the march toward "modernity" by grafting itself to the mother's language.

Taking the sand path brings the protagonist back to her childhood house, to the mother, and experience. Remarkably, when the Serigne takes another woman, the protagonist returns to her mother's, but still maintains her relationship with the Serigne and his wives: "Under the pretence of having something to do at home, I went back to my mother's, promising to return after a while" (189). Obviously, her mother's is a place of refuge. As she eats the sand on the path between her mother's house and the Serigne's, she further internalizes her culture, which coincides with a big sexual appetite. "The sand path that passed in front of our house and led to the Serigne's was always swept, sifted, and from time to time, sitting in front of our gate, I had many times had the need of eating some and I did. This sand would water my mouth and when I would swallow it, I would experience a strange sensation. This had coincided with a period when my libido was so to say wildly oscillating" (192–93). Those moments when she would eat the sand symbolize sexual awakening and her growth into a different woman. The path is also symbolic of her connection to her mother and her spiritual consciousness. Though saddened by the death of the Serigne, she is now a mistress of her self, and she grasps the full meaning of being an independent individual who is in control of her body and self. She no longer fears the future as she did in *The Abandoned Baobab* and *Cendres et braises*. She does not feel abandoned anymore, because she is fulfilled: she has become a woman who is self-confident, independent, and integrated in her society.

Riwan is structured around many issues that cannot be tackled in a few pages. One main aspect of this text is its stylistic features, which conform to basic conventions of oral literature. The text starts with a narration in the circular form of a folktale; the story itself both starts and ends on a Monday. This circular form symbolizes the narrator's quest, which restores sense to the "desacralized" body. With many repetitions, images, and metaphors, the text becomes more intense toward the end of the story, as the storyteller knows that she has the full attention of her audience. Later in the narration, the audience realizes that the novel is the author's interpretation of the story surrounding Rama and the Serigne because "il était impossible de savoir d'où avait surgi la parole" (it was impossible to know where the word had sprung from; 9). The novel opens with a dedication, which ends with: "à qui je raconte ceci aujourd'hui." (to whom I am telling this today), confirming the narrator's advice to "[tell] our own stories."

Not only does the novel unfold from the perspective of a storyteller, but the original story is appropriated in order to inform, privileging what the foremothers knew and how they conveyed it to posterity. Storytelling brings the women together, and it also insinuates that one can ask oneself what one can know that is essential and imperative for growth. Telling the story is not adequate, but questioning the content of the story is more engaging, and that is the narrator's preoccupation throughout this novel.

The story in *Riwan* observes no disciplinary boundaries; it encompasses history, sexuality, and politics. It also carries individual messages that go beyond polygamy and exploitation. It becomes sacred because of its language and because it involves a sacred figure, the Serigne, the spiritual leader. It also becomes a history to learn from, as the narrator learns from her mother, and her mother from her mother's mother, suggesting a women's history. The sacredness and strength of the text reside not in the language of the written text, French, or in its Western form, the novel, but in a *témoignage* that celebrates historical women such as the brave Nigerian newscaster Christina Anyanwu (73, 209); spiritual leaders such as Ahmadou Bamba Mbacké, who fought French colonialism; a politician and writer such as Ken Saro Wiwa (64); and legendary strike leader Ibrahima Sarr (113). Its strength lies also in its literary choices, which are poetic and contradictory, permitting an aggressive form of the text that allows the insertion of different texts. Telling the story with varied tropes moves the reader and makes her or him feel worth talking to, and the form of the tale and the speech marks orality, which is the popular register. The context of the tale itself is to bring people together because one narrates it to a live audience, thus bringing unity and togetherness.

Realizing how identities have been mired in problems and theorized, Bugul attempts to think through and evaluate ways in which women can be heard and hear themselves across borders and history. Beyond the style of the oral text, there are numerous mentions of different genres of female oral texts such as the "xarxar" (118), praise-poems (75), genealogies (101), and poems. By mixing the different genres and different languages such as Wolof, Arabic, Spanish, and English, the writer creates a new genre of intertextuality and a new language.

Ken Bugul's novels thus emerge from the oral tradition, which continues to provide the literary and cultural inspiration of many authors. At the same time, she mimics the novel, the foreign form that imposed itself on francophone texts through schooling and cultural diffusion. However, it is the oral form that provides *Riwan* with the signs that the narrator can now recognize, as well as the rich and colorful imagery and repetitions used to lift up the passions embedded in the subject.

Bugul's desire is to make the reader realize, with intensity and a passionate longing, the accuracy and importance of her cultural landmarks through the intertextuality of texts (oral and written) and the accumulation of repetitive details. By inserting the oral text in the novel, the narrator exposes cultural novelty and, at the same time, she avoids absolutisms and determinisms and recognizes herself as an African who has specific cultural landmarks. Since these have an intrinsic meaning, she and the rest of her community must connect to them. The frequent digressions in the narrative are connected with the orality of the legend of the tragic death of Rama and the vagaries of memory: "Il était impossible de savoir d'où avait surgi la parole" (9). These digressions can also be associated with her European education, which took her away from her African culture and environment.

Orality is also used for aesthetic reasons to suppress or discredit European cultural ethnocentrism. Since the French language does not convey the exact meaning or the vividness of what the author wants to say, she chooses different means, like the oral tradition and different languages. Doing so beautifies the European form and language, adding sophistication and flavor to the language and at the same time presenting a text that is neither French nor African, but a combination of both, thereby giving it a multiple identity.

The oral perspective demonstrates a need for contact with the mother, one's mother tongue, and cultural landmarks. By reviving her language as Ahmadou Kourouma did in *Suns of Independence*, Ken Bugul instates a body of a set of inscriptions that defines oneself. Understanding these inscriptions, then, helps in appreciating the self as an individual in harmony with the self and her community. In recognizing the conventional ways, she is able to debunk them as they hide certain realities that the narrator was unable to see before. In the end, the style of the text points to the author's disposition to embrace cultural phenomena with intersecting influences on the character.

Books play a role in *Riwan* ("Do not forget African authors, hold on, read *Le Cavalier et son ombre*"; 183) because education must be valued in order to know oneself.[3] The narrator walks around with a book without knowing why, but she seems to send a message that people must discover the content of books because they inform; she carries it because she inherited Western knowledge and because it provides information on women. By carrying it, she carries women and their history with her, and that is why she feels the need to contribute to that history and knowledge from an African woman's perspective. By writing the book, the author emphasizes the seriousness of the condition of women—"ce sont les problèmes de la femme posés par d'autres femmes" (those are a woman's problems as told by other women; 16)—and the importance for her to raise her voice, adding to the multitude of voices. The Serigne even encourages her to write when he buys her a typewriter (212).

Both the narrator and the Serigne are intellectuals. They are aware of what is going on in their locality and around the world. Most of the information given on the cultural background, such as marriages, ceremonies, deaths, sensuality, and spirituality, are part of the education she received. Books also mark the difference between the westernized and the unwesternized; there lies the rub.

To discuss Ken Bugul is to discuss tropes that characterize her personal life; her struggle with cultural differences, constructions, and translations as a woman; and, most of all, her outlook on "postcolonial" Africa, which finds itself entangled in issues of historicity, sexuality, and political and economic matters. Her novels circle around the question of denial and reconnection. Like the Cameroonian Calixthe Beyala, Bugul is not placid toward issues of sexuality that seem taboo in many African societies even though they greatly affect African women. Her generation of francophone women writers is forging a new discourse on sexual realism and identity issues to replace the hypocritical silences on sexuality that usually leave the reader thinking that African societies are asexual.

What Bugul offers here is not simply a reformulation of gender. She exposes the positive features available to her to express issues of identity, history, gender, age, class, and sexuality. Since every choice is a renunciation of something else, and since choice is a reflection of something going on inside, the narrator chooses to be part of polygamy, thereby rejecting some aspects of Western values that held her back in her search for identity. There finally is cohesion between the image she has of herself and the representation others have of her. The main task is to remain true to oneself and not be lost in the different categorizations.

The importance of Bugul's works and the diverse questions they raise point to an unprecedented determination in naming the direction that discourse on African theories on women, identity, and sexuality must take. Bugul defines a new ideology of literature by African women that incorporates issues of sexuality, traditionalism, and modernism and their connection to the mechanisms of history and

identity. These are important aspects of African life missed or ignored not only by African writers but by critics as well. Other female
writers such as Calixthe Beyala have certainly approached the issues
of sexuality, positioning, history, and identity, but Bugul's treatment
of the issues is quite different. She does not see them as separate issues; rather, she sees the interconnection of sexual, economic, political, and spiritual fulfillment as well as identity.

Interestingly, the author appears to encourage an intra- and multi-
cultural dialogue that ignores differences and so-called hybridity. For
Henri Lopes, "le destin de l'Afrique dépasse l'Afrique" (Africa's destiny goes beyond Africa; 44). This is reflected in the narrator's inspiration; she is locally, regionally, and internationally positioned and
has knowledge that ranges from history, culture, politics, economics,
and religion to gender relations. She solicits an international dialogue
that may destabilize the center, precisely because economic and cultural frontiers have already been blurred due to porous aspects of the
human mind and the natural tendency of cultures to borrow from one
another. Borders are artificial blockages and assumptions that widen
illusory gaps and abstractions that apparently divide. Bugul's vision
is to debunk these baseless spaces. Her perspective informs us that
the center of the world is everywhere, not in one place. That is why
she uses several languages in exposing this "socio-political satire,"
as Midiohouan mentions (1). Her point is that people may look different, think differently, and live in different environments, but they
have core principles that they all care about and that are important for
human survival.

Notes

1. The Mourid faith is based on a "path," or the "Order." Mouridism
is the African Islamic belief that "from God we descended, and to Him
we shall return." The founder of this brotherhood was the Senegalese
Serigne Cheikh Ahmadou Bamba Mbacké, who is worshipped by many
Senegalese who embrace this faith.

2. The historical organization of West African societies has created
some familial structures that allow individuals (female or male) within or
from a specific family to entertain people of their communities. Though
the author is evasive about Bousso Niang, one might well extrapolate
her status. Her inherited role is that of the individual who can use crude

sexual and body language to entertain. People may be offended, but they recognize that society grants the performer that role.

3. This text by the Senegalese author Boubacar Boris Diop tells the story of a woman narrator and storyteller, Khadidja, who, while narrating stories about an Africa that is torn between civil wars and corruption, vacillates between reality and madness.

Works Cited

Bourget, Carine, and Irène Assiba d'Almeida. 2005. "Entretien avec Ken Bugul." *French Review* 77 (2): 352–63.

Bugul, Ken. 1982. *Le Baobab fou.* Dakar, Senegal: Les Nouvelles Editions Africaines.

———. 1994. *Cendres et braises.* Paris: L'Harmattan.

———. 1996. *Riwan ou le chemin de sable.* Paris: Présence Africaine.

Diop, Boris Boubacar. 1998. *Le cavalier et son ombre.* Paris: Stock.

Kourouma, Ahmadou. 1981. *Suns of Independence.* New York: Africana.

Lopes, Henri. 2003. *Ma Grand-mère bantoue et mes ancêtres les Gaulois.* Paris: Gallimard.

Magnier, Bernard. 1985. "Ken Bugul oú l'écriture thérapeutique." *Notre Librarie* 81:151–55.

Meyer, Nicole E. 1999. "Silencing the Noise, Voicing the Self: Ken Bugul's Textual Journey towards Embodiment." In *Corps/Decors: Femmes, Orgie, Parodie,* ed. Catherine Nesci. Atlanta: Rodopi.

Midiohouan, Guy Ossito. 2001. "Ken Bugul: De l'autobiographie à la satire socio-politique." *Notre Librairie* 146 (October–December): 1.

Coda

African Women's Writing, Prospectively

Tuzyline Jita Allan

Since the 1960s, when literary works by African women were generally seen as isolated phenomena, a decidedly increasing number of works (and their authors) are regarded as phenomenal. According to the *Oxford English Dictionary* (eleventh edition), a phenomenon is "a fact or situation that is observed to exist or happen, especially one whose cause is in question," and *phenomenal* is defined as "remarkable or exceptional, in particular, exceptionally good." Long marginalized within the emergent body of postcolonial African literature, African women's writing seemed almost like an enterprise whose cause was in question. Ama Ata Aidoo summed up African women's increasing sense of alienation within the new literature at the Second African Writers' Conference, held in Stockholm in 1986. Drawing attention first to the shared imperatives of male and female writers in the wake of highly wrought fights against various oppressors, she added the following: "What we are saying though, is that it is especially pathetic to keep on writing without having any consistent, active, critical intelligence that is interested in you as an artist (or creator). Therefore, it is precisely from this point the African writing women's reality begins to differ somewhat from that of the male writer."[1] Similarly, Anglo-American feminist critics barely noticed the African female desire for self-reinvention even as they pored over the Western literary canon for signs of patriarchal misrepresentations of womanhood. Nonetheless, African women continued to write, driven by what Aidoo calls the "desperation," (162) enveloping their failing states, as well as by the artistic desire for soul freedom.

Criticism of African women's writing began in earnest as an oppositional discourse to Western feminism, which dominated the ideological landscape from the late sixties through the nineties. Womanist theory, devised simultaneously in Nigeria by Chikwenye Okonjo Ogunyemi and in the United States by Alice Walker, offered black/African female agency combined with a holistic sense of community to counter the universalist logic and gender-driven probe of feminist critique. Womanism reverberated throughout black America and most of the writing Third World, distilling notions of artistic and cultural differences between black and white women into an informal creed. But theories, as Ogunyemi admitted in a 1997 interview with Susan Arndt, "cannot explain everything."[2] And certainly, theory, including the current postcolonial contributions to the field, has done little to diffuse the fires of war, militarism, disease, poverty, and capitalist exploitation in Africa as the promise of new freedoms gives way to rising social and economic problems. Indeed, yesterday's fierce debates over womanism and feminism as models of intercultural criticism sound almost utopian today in the face of strangling local, national, and regional realities in many parts of the world. These realities resonate with great urgency in African women's writings, and the criticism responsible for delivering the values of these works will ultimately reflect a range of influences and approaches to mediate between Africa and the world at large.

By bringing together the pivotal texts of African women's literary production in a range of critical readings, this volume thus has a dual aim. It is first and foremost a testament to the implacable persistence of African women to write against all odds. The "desperation" Aidoo speaks of has given birth to a literary renaissance that signals women's imaginative authority to redefine themselves, their communities, and their nations. As these works illustrate, the urgency to write is variously inspired, but underlying the spectrum of themes is a collective understanding that as the stakes for African women's writing change, so they remain the same. Hence a portrait emerges of each writer trying to reconnect to the imperative of writing against the weight of history to provide new threshold beliefs about women and life on the continent.

In capturing the motivating energy of the texts, the readings illuminate the multileveled critical practice I referred to earlier as pointing to the future of the criticism of African women's writings. The assessments draw both difficult and hopeful lessons from the ideas that have fueled African women's creative imagination in the last four decades. It is hoped that these lessons and the methods of their illumination will enrich future pedagogical and intellectual debates on African women's creativity.

This volume therefore stands on a new threshold of possibility in African women's creative art. The penetrating (re)readings will inspire in writers, critics, and students a sustained commitment to women's literary production in Africa. There is no better time, then, to express an appreciation of the singular contribution of Chikwenye Okonjo Ogunyemi, endearingly called "Chi" by many of us who have known her over the years, to the literary criticism of African women's writings. As her name indicates, Chi has been a guiding spirit of the founding impulse to legitimize the new view of African women fostered by the writing women of the continent. Her aggressive interrogation of Western ideals, particularly when they are foisted on African social and cultural life, led to her groundbreaking essay "Womanism: The Dynamics of Black Female Writing in English," published in 1985.[3] The often-quoted essay has proudly taken its place in archives of contemporary feminist criticism. So too will her book, *Africa Wo/Man Palava: The Nigerian Novel by Women* (1995), a scholarly feat that blazed the path to understanding the expansive artistic talents of women in Nigeria.

Chi stands on a threshold as well. She has recently retired from many years of teaching in Nigeria and the United States. We celebrate her in this book, along with the women writers who have preoccupied her brilliant mind over the years.

Notes

1. See Ama Ata Aidoo, "To Be an African Woman Writer—An Overview and a Detail," in *Criticism and Ideology: Second African Writers' Conference, Stockholm 1986*, ed. Kirsten Holst Petersen (Uppsala: Nordic Africa Institute, 1988), 155–72.

2. See "Of Womanism and Bearded Women: An Interview with Chikwenye Okonjo-Ogunyemi and Wanjira Muthoni" by Susan Arndt, www.ishmaelreedpub.com/archives/spring_summer_2008/essays/.

3. *Signs* 11 (1985): 63–80.

Notes on Contributors

Tuzyline Jita Allan, professor of English, teaches African American, postcolonial, and women's literatures at Baruch College, City University of New York. She is author of the award-winning book *Womanist and Feminist Aesthetics: A Comparative Review;* coeditor of *Literature around the Globe;* and editor of *Teaching African Literatures in Global Economy,* a special edition of *WSQ: Women's Studies Quarterly.* Allan has published widely on the works of African and African American women writers. Her latest articles include "Feminist Scholarship in Africa" and "Modernism, Gender, and Africa." She is currently codirector and series editor of Women Writing Africa.

Margaret J. Daymond is professor emeritus and fellow at the University of KwaZulu-Natal. She has edited several volumes of fiction by African writers, including Bessie Head, Lauretta Ngcobo, Frances Colenso, and Goretti Kyomuhendo. She has also published many critical, feminist studies of writers, edited *South African Feminisms: Writing, Theory, and Criticism, 1990–1994* (1996), and coedited *Women Writing Africa: The Southern Region* (2003). She is a founding editor of the journal *Current Writing: Text and Reception in Southern Africa,* which is now in its twentieth year of production.

Nada Halloway received her PhD from the English Department at Stony Brook University, SUNY, and is currently an assistant professor

of English at Manhattanville College, Purchase, New York. Her publications include critical studies of Arab and African writers. Her fields
of interest include Victorian literature and Arab and African women's
writing at home and in the diaspora. She is currently working on the
different forms of resistance in the writings of women from Africa and
the Middle East.

V. M. (Sisi) Maqagi is a lecturer at the Nelson Mandela Metropolitan
University, Port Elizabeth. She teaches in the English Studies section
of the School of Language, Media and Culture. She has published
articles, chapters, and papers and was an associate editor of *Women
Writing Africa: The Southern Region*. In addition to writing poetry, she
has collaborated in running poetry workshops with aspiring women
writers in the Eastern Cape and coedited three volumes of *Nawe
Unakho* (You Too Can), a journal that resulted from the workshops.
Currently she is working with a colleague on a collection of critical
articles on Ellen Kuzwayo's writings.

Helen Nabasuta Mugambi is a professor of English and Comparative Literature at California State University, Fullerton, where she has
worked as acting coordinator of the Women's Studies Program. Her
research centers on issues of gender, identity, and postcoloniality in
oral and written texts. Her recent publications include "The Post-
Gender Question in African Studies," in *Africa After Gender?* edited by
Catherine M. Cole, Takyiwaa Manuh, and Stephan Miescher (2007);
and "Zimbabwean Feminist Art and the Politics of Representation"
(*Signs* 33, no. 2). She is on the editorial board for *Jenda: A Journal of
Culture and African Women Studies*.

Amira Nowaira obtained her PhD from the Department of English,
Birmingham University, UK, and is currently a professor of English
literature, Department of English, Faculty of Arts, Alexandria University, Egypt. Her publications include critical studies, translations
from and into Arabic, and creative writing. Her fields of interest include
English literature, Arab women's writing at home and in diaspora, and
comparative literature. She is a coeditor of the *Women Writing Africa:
The Northern Region* volume published by the Feminist Press (2009).

Chikwenye Okonjo Ogunyemi, professor of literature and the
founding chair of Global Studies, is currently faculty emerita, Sarah

Lawrence College, Bronxville, New York. She was professor of English at the University of Ibadan, Ibadan, Nigeria, and also taught African women's writing at Barnard College, Columbia University, New York. The author of *Juju Fission: Women's Alternative Fictions from the Sahara, the Kalahari, and the Oases In-between; Africa Wo/Man Palava: The Nigerian Novel by Women;* and *Richard Wright's* "Black Boy," Ogunyemi edited *Reading for Literary Awareness,* volumes 1 and 2, and coedited two special issues on Flora Nwapa and women's writing for *Research in African Literatures.* She has numerous publications on African and African American women writers.

Modupe Olaogun is an associate professor of English at York University, where she teaches African and postcolonial literatures. She has published articles on different genres of African literature. Her current research focuses on the aesthetics of African drama and on African literature and explores the subject of migration and dispersals from Africa. She provides a venue for the dissemination of African drama as the artistic producer of AfriCan Theatre Ensemble (Toronto), which she founded in 1998.

Chioma C. Opara is a professor of English and comparative literature and the former director of the Institute of Foundation Studies, Rivers State University of Science and Technology, Port Harcourt, Nigeria. With specialization in comparative literature and gender, her major research interests are women and cultural studies. She has published widely in scholarly journals and edited volumes, among which are *Writing African Women, Sisterhood,* and *Challenging Hierarchies.* Her books include *Her Mother's Daughter: The African Writer as Woman, Beyond the Marginal Land,* and *English and Effective Communication.* She is the editor of the *Journal of Gender Studies*—a multidisciplinary annual publication.

Nobantu L. Rasebotsa is currently director of Confucius Institute, senior lecturer, former dean of the Faculty of Humanities and former head of the Department of English at the University of Botswana. She received her PhD in English (Southern African Literature) from SUNY, Stony Brook, New York. She is one of the editors of the 2003 seminal book, *Women Writing Africa: The Southern Region.* She has researched broadly on gender issues, including work on HIV/AIDS in African literature. She is currently focusing on higher education studies and carrying out research on managing change as well as mentoring at the University of Botswana.

Aissata Sidikou is currently assistant professor in the Department of Language Studies at the U.S. Naval Academy. She is the author of *Recreating Words, Reshaping Worlds: The Verbal Art of Women from Niger, Mali and Senegal* (2001) and of several articles on African oral and written literatures and women's studies. She is coediting an anthology project on women's songs from West Africa with Thomas Hale.

Nana Wilson-Tagoe teaches African and Caribbean Literature at SOAS and in the MA Programme in National and International Literatures, Institute of English, University of London. She has written extensively on African and Caribbean literatures. She has published *Historical Thought and Literary Representation in West Indian Literature*, coauthored *A Readers' Guide to West Indian and Black British Literature*, coedited *National Healths: Gender Sexuality and Health in Cross-Cultural Contexts*, and written a forthcoming book on Ama Ata Aidoo.

Index